FELT
MISTRESS:
CREATURE
COUTURE

Felt Mistress: Creature Couture

Copyright © 2012 by
Louise Evans, Woodrow Phoenix
and Blank Slate Books

First published 2012 by
Blank Slate Books, London

Editor:
Woodrow Phoenix

Publisher:
Kenny Penman

Group Editor:
Iz Rips

Publicity and Marketing:
Martin Steenton

Publication Design:
SuperAdaptoid at Detonator

ISBN: 978-1-906653-32-3

10 9 8 7 6 5 4 3 2 1

Printed in Singapore
Keep up with Felt Mistress's work at
www.feltmistress.com.

Discover more about Blank Slate:
Internet: www.blankslatebooks.co.uk
Twitter: @blankslatebooks
Facebook: blankslatebooks

FELT
MISTRESS

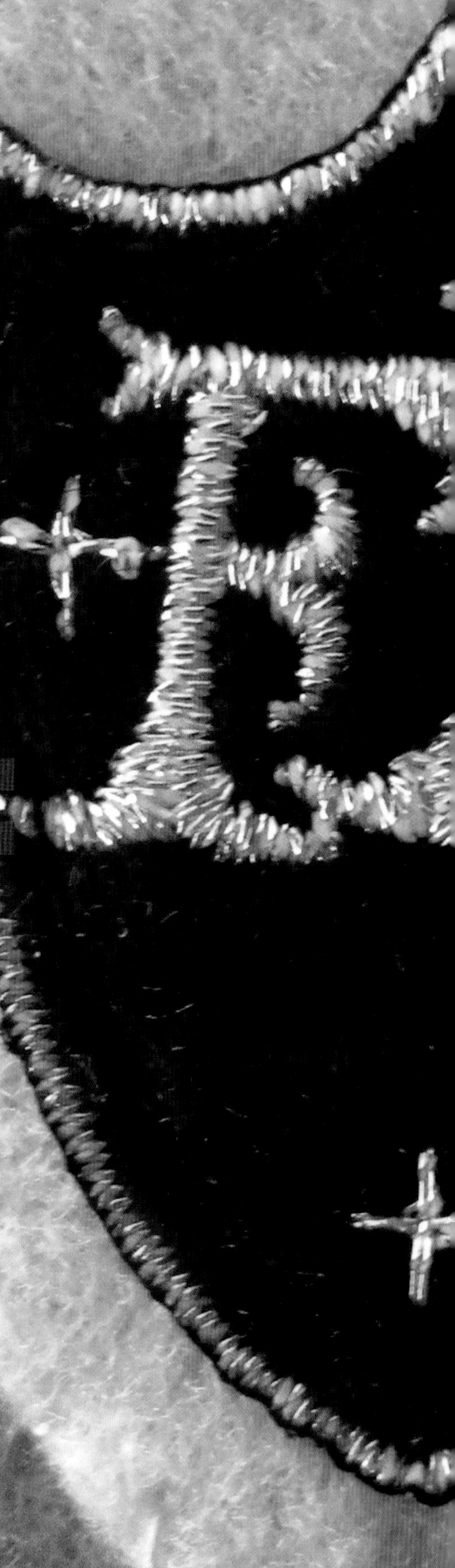

CREATURE
COUTURE

## Felt Mistress

## Collaborations

## Shows

# INTRODUCTION WOODROW PHOENIX

W hether working with her partner and long-time collaborator, Jonathan Edwards, working with a number of other talented artists, or working alone, Felt Mistress's creations are peerless, with method and style that have few, if any, precedents.

The work of Felt Mistress defies categorisation. The intersection of the creative drive and fabricating skills of Louise Evans with the pop-cultural preoccupations and loopy, delirious lines of Jonathan Edwards results in a uniquely individual, culture-clash expression that resists a single label. Somewhere in the midst of that mash-up you might get near what happens when two brains and four hands combine to shape an alternate reality into being.

Typically, handmade works are an aesthetic and practical alternative to the industrial finish of vinyl production. Plastic toys demand sculpts, casting, machining and factories. Cloth is much cheaper. In an area where slickness is the enemy and amateurishness is fetishised, the creations of Louise Evans are a felt bomb, a fabric deracination that clears the ground around it. Her meticulous, rigorously sewn pieces redefine the notion of what is possible, of the form human hands are capable of shaping, of what materials can express in and through the hands of one who has mastered them. Once a new paradigm is seen, everything else looks inadequate. Once we are aware of what is truly, excitingly possible, nothing else seems as interesting.

We have become so accustomed to looking at merely adequate work and calling it 'awesome' that we perhaps now lack the words to describe the output of a virtuoso. That term will embarrass Louise Evans, but there is no other way to describe what she does.

Her creations did not appear out of nowhere. They are the result of many years of focused and conscientious honing of the techniques and hand skills of a couturière that would normally find expression in exclusive salons. To apply those skills to much less rarefied, playful, contemporary artistic statements is a wonderful, radical act. This is what gives the creations of Felt Mistress their powerful charge. She is able to bring unlikely and fantastical ideas into being, to give them substance and credibility and validity with her absolute command of the materials at her disposal. The results are beautiful, impossible objects. They should not exist, but they absolutely, joyously do. A Felt Mistress figure commands authority by virtue of its pristine, faultless surfaces and demands to be dealt with on its own terms. This is the mark of a truly original creator.

Preoccupied as we all are with defining and categorising (how else would we know where we belong, where to put things?), encountering any really new idea brings a flood of questions, but perhaps, for once, no definitions are necessary. All we have to do is look, delight at what we see and revel in the collapsing of boundaries that Felt Mistress presents. There is so much more to come in the future. As astonishing as the contents of this book are, they are history now. Artists move forward in time. They take the lessons they have learned and apply them to ever more ambitious ideas in a constant levelling up of process and production. For those looking for a new aesthetic target, here is something to aim at. But you will have to look quickly, because tomorrow the target will have moved. Felt Mistress does not stand still. She experiments, refines, and innovates. Where does she go from here? As always, the answers will come not in words, but through her hands.

WP

FELT
MISTRESS
AKA LOUISE
EVANS

FELT MISTRESS (FM) I've seen photographs of my grandmother's dresses. My mum wasn't a dressmaker.

WOODROW PHOENIX (WP) Where did your interest in dressmaking come from?

FM It must have just come from watching my mother. She wasn't a dressmaker but she made things to sell at fund raisers for our local nursery school. When I was a kid I would make things out of plasticine, I wasn't so much honed-in on sewing. Also I was one of those awkward people who didn't want to wear what other people were wearing or do what everybody else was doing. I had to change it a bit. It was the only way I could get what I wanted. When I reached an age where I could choose my own clothes, I wanted something a bit different. I was quite tomboyish really, I wasn't a dressy kind of girl. My parents had two girls and I think I was definitely the more boyish of the two. My dad was a joiner – there was lots of sawing wood, making things out of balsa wood, go carts, going on at the same time as making little felt things. Not really embroidery or anything cute like that. Practical things, things that I could play with after they were made which is probably

*see page 14, top right   why I made my first plush rabbit,* so I could use it to make pretend stories.

I did sewing in school and the first item of clothing I would have made was a straight skirt from a pattern, you had to cut it out and decide whether you wanted a pleat at the front or a split at the back. Basic stuff. I was probably 12 or 13, my friend's dad was a security guard and his jackets were quite military with epaulettes and all that, I cut one of those into a box jacket to wear. I'd cut jeans up into clothes to wear.

WP What kind of patterns did you use?

FM I didn't have any patterns. I just made them up. I don't know where I got the styles from, it must have been something that I had seen, but it was just messing around. I didn't know anything about dressmaking until I went to college. I had no knowledge of that.

Before I went to college I did a diploma. It was called fashion and clothing technology but it was very technical, so there was a lot of pattern cutting which actually amazed me. The first day we got to understand about dart manipulation and that type of thing, I just went crazy, I thought "Oh my god I know how this works now, I can do this!" It was really exciting.

When I left school, I went to work at Laura Ashley thinking that I would be able to sew there. Being really naive, not realising that I was going to work in a factory and it was going to be quite hard. I managed to last 12 months there. Even though I didn't like it because of the environment, I think it was really good because I learnt how an industrial factory would work, how sewing machines were threaded.

WP What was it like working there?

FM Training at Laura Ashley at that time was very, very particular so I learned a lot, like how to insert zips, how to do a placket on the front of a shirt. Cuffs and collars. They put you in two camps. You could either be an over locker or you could be a lock-stitch machinist. They watched how you handled the machines and decided which one you were best suited to. I did lock stitch and that was when I started to make more clothes.

But what really shocked me about working there was that nobody there made anything for themselves. They were taught one job and they knew how to do that job really quickly and efficiently, but anything straying from that they had no interest in. It was a job and they didn't do it because they had an interest in sewing, which was sad for somebody who did have an interest in sewing. I would get really excited and say "this is great, we can do this" but there would be no enthusiasm from my colleagues. So then I thought, this is not for me, I'm going to have to go to college.

So I did the diploma in clothing technology, I did pattern cutting, which opened up a huge amount for me, the construction, all the paperwork that went with mass producing a garment. Right from the start you'd be researching mood boards, themes, all the way through to how to finish a garment. Towards the end of that I got really interested in making hats because I discovered Philip Treacy. By the time I finished that diploma, I thought 'right, I really want to do millinery, it's all hand sewing and hand finishing. Even though I like clothes I'm still going to do it'. I couldn't really see an opening to make something as a one-off in the clothing business. I kept thinking I'd have to get a job working for a company doing mass produced stuff if I went down that route. Whereas if I went down the millinery route I could perhaps do things for people for special occasions and it would be a one-off piece and I could spend ages on it and hand sew it.

But unfortunately there weren't any millinery courses at the time. So I went to Epsom, but I wasn't happy there. I couldn't settle so I transferred to a college in Manchester and although they didn't have a millinery tutor, they introduced me to a lady who had taught in the college years ago. She had retired, and was now in her 70s. Her name was Mrs Payne. She was happy to teach me privately – for free! – as she wanted to share her skills, worried that they were dying out.

There were two people who were key in my life, one of them was Peter who taught pattern cutting in Wrexham at diploma and the other was Mrs Payne. I'd go to her house two days a week during my free period. It wasn't part of the course but they were happy for me to do it because it was millinery. She was so

strict! She hated all these new manufacturing ways of using glue – which is why I'm crazy about the glue aspect! If I had sewn something and it wasn't quite straight, even if it was quite neat but wasn't perfect, she would just undo it. I'd have to start again. I might have gone all all the way round the brim of a hat and it was okay, but there might be one little bit – she would just undo the whole thing and say, "I'll go and make us a cup of tea and you can undo that and do it again."  The relationship wasn't like a teacher/student where I'd hate her because of that...

wp Was it more like Luke and Yoda?

FM Yeah, because I really respected this woman and I was old enough not to be childish about it all, but it was like "my goodness you're making me undo it just for that...!"

wp Did she demonstrate what she wanted from you? Did she show you the kind of stitching she expected?

FM Oh yeah, yeah. When she learned to do millinery back in the forties it took something like five years, I think, before you were allowed to work on a hat as an apprentice milliner. You'd spend a lot of time just watching people then they'd let you do trims, she said. She spent ages showing me how to make felt trims, little felt flowers that they would have because they always needed lots of spares of those, so that's what most of the apprentices did. So again I think that's why working with felt came out of me later on. I've actually got interviews with Mrs Payne that I did for my dissertation where she speaks about her apprenticeship.

wp So you spent a lot of time quizzing her about these things.

FM Oh yes. It was great. She'd make a cup of tea, she'd always baked a cake and it was just like visiting your grandmother really. She wanted me to do really well and gave me so much stuff, she donated all her wooden hat blocks to me, so many feathers... I have got an attic full of stuff that she gave me when I left, "you can't get these any more!" she'd say.

When I left college I had this big dream that I was going to make hats but I got a job making wedding dresses. It was amazing that I got a job as soon as I left college, a design job, whoa! But I never would have done wedding dresses really, it was such a strange thing for me to do. Working there, working with different body shapes, learning about corsetry I managed to make it into something interesting. Besides the problems that came with a 9-to-5 job I did enjoy the actual working side of it.

wp Describe a typical day in the wedding dress shop.

FM Get in, in the morning, have a look at who's coming in for a fitting, check what point their dress is at, there were lots of consultations with brides to find exactly what they want because we did one-off dresses, they weren't mass produced. Fittings were done with a full canvas toile to fit on the bride when she came in so she could see the style of skirt, so I could see whether it fitted her in the bust, the waist, all those type of things. Because brides get married from January to December and the dresses were all at different stages, you could be working on a toile in the morning and sewing the last button on somebody's dress in the afternoon. I had to control the process straight through from when I first saw them when they came in through the door, to when they collected the dress at the end. I didn't press the dresses, I had somebody who did that because I was rubbish at pressing. I'd see these women for 12 months, 18 months, so it was quite a relationship, it involved quite a lot of trust.

wp Were they picking their dresses from a pattern book?

FM No, because I worked for a company that manufactured as well, there were dresses to go into shops. As a result there were always samples that they could try on before they made any decisions so they could say "I like a full skirt" or "I want a straight skirt". But most brides, when they come through the door, have an idea of whether they want a big dress or a small dress, a long dress or a short dress. It has to fit where they're getting married, maybe they are going abroad...

They don't think they know what they want, but when you start asking them questions, they do. Because they've got a problem with their arms, so they've got to have sleeves. Or they've got a tattoo that they want to hide – or show – so all these little things then narrow it down. So we would start doing design work, really bad sketches because I'm rubbish at that. I much prefer to get into calico, get them to trust me to make something in calico I can put on them and say "this is what it's going to look like", then they can see the shape.

wp You create using the material right there, like a sculptor would, making a dummy, a prototype?

FM Obviously, for dresses, but when I do the character pieces, I've even been known to make them completely out of paper. Just cut shapes out of paper and sellotape them together so I can actually see what they look like. This is partly because I don't want to stitch something and waste fabric, I can just see what this head would look like. Cut out the pattern pieces flat, see the scale of it. I used to work more that way than I do now, figuring out how to make a ball, how to make a cylinder, because as you do more and more you can almost be safe enough to go straight into fabric, straight into paper to make a pattern because you know the widths and the shapes.

WP Would you say that by working in this place, making all these dresses, you pretty much covered every kind of construction there was, every kind of style, dresswise?

FM Yeah, I had to solve pretty much every problem along the way. My knowledge of full tailoring isn't as strong as my knowledge of dressmaking.

WP Explain the difference.

FM In tailored jackets there are many layers, different underlayers and the padding, interlinings and all that type of thing, how a jacket is properly constructed. I have an idea of that, but it's not something I've ever worked on. I can make a jacket for a figure, but making one for a full-size person isn't something I've done a lot of.

WP But you've made many jackets for brides. What's different?

FM They would be tailored, in the sense that they would be fitted, but the fabrics are different: silks, softer fabrics, you're not using tweed. Perhaps you'd get a tailored sleeve on something, shoulder pads, obviously, but you wouldn't get the layers of interlinings like on a tailored jacket, very few rever or reefer collars.

WP But the amount of construction that goes into making a jacket isn't more than what goes into making a dress, is it?

FM No. I have a basic understanding of it but it's probably the thing that I know the least about as far as sewing is concerned. I have my own way of doing it but if I speak to a tailor I think they'd probably go, "What! Why are you doing it that way?" I might be doing it perfectly right, mightn't I? I don't know!

WP Isn't the garment itself the proof? Does it matter what method you used to make it?

FM True, but I'm not making anything that's having a lot of wear, am I? So there's things like that you have to take into consideration. I mean, I've made jackets for myself, and worn them —

WP You've made coats for yourself!

FM Yeah, I've made coats...perhaps I'm being cruel to myself.

*see page 285

WP Just a little modest. Let's talk about when you began making presents for people. I remember Pants Ant arriving in the post at my studio and being utterly flabbergasted by it*. I did not know what to say. It was so perfectly done. It looked like it had come from a really wonderful model-making, special-effects house that had studied my comics, that had been given plans and turnarounds by me, that I'd told them what I wanted: the contours have to conform to this specification, the folds go here and the lines of the robot legs follow this style...and you had just done all that by studying the comic. It was like you had been inside my head and read my mind. I didn't know how to evaluate it. I sat there, looking at this Pants Ant figure, honestly for about an hour. Turning it over and over, looking at this detail and that detail from every possible angle. In the end, Carl and Ed came and took it away from me because they said I was freaking them out! I was just sitting at my desk, staring and staring at this object. I was stupefied. I couldn't get over it.

That ability that you've got to take a 2D plan, analyse it and translate it into three dimensions is really quite astounding. Where does that come from?

FM I think that's from working with lots of different body shapes, from making wedding dresses. No two people are alike. You get some crazy variations in body shape. And when you're making something as fitted as a wedding dress every piece has to fit, has to be comfortable. And if you need it to curve here or flare out there, you know what to do. I do think that's helped an awful lot, that's what I put it down to anyway. I look at it in a similar way. If that shape was a bride, how would I get the dress to fit her? It would be a very bizarrely-shaped bride, but I suppose that's how my brain works now! As soon as somebody walks in the door...

WP You start mapping them! You scan them.

FM Yeah, totally. I do that now when I read things. I think how would that work, how would I make that, what would it look like from the back. I don't see things flat very easily at all. I don't draw, if I tried I don't know how it would work. There's gotta be different wiring in the brain. I can't do flat work.

WP But you are working with flat things, you're extrapolating points into vectors and filling in the shapes and it's an amazing and unusual ability to transform one thing into another like that.

FM Yeah. I've never done upholstery but I've covered a chair. I took the same approach, like if the chair was a person how would I dress them, so you can lend that to all sorts of things. It's really hard to explain when it's just what you – it's just how I think. I never really question it or think about it so I don't know, I've always made things. I did as much colouring-in and drawing as other children but I did much prefer to build something. Knock a nail into two bits of balsa wood or glue something to something.

WP It fascinates me because artists try to manipulate Z space. Drawing is about transferring the essence of 3D objects onto a 2D surface and trying to create the impression of depth, trying to make it feel as if a drawn object has volume even though it's just flat. Whereas you do the opposite. You take a drawing and you make it real. So you're a living Z space generator! That's magic to someone who makes pictures because although our output is flat, the characters are quite solid in our heads. And I imagine most people you collaborate with have the same experience of what you do: to see their flat imaginary concepts brought to life in 3D is enormously exciting and gratifying.

FM I get lots of Twitter followers who are illustrators. I think you might be right, they want to see their work in 3D. That's why vinyl toys are so popular and everyone wants to have a vinyl toy out or a plush toy. But I wish I could draw all nice as well, so it works both ways. I wish I could sit here and do a really beautiful drawing that people are going to want. I envy my artist friends because all you need is a pen and a piece of paper, you can go into a cafe and you can sketch, and you've made something. I don't know what the equivalent of sketching is for me.

WP Isn't it a toile?

FM It is, but you can't do one anywhere. You still need your stuff with you, quite a lot of supplies. It's not the equivalent of the progress from a sketch to a finished artwork. It's being able to get an idea down really quickly, on the bus or somewhere, I regret not having that. I can write notes, I can get excited about the idea of making that but I still have to wait till I get home. Perhaps I should start carrying felt in my pocket! Have a needle and thread and start improvising while I'm out and about.

WP Then it's not actually the drawing as much as being able to fashion a prototype quickly and easily using paper. Like a lot of artists, I am often much more enamoured of the rough than of the finished drawing because there's an energy there, you feel closer to the artist's thought. A finished drawing is perfect but there is something...

FM ...it hasn't got the life. I think I'm like that with clothes. I love toiles, when I make toiles for dresses I sometimes much prefer them to the finished item. But I don't feel that way when I'm making characters or other sculptures because they're not finished as fully. There's something about clothing in calico, looking at it all in one colour and there's nothing interfering, you can see all the pleats and the seams...

WP There's a purity to it.

FM There's something really lovely about it. Sometimes I'm really disappointed when I've made the finished article. I don't feel that way about the toiles for the pieces. Sometimes you make a really nice shape and it feels good because it's an unusual shaped head or something but an unfinished piece in toile never has the same feeling as an outfit.

WP When you started making presents for people, what was your motivation? Did you think, wait till they see this, or were you testing your abilities? Why did you do it?

FM The impulse was, if I'm honest, I was going to comic conventions, my friends were putting zines together and I couldn't get involved. I made The Thing for Jonathan and we photocopied a picture of it which went into a zine at this small press event. I was involved. I was able to take my skill and join the gang. I couldn't

draw, but I could look at the characters you all were producing and I could make them. I was doing something creative rather than come along to these things but not get involved because I make dresses for a living. I never thought I might stop making dresses and have a career doing this, it was the need to be involved. Because EVERYBODY that surrounds me draws, designs characters. People that I mix with. Peer pressure!

wp But there was a point at which, rather than inserting yourself into other people's worlds, you started to create your own world.

fm It was because I'd made things and they were successful that I began to get excited about character designs, making a world, like you said. All the birthday presents, they were quite simple. Yours was the first related to something that was quite complex. Urbane Gorilla and Pants Ant, they had lots of detail specific to them, they weren't like the JAKe doll or The Thing that I'd made previously. But the first toy design that could be sold was the Kaiju.

wp So how did you come up with that?

fm Jonathan was doing some designs for a clothing company with monsters on them. He'd drawn one in his sketchbook and I thought "I'm sure I can make that." It was such an interesting shape. I don't like things that don't stand, I like things to stand up, not two pieces that are flat. I wanted to make a real three-dimensional thing with a tail, so I just worked out how to make a basic shape.
   I went to college with the lady who was employing Jonathan at Sportax and she asked me to make some Kaiju for the stand, to display at the trade show they were selling these clothes at. The monsters would be promotional items to get people to visit the stand. I had to do it then. So that's how the first few came to exist. I think Jonathan said we should try selling these, and I can remember thinking: "Who's going to buy these? What would we sell them for? £20? Who's going to pay £20 for these? Who's going to do that?" We went into a shop that was near to us that sold Japanese import items and they loved them, "ooh yeah, we'll sell them", they said. And they just kept selling! I wasn't making any money on them but it snowballed and they kept selling.
   I got bored with that though and I wanted to tie in the clothing side of it. I was thinking, I've done the characters and I want to start putting clothes on them. So the politicians were the first that were dressed and they actually had clothes that had been thought about.

wp I remember being dumbfounded by the level of detail and thinking and depth of craft that had gone into making the politicians. They had distinctive personalities and the tailoring was very precise. Real clothes with fastenings and linings…which was a bit mental. It was like they had come from some alternate universe.

fm That was because I couldn't make clothes any other way. Coming from the angle of having to make expensive very high-quality silk dresses, bespoke clothing, it was really hard to undo that 'this jacket has to be fully-lined, the pocket has to be welted' thing. It was really hard not to do that because that's what I knew. Even with the jackets, nobody was going to take them off to know if they were lined. It's really stupid!

wp I think people WILL undress their Felt Mistress creatures to see what's going on underneath there…

fm But even so I don't think anybody would say "My goodness, she hasn't lined this!" Perhaps they would now, knowing how I work! At the time it didn't really need to be like that, but it was important to me.

wp There is a certain level of completeness when you make something; you want to make all of it. It's not like a theatre flat where there is nothing behind it. If you go around the back, the back is all there and completed in the same way as the front.

fm I hate buying a doll that has a coat on and when you open it there's nothing there, just paint. It was dead exciting if they had a pair of knickers on. That's what you would do if you got dressed in the morning, you would put those clothes on. And if anything is missing…

wp …Then it's a toy and not a real thing.

fm And when you're playing with it you might want to put it in its pyjamas at bedtime because that's what people do. So it is important to me, and to go back to training: if I had been trained in a different way, perhaps I would approach it differently.

wp Your approach takes them out of the arena of toys doesn't it? It takes them somewhere else. Where are they?

FM I've never wanted to sell them as toys because I didn't like those restrictions. As soon as you put that label on it, it's got to be safe for children and if there are little details it restricts what you can do with it. I just want to do what I want to do. It's really frustrating if I can't do it how I want to do it. So they don't fit into that category. Toy industry people seem to think of me as being more in the art and fashion area but I wonder whether that's because I know that world better.

I'd like to think that they are art objects. And the people who buy them appreciate them the same way they love everything else they buy.

WP What interests me about what you do is that most people will never see or wear handmade clothing because it's so expensive it is completely out of their reach. Generally the only way we can encounter it is to go to a vintage shop and buy something old, that someone has left behind. So what you do is in a place very far away from those people who typically make plush toys because it's all they can afford to do, they don't have any training and their skills are somewhat rudimentary, their stitching is not perfect and it's all very home-made looking.

FM They are creating something for different reasons though, aren't they? I get enjoyment from the details, I mean if you have checks on two pieces and the checks marry up, I just love that, that's great. Finding the perfect braiding that matches the tweed you're using when making a fake Chanel jacket for a creature, that's what makes me tick. It's all about improving, I want to get better at this, still keeping the personality and not losing any of that. I wouldn't want to pretend that I can't sew in a straight line. That kind of thing can be charming but it's not me, is it? I have been made to undo things time and time again to get them right.

WP Surely anybody who is going to create an object wants to make it as well as they can? If the majority of the stuff we see out there is badly made and wonky and a bit shonky it's not because the people making it want it that way, it's because they don't have the ability to make work any better than that. I hope!

FM I hope that's true. I do get an awful lot of people asking me if I've bought children's clothes for my creatures! I'd like to see a child wearing anything like some of the things I have made! As if I buy clothes and just restyle them instead of making them.

WP But that's a compliment! It just means they don't understand how this works. They don't understand the skill you have or how it comes about. What you do is very complicated and from the outside it looks like magic. It's so precise and so flawless there is no way to see how it is done.

FM It is a compliment – depending on where they think I bought the clothes from?! It's so strange. I have sewn for so long now. There was and is no shortcut to get to where I am now, just constant practice. I find it hard to explain how I do what I do. When I first started sewing I was like everybody else. I made plenty of things that were bad. But you have to be interested. I like things to look right.

WP Is it like solving puzzles for you when you are making your creatures?

FM Definitely yeah, yeah. Working out how to do things. The process of how you are going to make them and how you are going to dress them. We can put our clothes on over our heads but if their heads are four times as wide as their bodies they can't do that! I wake up in the night thinking "that's not going to go over his head, I'm going to have to put an opening on the shoulder or I won't be able to dress him..." When you've worked in an industry producing clothing there is a system, an order that things have to go in. You have to put the pockets on the jacket before all the other panels go on. This works exactly the same way. You just have to break things down - put the legs on first before you attach this bit... It is like a puzzle, how to physically sew them together, how to draft the patterns for them, which piece will make the fabric wider, what if I put a curve here, is that going to make a bump or will it be smooth? It's exactly the same as if you had to fit somebody with a bigger bust. I'm constantly referencing things like that. It's really similar, I think so anyway.

WP When you decide you want to make some new thing, do you commission Jonathan to draw it for you? Do you look through his designs and decide "I want to make that one?"

FM With the politicians Jonathan was just sitting in front of the TV drawing all the bad 70s fashions. He had done this series of drawings in his sketchbook of wide-lapelled suits with high collars and I just thought "my goodness that's going to look amazing". They weren't designed to be made, they were just drawings. Other times we've seen somebody walking down the street and we've thought they've got such a great style, we've got to make a character who looks like that. I say to Jonathan "draw what his hair would be like", we design them together and they are fully formed before they are made.

I might make a shape that I like and say to Jonathan "what type of face are we going to put on this?" Because we have worked together for so long—we've been together for so long—I know exactly how he works, I have seen so many of his drawings, we know what's possible. And Jonathan has seen my techniques to make things so he can say "that would look really great if you make this coil like that", and so we can design something that's going to be perfect. Because not all flat artwork will translate into 3D and vice versa.

There's a lot of, not arguments, but I'll say "this is impossible to do because you can't get it that pointy, fabric isn't going to do this, felt isn't going to do that". And Jonathan might come up with a character that has the clothes and personality worked out but not the shapes, the essence of them is there but they're not fully formed yet. I can visualise them much better if they are drawn on paper so I might give Jonathan a really naff drawing to fix. I always want to make them when they're drawn really nicely, then I can really see them. It will take me a lot longer to work out something if I haven't seen it drawn flat. It is much easier having an illustrator in the house who can draw something because then it makes you want to make it because you know it will be beautiful.

WP Does he help you with the beetles?

FM Some of them I make by myself. One of the bigger ones, you can see there's a face on the back of it. I knew I wanted to have the face but I didn't know how it was going to work so I needed to map it on paper. There's lots of things like that. And some of the lines on the beetles' backs, Jonathan will say "this pattern looks really nice, you can flow this colour into that colour…" I have also sat there with the felt all around me, no paper or any patterns, cutting pieces out, placing them on top of the beetles and working it out like that. The first one, Jonathan drew as a round ladybird type. We found that round ones are much more popular than any other shape. In Japan, people say "maru maru" which means round, apparently it's a more pleasing shape for people's eyes. But the other shapes, again, are not made in paper they're just cut out and stitched, I don't plan them. The three parts of the body of the beetle, I cut a load of them, stick them all on a tray I've got, I go downstairs and put the TV on. Decisions like where the embroidery thread goes, that just happens organically. The beetles are not drawn like the other things that we do, there's more freedom for them to just happen.

WP I get the impression that the way they are made, with lots of layers of colour, is you freestyling…

FM Definitely, layering felt and seeing what works and saying to Jonathan "What about this? What colour shall I put with this?" Certain times, like if there's a petal shape and I can't quite get it right I will say to him "just do a shape for me, it needs to fit into this space, and your curves are nicer than mine." When you are making a big figure you really have to think ahead. What are you going to do? Is there wire in their arms, is there wire in their fingers? Whereas with the beetles it's quite therapeutic and quite nice, I find it really peaceful making them, they're little and I like the fact that people can just take them home and put them on the wall. A lot of people who buy my big pieces have to have cabinets made, it's a purchase that you've really got to think about, where is it going to fit into your life? People who want a piece of my work but just don't have the room, the beetles are nice for them. We're doing a show in July and I just want to fill a wall with beetles, I think they look much better en masse.

WP Collaborating with other artists is different than working with Jonathan, isn't it? With him there's a lot of backwards and forwards but with other artists – I get the impression they give you a drawing, you make the figure, and that's it.

FM I'm not very good with the people getting involved and telling me how to do this, "Why don't you do it this way?" I'm okay with that input at the very beginning but once I begin to create it, if I show somebody a part-made thing and say "what about this?", if they're not 3D literate they'll just say things that will confuse the process and mess it up. So what's happened with all my collaborations is that they send me drawings; Pete sends me turnarounds, Jon sends me turnarounds occasionally, I'll have a look at the plans, then if I have any questions – normally to do with what colours they are – I'll ask those before I even start. I may send a fabric swatch if there's a particular colour it needs to be. Or sometimes Jon B. rings me and tells me that Port Salut cheese is the closest to the yellow he wants! And then they won't see anything until it's finished. And I'm happy with that.

If people want to collaborate with me, I don't want them telling me exactly what they want me to do and how to do it because then I'm just work for hire. I'm translating their drawing and it's my job, I want it to look like mine. I'm not good with… I don't think I could collaborate with somebody else who sews, which is bizarre. I would want to do it all myself. So when I work with somebody who doesn't do that it's nice. They can do their bit, I can do my bit, and there's no interfering, no back-and-forwarding. I don't know how to draw and they don't know how to sew! It just gets all confusing if you don't keep it separate. We can talk about things over the phone but I don't show them anything until it's finished. That's how I prefer it.

WP The level of collaboration is up to you to set, isn't it? If you don't need any more input than the drawing then that's fine. I just wonder what happens when the drawings only show one angle and you have to work the rest out. That's not a problem for you – you don't dislike that?

FM Occasionally I have to ask: "Does X have a tail at the back? What's going on at the back of the jacket? Is the pattern continued all the way around, or if they've got spots, have they got spots on the back?" But most of the time I say "No no, I don't need that." One of the shows I did with Burgerman, he sent me one of the paintings that he had done, circled an area of it in highlighter and said "Can we make this?" It was for his Brain Drain show, he wanted it to look like the pieces interlocking. That wasn't a character design, it was just part of a painting.

There was probably more back and forth from a technical point of view when I made the puppets for The Stuffs because they were going to be filmed. I had to know what the puppeteer needed because there are certain demands to make it comfortable to work with and what they needed the puppet to be able to do. That didn't have anything to do with the design but with the construction, you have to make the hands a certain size, because they need to be able to hold things while filming little jokey sketches and stuff.

WP Burgerman's drawings are about flat logic, a line intersecting with another line because that is a pleasing shape. You have to take those lines and transform them volumetrically which changes that logic. You create impossible objects that shouldn't exist, don't you?

FM The first pieces I did for his London show 'I Can't Sit Still', Sprouthead and Tickler, they looked like character designs when they came through. John had done vinyl toys and they did look like toy designs. I think if he had just given me one of his paintings to work from at that early stage I would have thought "What on earth? How can I do this?" But because I had spoken to him a lot for those first three and I had come to understand a little bit more, as time went on and I worked with him more it seemed to be quite easy to do. His work translates well to felt because of the bright colours and shapes, although he does keep me on my toes.

Like the last one, the Aubudo burger, that's quite crazy actually, when he first sent me that one it was like, "Gasp!" The paint was dripping, he was using three primary inks so where Burgerman usually crosses his lines he was crossing the blue and yellow to create green in the middle. Trying to recreate that in felt, which is not translucent enough to do colour changing on its own, you've got to do it with another colour. So I tried to do things with embroidery thread with knots on the end to represent dripping paint. We did talk about him painting the felt but because he's in New York and I'm in Wales it wouldn't have worked. When I first saw his work, everything is asymmetric, you can't cut one arm and then cut another one exactly the same, you have to make two separate arms. But that's great for handmade stuff because that really works, and it works really well in the felt.

WP And it has extended your vocabulary of gestures in felt. Different kinds of stitching, different closures...

FM Going back to what you were asking about working with other artists, what I can't do... Jonathan laughs at me, and says "You can't tell Jon Burgerman 'I don't want to do legs like that'!" Because he's already drawn it and it's going to be in a show so I just have to work through until I have done it. It's easier for me to say to Jonathan "Make the legs wider because it's going to be awkward." It's a little more dangerous for me to get my input into the actual design of it when I'm working with Jonathan! With anybody else, it's their design; I need to translate it into my way but I can't really change it. I can't ring up and ask, "Can you change the ears?" with anybody else, they are like that for a reason.

WP There's a certain compulsive aspect to making a whole world of creatures, isn't there?

FM I like to see groups of characters, I think they really come to life when they are in a group, you can imagine that they are a gang, that they hang around together. Doing one character is really nice but there's something really satisfying when there's a group. To go back to Burgerman, when I did his group of hipsters for his New York show, having all of them together, all seven lined up...There's something nice about having that many characters who can interact with each other.

WP They reinforce each other.

FM Definitely, it adds to their personalities, their stories and their bios. Like there's a supermodel and a photographer and the photographer had to exist because the model needs somebody to take her photograph! Things like that just make them more real. Jonathan is much better than me at naming them. Occasionally a name comes on the TV and I really like it so we write it down. We've done a few like that. We usually sit down with a long line of names and pick or else they just instantly look like somebody, just look like a name. We have got spare names which we've not used yet, but Jonathan takes full responsibility for naming them,

he likes them to sound... he's much better with words. Occasionally, they may have obvious monster names but we don't always want to do that, calling them Groobo or whatever. You've got to have a few Hesters in there, proper names. The names dictate the personality.

Creatures who aren't fully clothed have more monstery names, whereas the ones that are completely dressed, with refined clothes, have refined names.

WP Your working process has evolved but it is still essentially the same – you are making distinctive, one-off, individual creations. Are you interested in anything else?

FM Do you mean mass production? The figures are made and they exist and they go to shows, they get sold. I would like them to hang around a little bit longer. That might mean being used on other things, on cards, in photos. They take so long to make it would be nice to have them doing something else, to explore their lives a bit, see what they do. I'm not sure how we're going to achieve that but that's the kind of thing I'd like to do.

Regarding mass production, I don't know, that's really difficult. Perhaps if I could get something that looked right. But then I don't want to run a business. I want to be able to make things for a living and if I'm just making money by designing one item and then directing people to remake it, I'm a business person, I'm not creating anything. I would rather be working this way and have no money than have lots of money but have that bit of the process taken away from me. I could get someone in to help me but to assist me they would take over the bits that I like doing and I don't really want that.

It would be good to be able to make them more affordable for people by having alternative versions of some of the characters but it certainly wouldn't replace anything. I have yet to see a mass produced item I am really happy with. It would have to look like my work. There are certain things that would be required. Setting factories up to do hand sewing around the eyes, to do all the details, I don't know enough about that side of the industry to completely say "It's not gonna work." There are obviously some great manufacturers out there who say they can make it look exactly the same. I'm sure there are, and I never say never.

WP The process of making these creatures is a very fulfilling one for you.

FM Exactly. It's what I like and it makes me happy and having worked for years and years not doing this, I don't want to let it go and go back to doing 'proper' work. Ha ha, no way! I'd rather make just enough money to live and have this fulfilling life than be loaded but not have that self-fulfilment.

WP Getting your brainchildren out into the world?

FM Yeah, it's gotta be done hasn't it. As I get older it becomes more important to me. Life's too short to be doing stuff for other people, it's time to do stuff for yourself, to get it out there and to be happy about it.

WP What I think is wonderful about what you do is that there aren't any precedents for it. Do you think that has anything to do with the way that you and Jonathan are away from the mainstream, living where you do?

FM We've discussed that quite a lot. Obviously you can't say that we're not aware, we've got the Internet, we can see everything, if we didn't have access the work wouldn't look like it does. I don't know why there isn't anybody who does something similar... I don't know! It does confuse me. When people say "Do you have a plan? Do you have someone you compare yourself to?" I don't know who that would be really. We're such a weird mix, it just sort of...happened.

I think sewing and making craft things is obviously becoming more popular but there's still a difference between what I do and the craft world so I don't fit in with the toy camp and I don't fit in with fine art. I seem to be bordering a lot of these areas. I've got a foot in each of them but none will actually say "Yeeeaah! You're one of us."

WP In the Felt Mistress venn diagram your circle intersects with lots of sets but it stays uniquely itself.

FM That's not intentional, but there are certain things I don't like about each of those areas so then I am glad that I'm not a part of that, because there are things that I see and I think "Ooh no, I don't want to do that." It's purely selfishness, my wanting it to be how I want it to be and not trying to do what anybody else wants it to be. It could be the downfall of me, but I'm hoping I will get people around to my way of thinking eventually.

CR
COUTU

EATURE
RE

Stylist, blogger, "It Girl" and heiress to the De Lorian French Fancies fortune, Amphibina's latest venture is a range of gilets for squirrels.

**Amphibina De Lorian**
900 mm x 320 mm
Made for "Hey! Who's This Guy?", Nobrow Gallery.

Amphibina wears black "Chip" kinetic glasses by Kirk Originals, an aubergine slash-neck knitted jumper with button detail at neckline, a paisley-printed silk scarf, skinny indigo jeans with turn-ups and white lace-up brothel creepers.
Mixed-fibre felt, card, plastic safety eyes, wire and polyester fibre filling.

Owner of Lemon Goon
Records. Signings (amongst
others): the bands Hot Mortar,
Pale Nancy, Bag For Life and
Ian's Dream.
If you've heard of a band then
chances are he doesn't like
them.

**Anton Trenche**
1120 mm x 300 mm
Made for "Hey! Who's This
Guy?", Nobrow Gallery.
Anton wears white
"Stallion" kinetic
sunglasses by Kirk
Originals. A white cotton
wide collared shirt with
deep collar and cuffs, a
knitted yellow and grey
striped tie, a grey, two-buttoned jacket with narrow
lapel, single back vent, welt
pockets and 3- button cuff
detail. Narrow legged black
denim jeans with turn up,
pointy black heeled boots
and a yellow leather belt.
Button badge by SeaHawks
music. He smokes a
cigarette.
Mixed-fibre felt, card, wire
and polyester fibre filling.

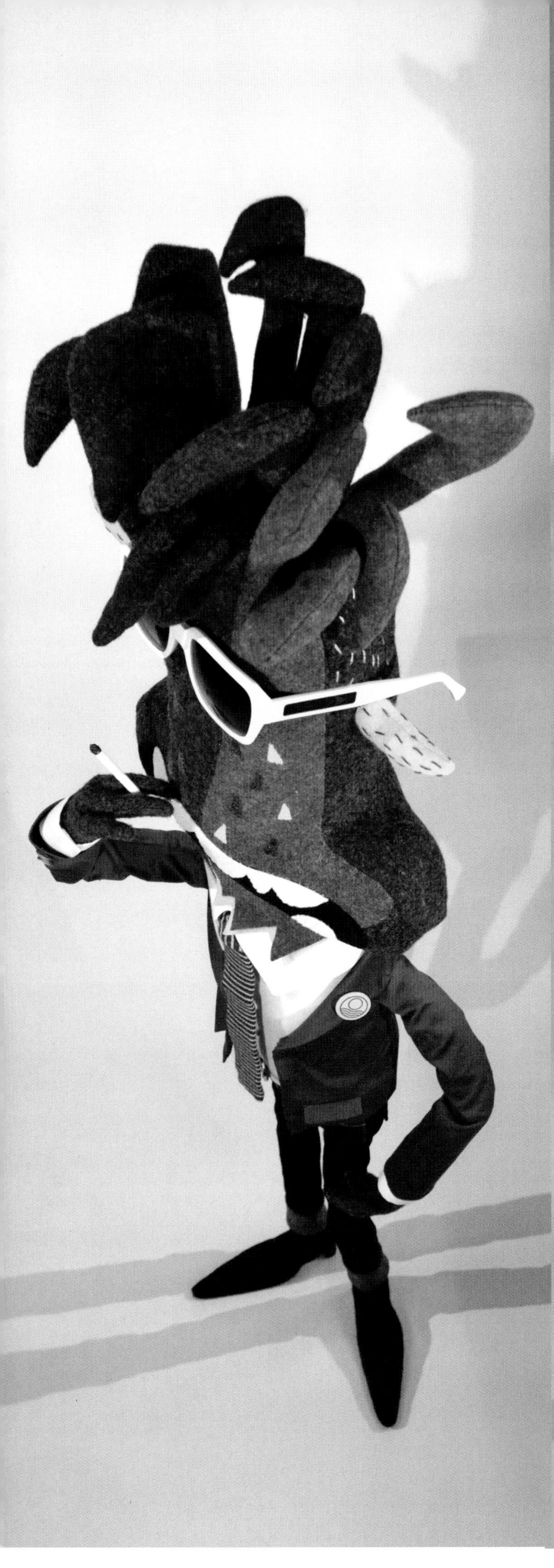

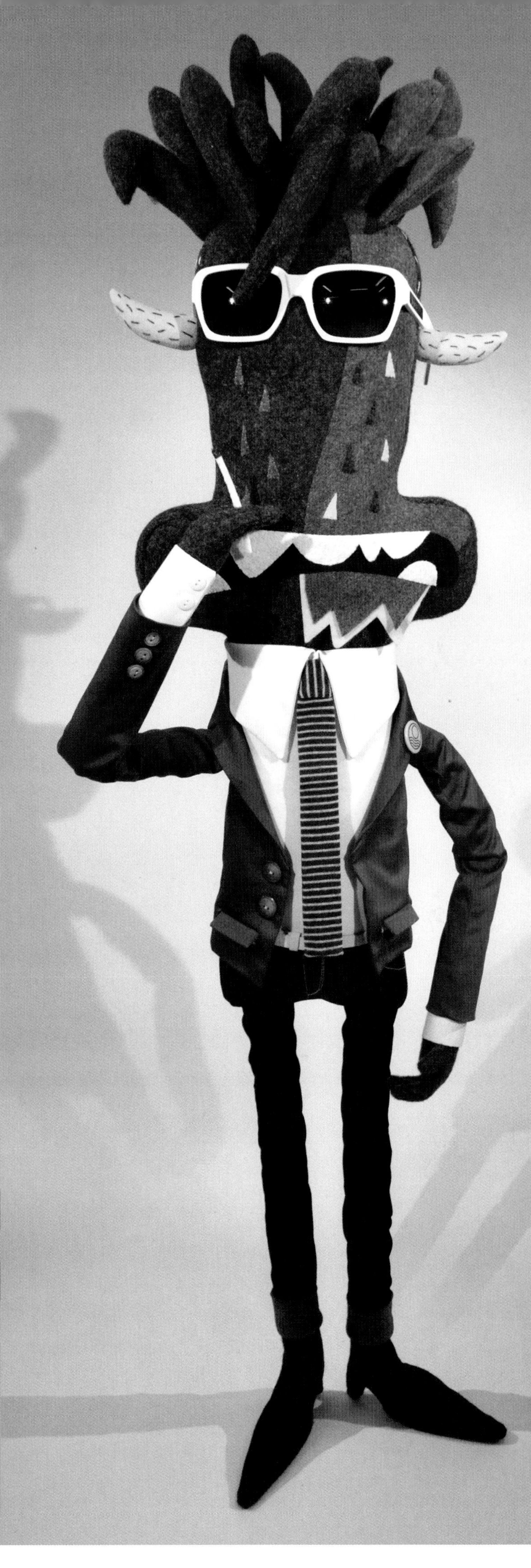

A-List: Anton Trenche —— 2012

A serene, blue dude, G'goob believes inner enlightenment can be achieved through the consumption of Tunnock's Teacakes and the music of Boney M.

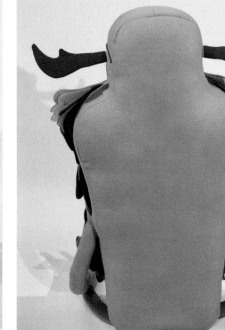

**G'goob**
1380 mm x 480 mm
Made for "Hey! Who's This Guy?", Nobrow Gallery.
G'goob wears Turquoise "Marvin" glasses by Kirk Originals and nothing else but his beard.
Mixed-fibre felt, card, plastic safety eyes, wire and polyester fibre filling.

A keen entomologist and professional grumph, Hector lives in a 400-year-old oak tree with a bay window (in which he can be found all day long, waiting to admonish unruly passers-by).

### Hector Bunford

1000 mm x 430 mm
Made for "Hey! Who's This Guy?", Nobrow Gallery. Hector wears brown "Janus" glasses by Kirk Originals. Wool tweed three-button sports jacket with patch pockets, a single back vent and elbow patches. Light brown knitted polo-neck. Green needlecord straight-legged trousers and brown dealer boots. He smokes a pipe. Mixed-fibre felt, card, plastic safety eyes, wire and polyester fibre filling.

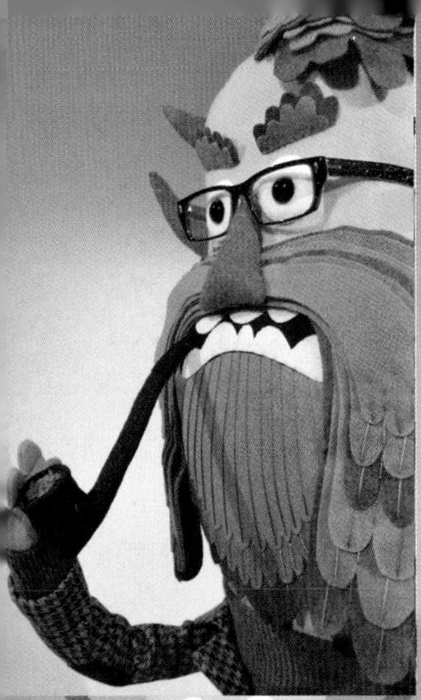

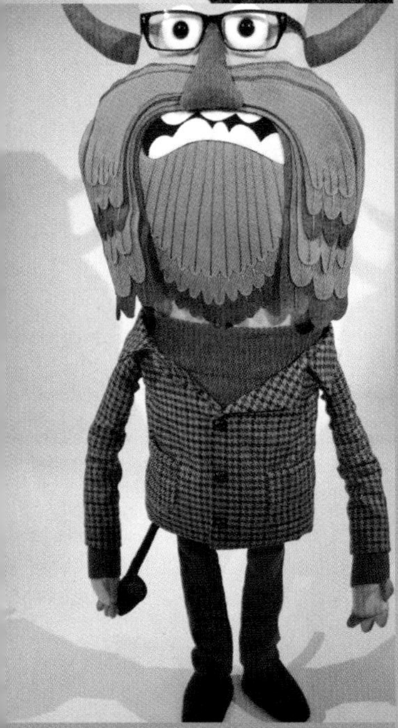

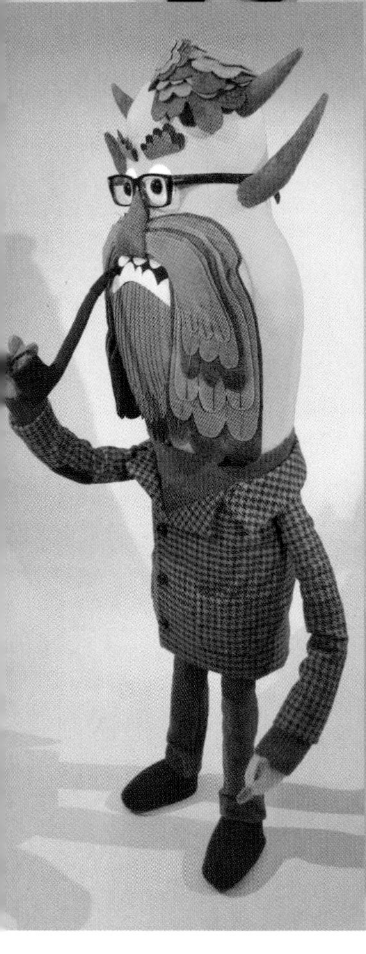

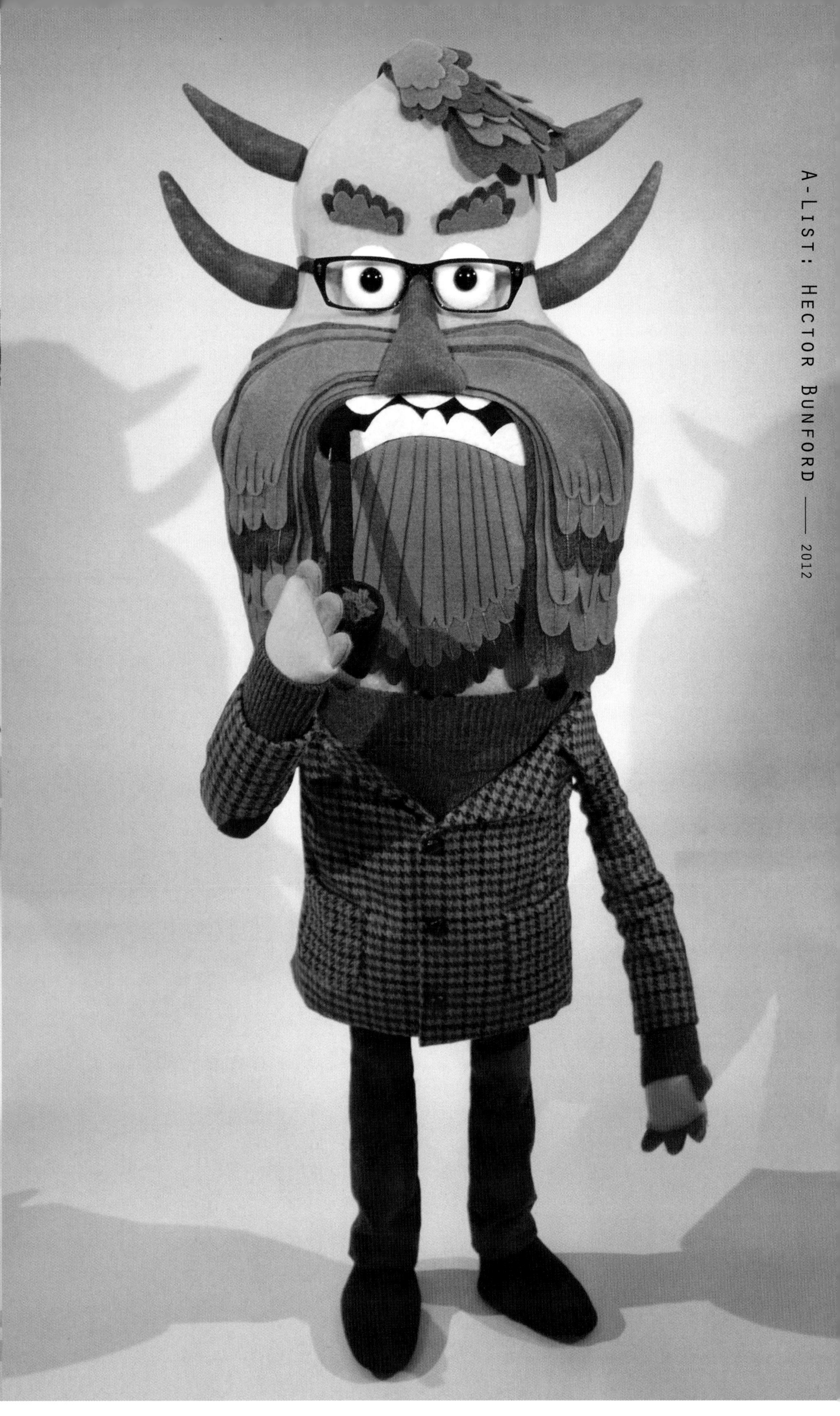

A-List: Hector Bunford —— 2012

Together with her husband Lester, Hester is the founder of London's influential Furious Rhomboid gallery.
They currently share a converted wheelie bin just off Brick Lane.

**Hester Flent**
1070 mm x 340 mm
Made for "Hey! Who's This Guy?", Nobrow Gallery.
Hester wears orange "Dione" glasses by Kirk Originals. Black crepe a-line, button-back dress, with long fluted sleeves edged with lace and vintage button detail. Black petersham ribbon belt fastened with vintage button. She also wears her orange live tentacle scarf/pet.
Mixed-fibre felt, card, plastic safety eyes, wire and polyester fibre filling.

Husband of Hester,
co-founder of the
Furious Rhomboid
gallery, Lester believes
in the power of the
continuous line.

Lester Flent
1240 mm x 450 mm
Made for "Hey! Who's This
Guy?", Nobrow Gallery.
Lester wears orange
"Janus" glasses by Kirk
Originals. Black, high-
fastening double breasted
suit with large lapels, welt
pockets and single back
vent. His trousers have a
slight flare. Also wearing
orange gingham shirt with
wide collar and cuffs, black
satin bow tie and black,
shiny pointy boots with a
heel.
Mixed-fibre felt, card,
plastic safety eyes, wire
and polyester fibre filling.

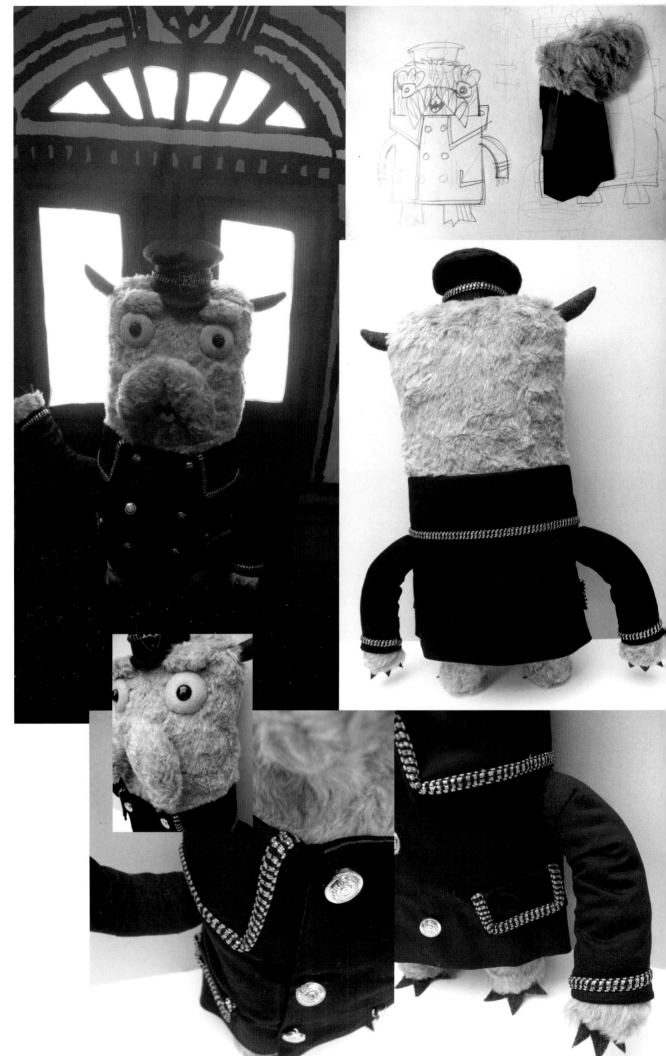

Alfred works as a doorman outside Felty Towers and dreams that one day they will let him stand inside.

**Alfred Krimpling**
350 mm x 300 mm
Alfred wears black double breasted uniform jacket with gold buttons and braid trim, felt, peaked hat with embroidered FM patch and gold braid.
Mixed fibres, fake fur, felt, plastic safety eyes, card, wire and polyester fibre filling.

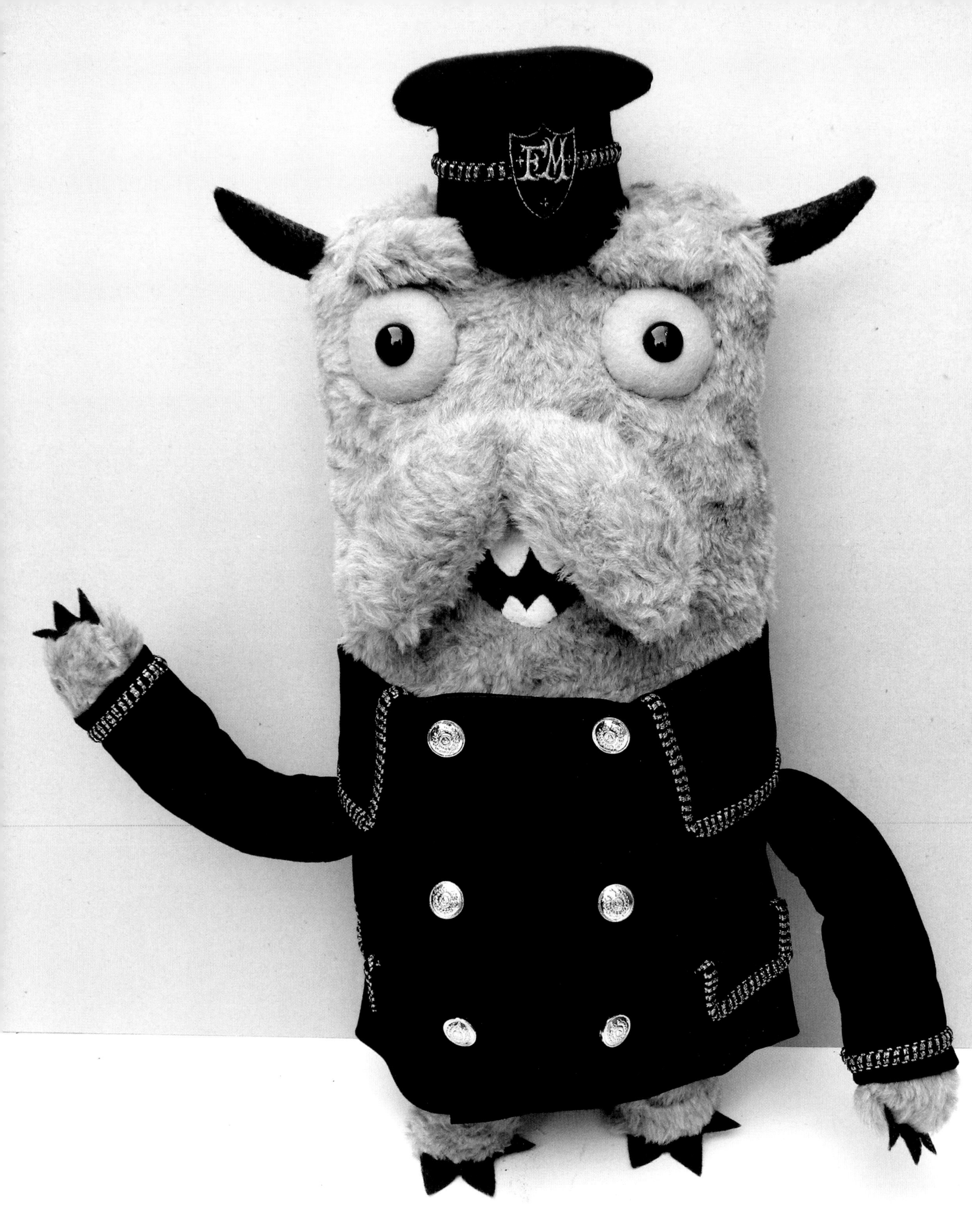


Alfred Krimpling —— 2010

Despite being mostly subterranean, Alfonso never appears without a hat, due to his fear of soil and male-pattern baldness.

**Top and Left**

**Angry Squared**
250 mm x 340 mm
Made as a present for Jonathan Edwards.
Black polyester fleece, Mixed-fibre felt, embroidery thread, card, wire and polyester fibre filling.

**Bottom**

**Alfonso**
260 mm x 190 mm
Alfonso wears black felt top hat with polkadot bow.
Mixed fibres, fake fur, felt, plastic safety eyes, card, wire and polyester fibre filling.

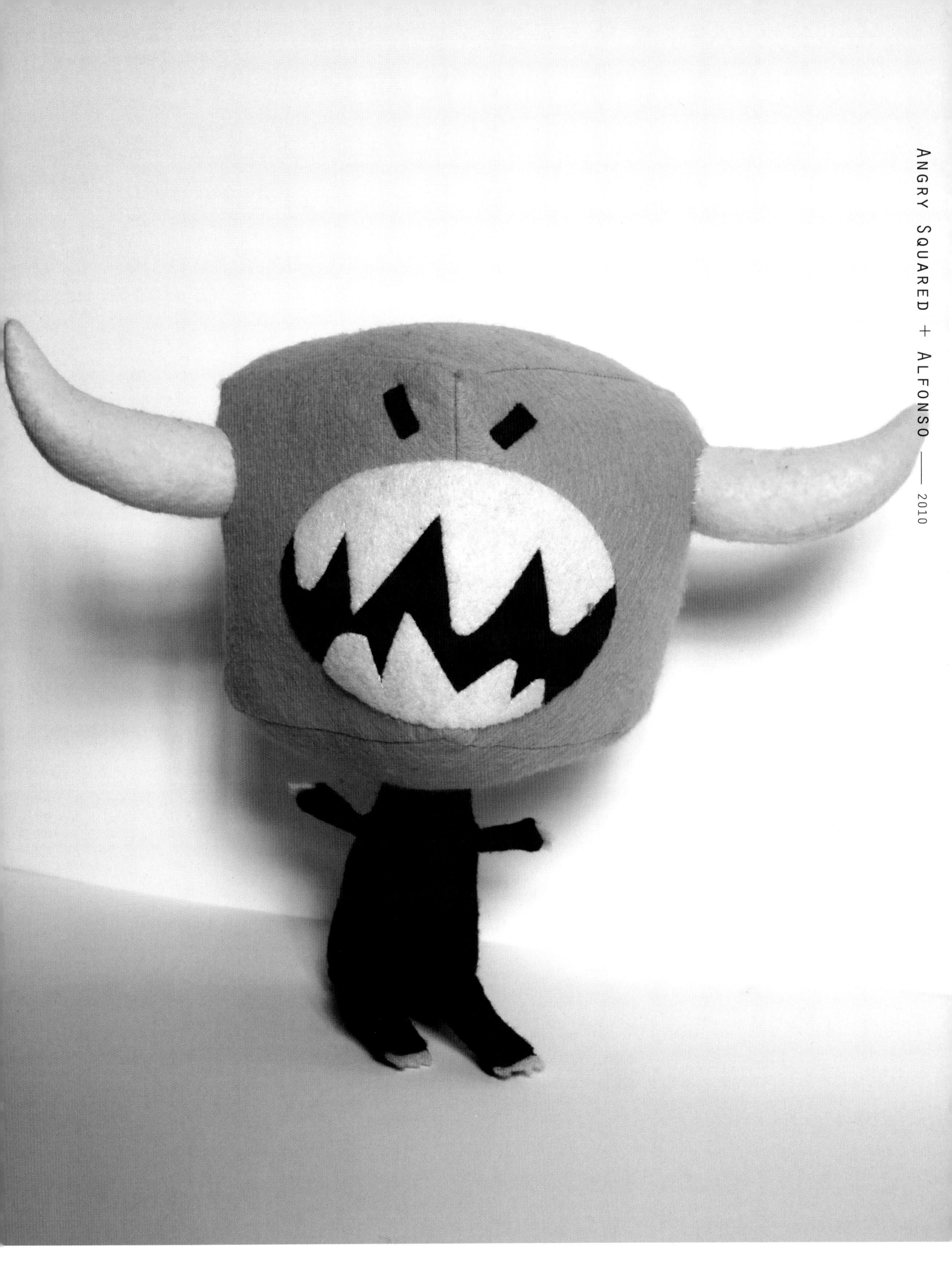

ANGRY SQUARED + ALFONSO — 2010

# JAKOB WESTMAN
# KÄRNHUSET SWEDEN

I've known about Jonathan and Louise's work for a few years and have always been on the lookout for an excuse good enough to get to work with them. The Arla poster series seemed like the perfect match! I'm a big fan of illustration, and that's how we approached this, like illustration deluxe. There's been a healthy interest in crafts and textures in graphic design and illustration in the last few years, and a big boom in retro-photography with apps like Hipstamatic and Camera+. We wanted a surreal (but non-retro) look and we were very keen on having the handmade look come through.

I get such a kick from seeing the textures and the wires, to see that it's NOT 3D-generated, and that there are a bunch of imperfections in there. I also get a kick from the scale of it, that we were able to work with actual props. The candles on the cake are actually burning, the balloons on the ground are real and the clasps on the farmer's dungarees are actual full-scale clasps. That's something you don't get with CGI or traditional illustration and it brings a whole other level to the final poster and makes it so much fun to look at.

It was also great to see what the photography was able to add. The photos I'd previously seen of Felt Mistress' characters had been more documentary in style and I think we were able to make them a bit surreal and trippy while still having the handmade qualities show. It's been really rewarding to see how everyone involved has taken something already great and made it even better.

*Arla Milk Campaign*
**Series of posters for milk vending machines and cafeterias in Swedish schools**
Commissioned by Kärnhuset Sweden

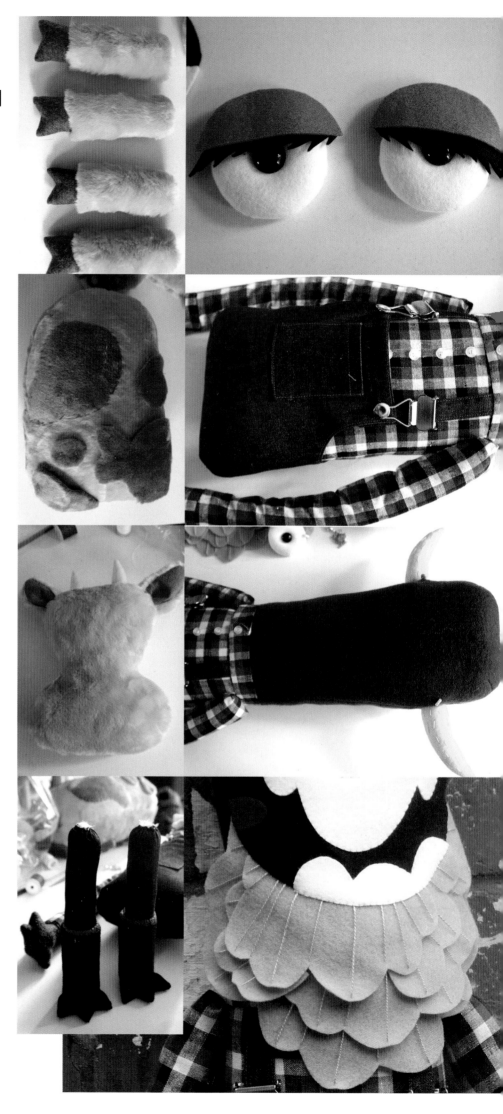

**Farmer**
900 mm x 320 mm
Farmer wears blue denim
dungarees, cotton checked
shirt and trucker cap.
Mixed fibres, felt, plastic
safety eyes, wire, card and
polyester fibre filling.

**Cow**
550 mm x 450 mm
Mixed-fibre felt,
embroidery thread, plastic
safety eyes, card, and
polyester fibre filling.

**Cat**
300 mm x 190 mm
Mixed-fibre felt,
embroidery thread, plastic
safety eyes, card, and
polyester fibre filling.

**Bird (large)**
300 mm x 260 mm
Mixed-fibre felt,
embroidery thread, plastic
safety eyes, card, and
polyester fibre filling.

**Birds (small)**
250 mm x 180 mm
Edition of two
Mixed-fibre felt,
embroidery thread, plastic
safety eyes, card, and
polyester fibre filling.

**Rabbit**
300 mm x 120 mm
Mixed-fibre felt,
embroidery thread, plastic
safety eyes, card, and
polyester fibre filling.

**Ground Dwellers**
250 mm x 150 mm
Edition of two
Mixed-fibre felt,
embroidery thread, plastic
safety eyes, card, and
polyester fibre filling.

**Big Arm/Hand**
700 mm x 200 mm
Mixed-fibre felt,
embroidery thread, plastic
safety eyes, wire, and
polyester fibre filling.

Austin Flisk and Skeechy Dwippford. Hosts of the best parties, makers of the best espresso, wearers of the sharpest threads. Why sit when you can dance?

## Austin Flisk

750 mm x 340 mm

Austin wears four-button, red-striped single-breasted blazer with single back vent and two welt pockets. Black cotton shirt with narrow button-down collar and silver jacquard tie. Black narrow legged trousers, black pointy boots and thick framed black sunglasses.

Mixed fibres, fake fur, felt, plastic safety eyes, card, wire and polyester fibre filling.

## Skeechy Dwippford

600 mm x 400 mm

Skeechy wears skinny black polo-neck, dogtooth check tweed dress with side bow and vintage buckle, matching bow hair clip, black shoes with black and white double button detail.

Mixed fibres, fake fur, felt, card, wire and polyester fibre filling.

Chet Krink is a poet and part of an existentialist, beat collective: a bunch of Rive Gauche dwelling, espresso-sipping, jazz-loving, poem-writing Bea(s)tniks. Chet is never without his copy of "Growl" by his hero, Allen Grimsberg.

Jean-Paul Schmunkle is a jazz trumpeter and his most highly prized possession is his copy of "Five Horns" by Munchy Gribbs & The Jazz Brutes - his Jazz svengali.

### The Beastniks made for "Plush You" Show, Seattle.

L to R
**Andre Krunkle**
500 mm x 250 mm
Mixed-fibre polo-neck jumper, straight-legged black denim jeans with turn-ups. Carrying port-folio of work (original ink drawings by Jonathan Edwards).

**Jean-Paul Schmunkle**
660 mm x 200 mm
Jean-Paul wears acrylic polo-neck, straight-legged black jeans with turn-ups. Carrying LP - "Five Horns" by Munchy Gribbs and The Jazz Brutes. Cover artwork by Jonathan Edwards.

**Chet Krink**
240 mm x 180 mm
Chet wears woollen polo-neck ribbed jumper and black denim straight-legged jeans with deep turn-ups. He carries a poetry book, "Growl" by Allen Grimsberg, with original poems written by Jonathan Edwards, Jon Burgerman, Drew Webster and Darryl Cunningham.

Mixed fibres, fake fur, felt, card, wire, plastic safety eyes and polyester fibre filling.

sidewalk cracks
up
at fire hydrant
he's gotta
good flow

—grimsberg

Felt Mistress: Creature Couture

Stripy-Legged Paku-Paku Beetle

Smoke-frilled Maru Maru Beetle

Flame-frilled Red Ember Beetle

Curl-toed Sweetheart Beetle

Frilled Arizona Saloon Beetle

Hot-Footed Booted Beetle

Monochromatic Chelsea Beetle

Party-footed Petal Wing Beetle

Gold-frilled Cherry-hot Beetle

Scalloped-wing Cherry Heart Beetle

Purple-hearted Petal Beetle

Wide-eyed Mint Winter Beetle

Previous page/top
**Smoke-Frilled Maru Maru Beetle**
250 mm x 250 mm
(Framed)
Mixed-fibre felt, embroidery thread, card, wire, and polyester fibre filling. Wooden glass-fronted box frame.

Previous page/bottom left
**Scalloped Wing Cherry Heart Beetle**
250 mm x 250 mm
(Framed)
Mixed-fibre felt, embroidery thread, card, wire, and polyester fibre filling. Wooden glass-fronted box frame.

Previous page/bottom right
**Curl-Toed Sweetheart Beetle**
250 mm x 250 mm
(Framed)
Mixed-fibre felt, embroidery thread, card, wire, and polyester fibre filling. Wooden glass-fronted box frame.

This page
Top
**Ruby-Booted Petal Wing Beetle**
250 mm x 250 mm
(Framed)
Mixed-fibre felt, embroidery thread, card, wire, and polyester fibre filling. Wooden glass-fronted box frame.

Bottom
**Purple Hearted Petal Wing Beetle**
250 mm x 250 mm
(Framed)
Mixed-fibre felt, embroidery thread, card, wire, and polyester fibre filling. Wooden glass-fronted box frame.

Previous page/top left
**Ice-Winged Polar Beetle**
250 mm x 250 mm
(Framed)
Mixed-fibre felt,
embroidery thread, card,
wire, and polyester fibre
filling. Wooden glass-
fronted box frame.

Previous page/top right
**Monochromatic Chelsea
Booted Beetle**
250 mm x 250 mm
(Framed)
Mixed-fibre felt,
embroidery thread, card,
wire, and polyester fibre
filling. Wooden glass-
fronted box frame.

Previous page/bottom left
**Stripey-Legged Paku
Paku Beetle**
250 mm x 250 mm
(Framed)
Mixed-fibre felt,
embroidery thread, card,
wire, and polyester fibre
filling. Wooden glass-
fronted box frame.

Previous page/bottom right
**Frilled Arizona Beetle**
250 mm x 250 mm
(Framed)
Mixed-fibre felt,
embroidery thread, card,
wire, and polyester fibre
filling. Wooden glass-
fronted box frame.

This page
Top
**Wide-Eyed Mint Winter Beetle**
250 mm x 250 mm (Framed)
Mixed-fibre felt, embroidery
thread, card, wire, and
polyester fibre filling. Wooden
glass-fronted box frame.

Bottom
**Flame-Frilled Red Ember
Beetle**
250 mm x 250 mm (Framed)
Mixed-fibre felt, embroidery
thread, card, wire, and
polyester fibre filling. Wooden
glass-fronted box frame.

Opposite page
Top left
**Prototype Beetle 1**
120 mm x 70 mm
Mixed-fibre felt, embroidery
thread, card, wire, and
polyester fibre filling.

Top right
**Gold-Frilled Cherry Boot Beetle**
250 mm x 250 mm (Framed)
Mixed-fibre felt, embroidery
thread, card, wire, and
polyester fibre filling. Wooden
glass-fronted box frame.

Bottom
**Prototype Beetle 2**
230 mm x 100 mm
Mixed-fibre felt, embroidery
thread, card, wire, and
polyester fibre filling.

Left
**Giant Cavalry-caped Kitchener Beetle**
520 mm x 520 mm

Right
**Giant Japonica Yosemite Ocular Beetle**
520 mm x 520 mm
Made for "Hey! Who's This Guy?", Nobrow Gallery.
Mixed-fibre felt, embroidery thread, card, wire, and polyester fibre filling. Wooden glass-fronted box frame.

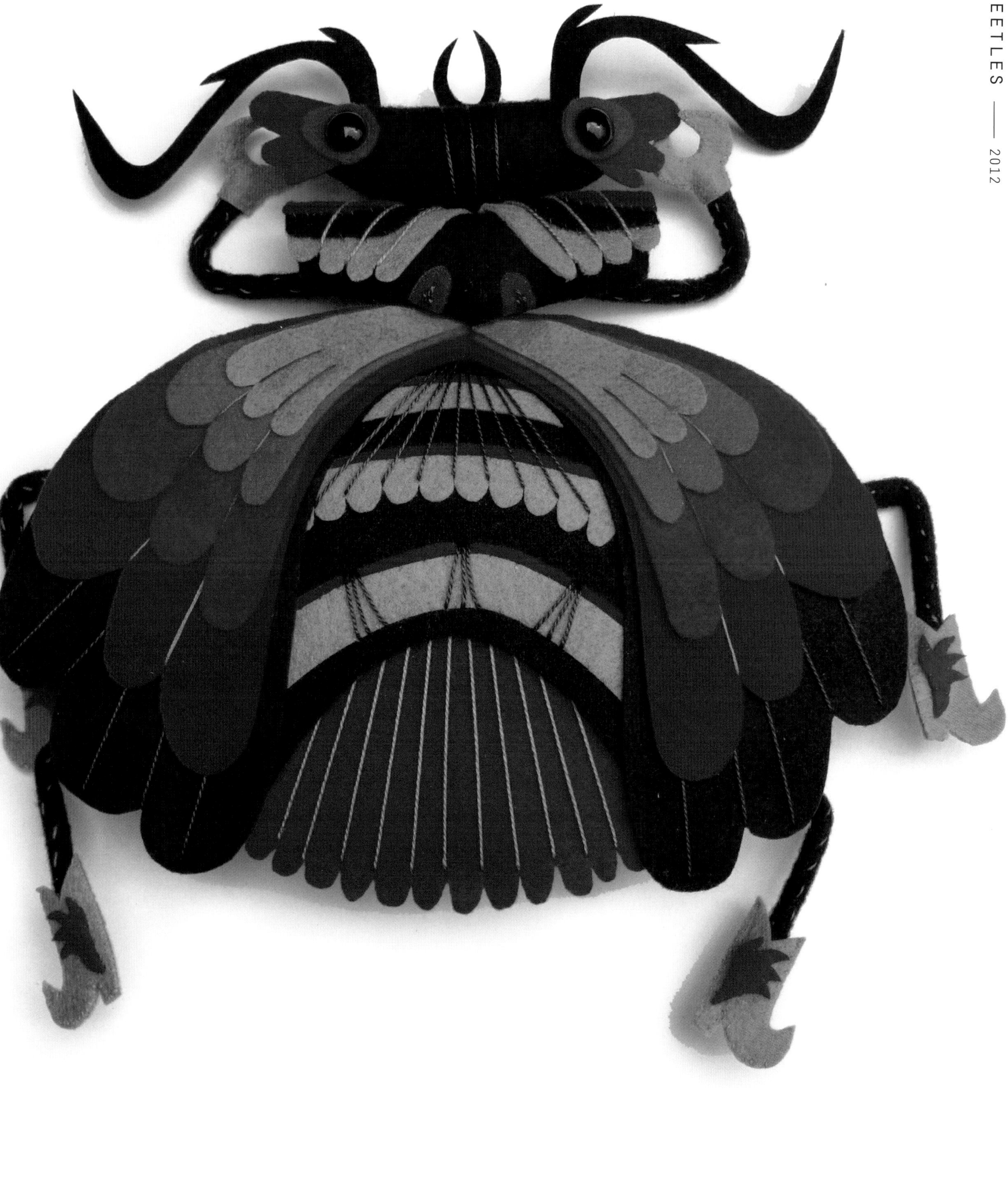

BEETLES — 2012

Left/top
**Grey-tongued Lichen-licking Beetle**
250 mm x 250 mm
(Framed)
Made for "Hey! Who's This Guy?", Nobrow Gallery.
Mixed-fibre felt, embroidery thread, card, wire, and polyester fibre filling. Wooden glass-fronted box frame.

Left/bottom
**Sighing Cyan Serrated Sundown Beetle**
250 mm x 250 mm
(Framed)
Made for "Hey! Who's This Guy?", Nobrow Gallery.
Mixed-fibre felt, embroidery thread, card, wire, and polyester fibre filling. Wooden glass-fronted box frame.

Right/Top
**Heliotrope-headed Honky-tonk Beetle**
250 mm x 250 mm
(Framed)
Made for "Hey! Who's This Guy?", Nobrow Gallery.
Mixed-fibre felt, embroidery thread, card, wire, and polyester fibre filling. Wooden glass-fronted box frame.

Right/Bottom
**Reckless Running Rhomboid Beetle**
250 mm x 250 mm
(Framed)
Made for "Hey! Who's This Guy?", Nobrow Gallery.
Mixed-fibre felt, embroidery thread, card, wire, and polyester fibre filling. Wooden glass-fronted box frame.

Left
**Crimp-frilled Kayamori
Kicking Beetle**
520 mm x 520 mm

Right
**Silver-booted, Midori-winged
Sakurai Beetle**
520 mm x 520 mm

Mixed-fibre felt, embroidery
thread, card, wire, and
polyester fibre filling. Wooden
glass-fronted box frame.

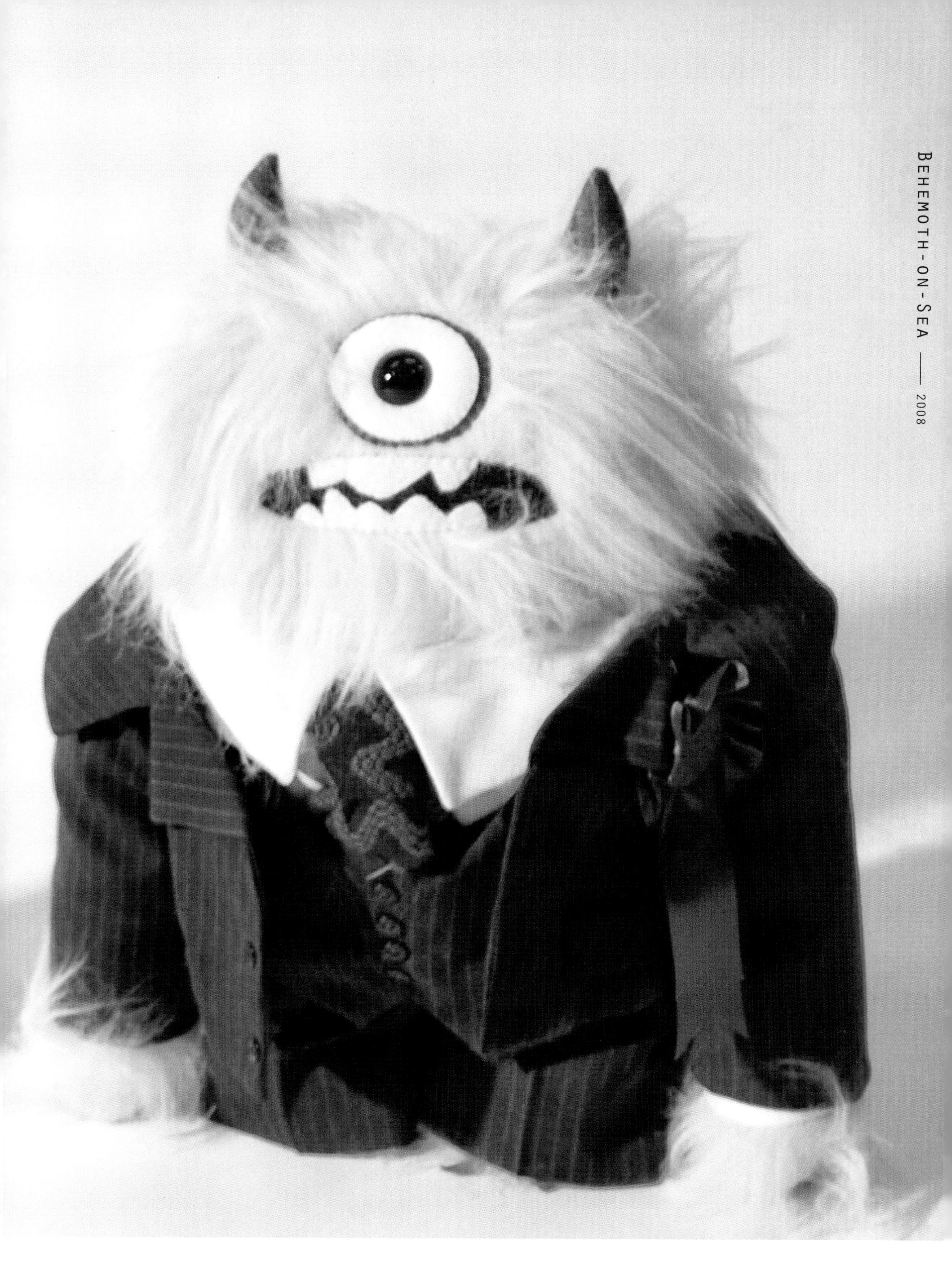

Behemoth-on-Sea — 2008

The candidate with the largest horns in the Behemoth-on-Sea by-Elections. Hugh states his interests as fly-fishing, fly eating and Man at C&A (1972–1981 "The classic years").

**Hugh Scruntin**
350 mm x 190 mm
Party Political candidate for the Behemoth-on-Sea By-Elections.

Hugh wears striped polyester, fully-lined two-buttoned single-breasted suit, welt pockets, trousers with crease line and slight flare and white, cotton, wide-collared shirt with deep cuffs, printed rayon tie with large knot. Satin ribbon rosette. Brushed and plain mixed-fibre felt, plastic safety eyes, card, wire and polyester fibre filling.

The only female candidate in the Behemoth-on-Sea by-Elections.
Lady Jemimarraggh is descended from a long line of Grunks. If voted in, she planned to privatise Bigfoot.

**Lady Jemimarraggh Grunk**
460 mm x 170 mm
Party Political candidate for the Behemoth-on-Sea By-Elections.

Lady J wears white cotton broderie Anglaise blouse with high-neck frilled collar and frilled cuffs. Fully-lined vintage tweed wool box jacket with braid detail and matching lined A-line skirt with back split and braided hemline. Carrying felt, clasped handbag.
Satin Ribbon rosette.
Brushed and plain mixed-fibre felt, plastic safety eyes, card, wire and polyester fibre filling.

The winning candidate in the Behemoth-on-Sea by-Elections. Leonard loves his constituency, cold climates and pies.

Leonard Groyle
300 mm x 300 mm
Party Political candidate for the Behemoth-on-Sea By-Elections.

Leonard wears mixed-fibre single-breasted pinstriped three-piece satin lined suit (unfastened) with wide collar and welt pockets. Trousers with crease line. Satin backed single-breasted waistcoat, white cotton wide-collared shirt and vintage tweed tie. Satin ribbon rosette. Brushed and plain mixed-fibre felt, plastic safety eyes, card, wire and polyester fibre filling.

**Professor Roofle Dwent**
520 mm x 330 mm
Prof. Dwent wears a beige lightweight three-button suit jacket with single vent and welt pockets, brown woollen jumper, brown needlecord straight-legged trousers and bronze oval wire-framed glasses. He carries his pipe.
Mixed fibres, fake fur, felt, plastic safety eyes, card, wire and polyester fibre filling.

Part of the St Grunks' faculty, alongside Wilbur Grumph, Roofle Dwent and Gussy Flenderman. Pumford was voted pipe-smoker of the year at St Grunks' in 2010, and answered the winning question as part of their Eggheads team.
His hobbies include cataloguing dust, pipe modification and brewing his own "real ale" (Pumford's Musty Infusion).

**Dr. Pumford Russett**
750 mm x 350 mm
Dr Pumford Russett wears a brown, striped, three-button sports jacket with single back vent and welt pockets, beige jumbo corduroy straight-legged trousers, white cotton wide-collared shirt, vintage tie and square black-framed glasses. He carries his pipe.
Mixed fibres, fake fur, felt, plastic safety eyes, card, wire and polyester fibre filling.

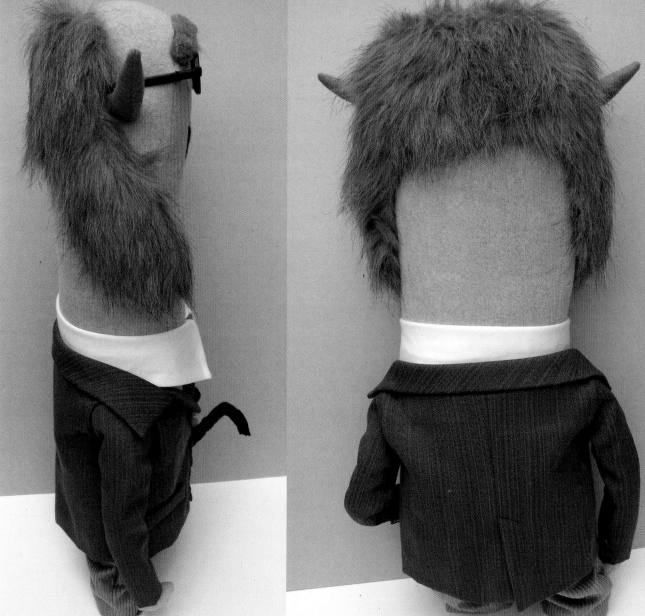

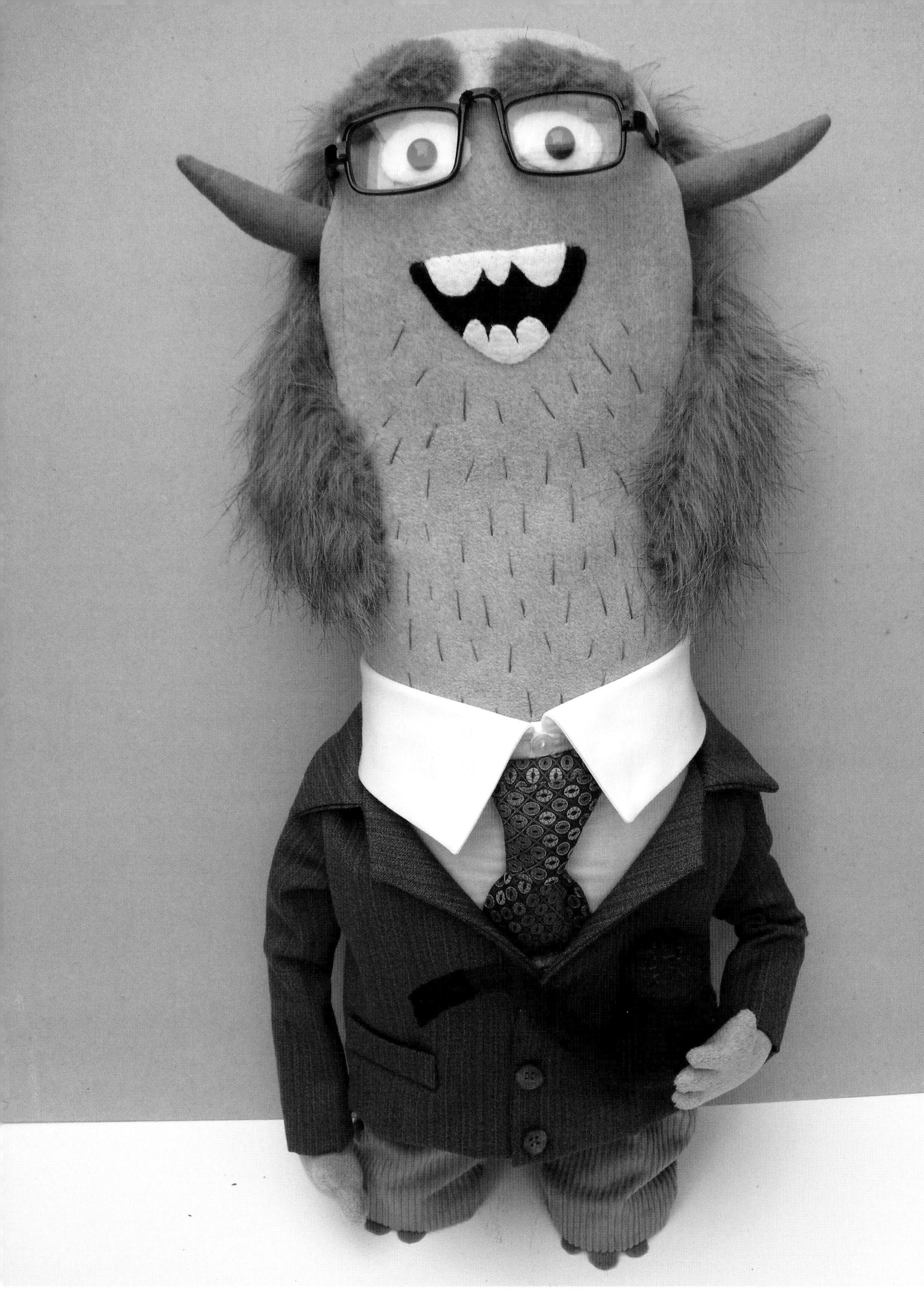

The Boffins/Dr. Pumford Russett —— 2010

Gussy is a professor of Edwardian fungus (specialising in lichen). He also enjoys the music of Steeleye Span and relaxing in a pool of shallow ditchwater.

**Professor Gussy Flenderman**
600 mm x 290 mm
Prof. Gussy Flenderman wears vintage herringbone tweed three-button sports jacket with single back vent and welt pockets, white cotton shirt with vintage tie and dark green needlecord straight-legged trousers.
Mixed fibres, fake fur, felt, plastic safety eyes, card, wire and polyester fibre filling.

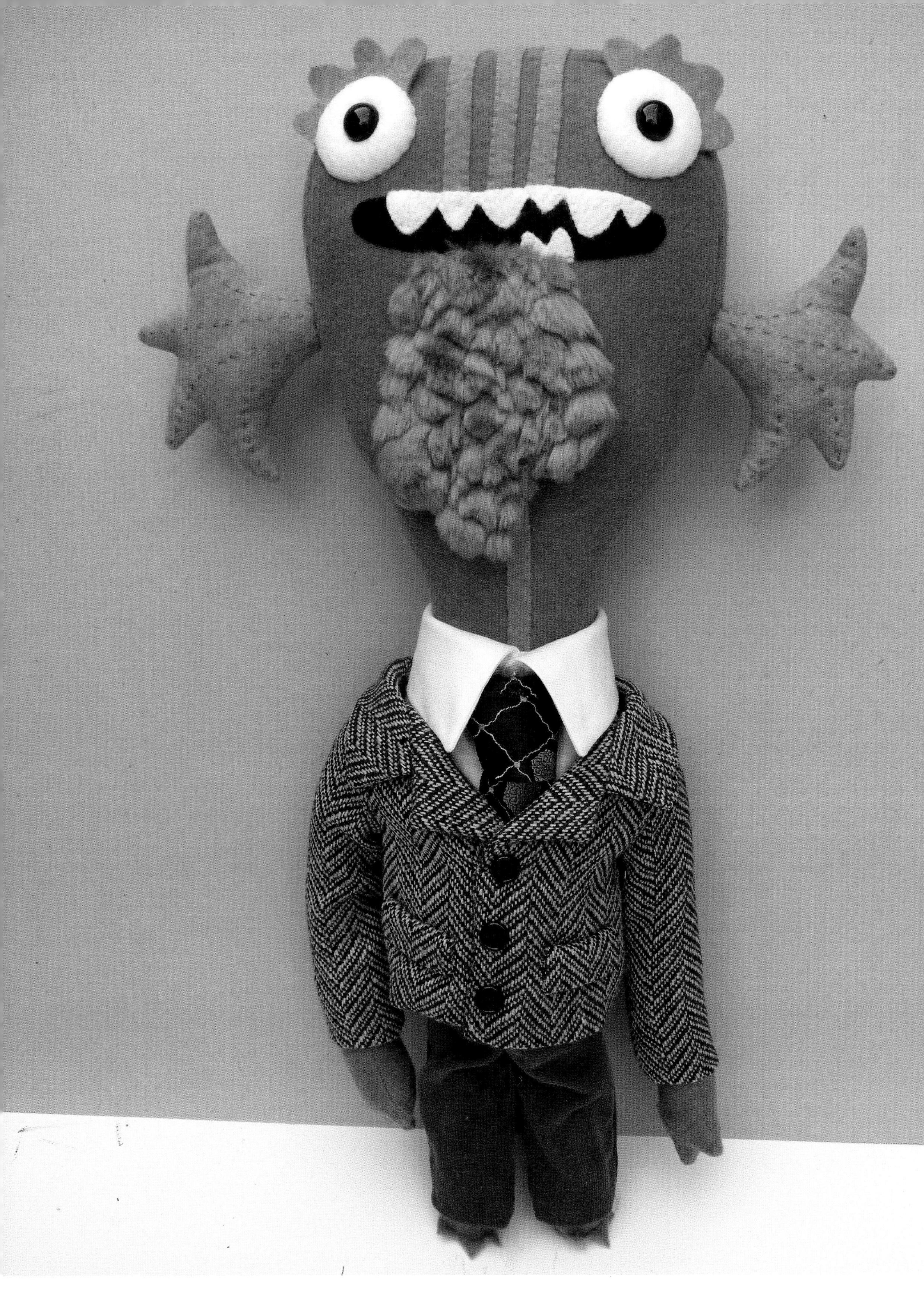

The Boffins/Professor Gussy Flenderman —— 2010

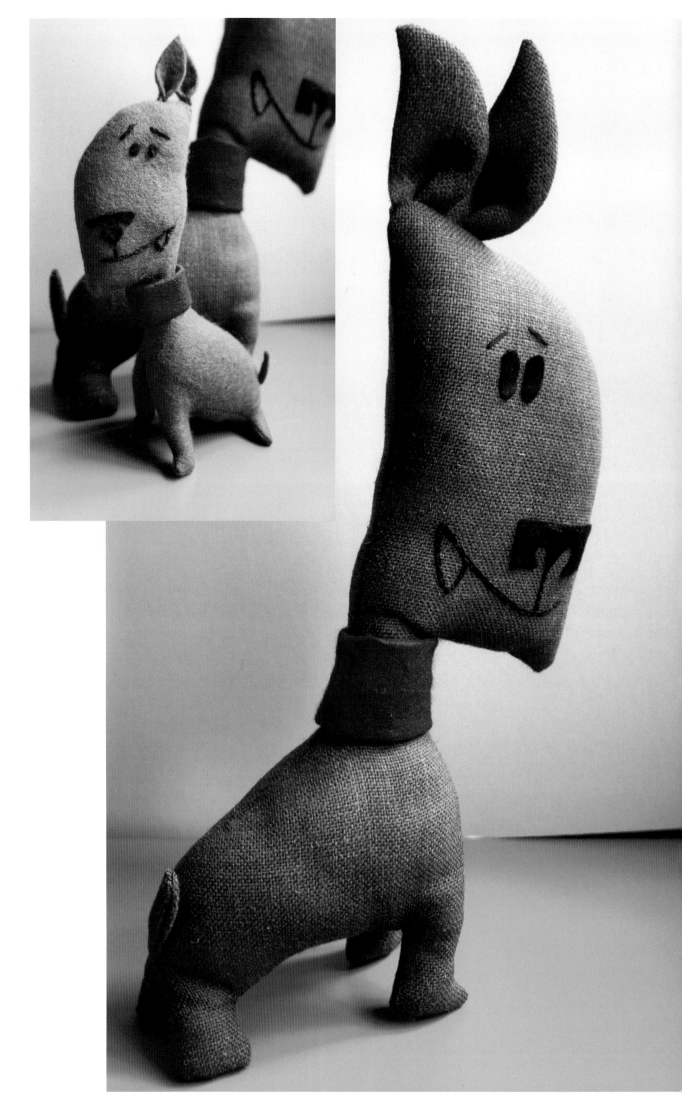

Bongo Lewis, King
of Dogs (large)
280 mm x 180 mm
Large Bongo wears
a scarf of Mixed-
fibre felt.
Vintage brown
wool tweed,
embroidery thread
and polyester fibre
filling.

Bongo Lewis,
King of Dogs
210 mm x 170 mm
Edition of five.
Made as Christmas
presents.
Mixed-fibre felt,
polyester fibre
stuffing and
embroidery
thread.

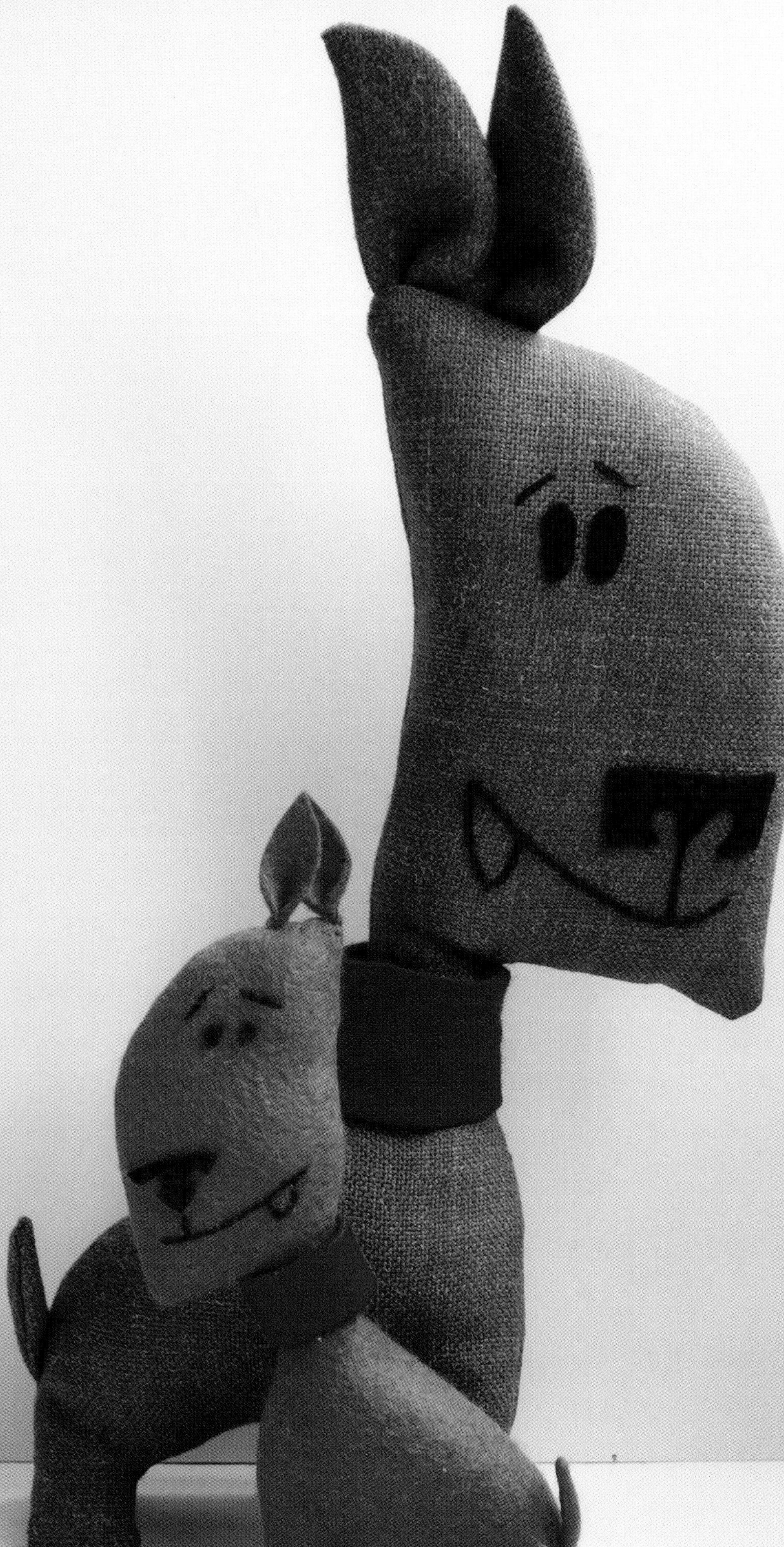

Bongo Lewis, King of Dogs —— 2007/1998

Brunhilde was private schooled in a hollowed out tree trunk by an owl. After leaving the Tree Trunk Academy she spent a number of years living in Tokyo (specifically Harajuku) working as an assistant to a prominent Japanese Yokai, where she developed her love for stripey tights, crepe soles and stag beetles. On returning to her Woodland home she found Little Geoff, her six-legged frug, from whom she is never parted.

### Brunhilde
1000 mm x 300 mm
and **Little Geoff**
150 mm x 180 mm
Brunhilde wears a high-collared printed cotton dress, short puff sleeves, a gathered skirt, nipped-in at the waist with grosgrain ribbon tied in a bow. Her hemline, sleeve edge and collar are trimmed with white rick-rack braiding. A silver metal skull and crossbones decorates the neckline, as well as a neo-prene choker with square studs. She also wears striped knee-length socks and white lace-up brothel creepers. Her undergarments include lace pants and a net petticoat. Geoff wears a leather collar and chain lead. Mixed fibres, felt, fake fur, metal, wire, card, wooden doweling, plastic safety eyes, leather, studs, and polyester fibre filling.

Bunko is Kaiju's country cousin. Kaijus like those crunchy high-rise blocks. They're never happier than when they're stomping around Tokyo or Osaka, biting clumps out of the buildings of Aoyama or slurping water under Rainbow bridge.

Bunko likes the chewy trees.

**Bunko**
260 mm x 300 mm
Edition of fifteen.
Black body and contrasting horns with details in either orange, yellow, red or green.
Polyester fleece with Mixed-fibre felt details, plastic safety eyes and polyester fibre filling.

**Bunko**
260 mm x 300 mm
Edition of fifteen.
Black body and contrasting
horns with details in
orange, yellow, red or
green.
Polyester fleece with
Mixed-fibre felt details,
plastic safety eyes and
polyester fibre filling.

**Arctic Bunko**
260 mm x 300 mm
Edition of six.
Cream version of Bunko
with details in turquoise
and grey.
Polyester fleece with
Mixed-fibre felt details,
plastic safety eyes and
polyester fibre filling.

# JON BURGERMAN

When I lived in Nottingham, Louise and Jonathan would come when they'd be passing through. We'd meet up and have tea and cakes and things and we became friends. It just seemed very natural to suggest a collaboration with Felt Mistress, it made sense to do it. I can't remember, really, it being a big deal. I wasn't taking a risk asking this person about doing something, but asking a friend if they wanted to experiment doing something. I was very clear from the outset that if we were to work together it wouldn't be me, drawing and saying, "right, do exactly what I say to turn this into..." it was more like "This is my idea for a character that could work, what do you think?" It was very much a collaboration, and not a production job. I wanted to work with her, not have her work for me. It turned out really well, so we started doing a whole bunch of projects together.

The first few ones we did were straight characters reinterpreted into the magic of felt, and I think maybe my favourite ones she did were the Brooklyn Hipsters. They were phenomenal because for the clothing on the characters, she'd cut up shirts and jackets and denim to dress the characters in. They looked fantastic, they had sneakers on and lots of little details. Once we'd done that – and as is my practise – I didn't want to do the same things again. So we wanted to keep working together but on different things. Obviously Louise is amazing at making things, so I wanted to try and do something that we were not quite sure whether it will be amazing or even whether it will work. That's just how I am. If I know I can do something then I don't want to do it. It may be a little perverse but otherwise it's just milking a winning formula.

As we started to work together and do more stuff, Louise started to do similar things with other artists. From my perspective, we should be doing something more specific to our relationship, what I do and what she does, rather than just reinterpreting someone's character into felt.

I had an exhibition called Brain Drain in Winchester, it was still going to be character-centred but was based on a more sculptural idea: how can we make something out of felt as an object that echoes the intertwined lines and features that my 2D drawings have. How can we interpret that? That was the challenge. So that was the first time we made something a little weirder than just a character. That worked pretty well. That was the three eyed bunny. We changed the colour palette as well. I made three pieces of work and then we took some of the key characters from those artworks and we turned them into sculpture. There was a relationship between those things instead of just making mascots of the characters in my work. I wanted to make a piece of work and there was a distinct difference between those two things.

Jim & Jon Anxieteam
Hand Puppets
400 mm x 230 mm
Made for Anxieteam
Music Video.

John carries a microphone and
Jim a Ukulele.
Mixed fibres, felt, card,
embroidery thread and
polyester fibre filling.

Seeing what Louise could do opened up all these opportunities. All of a sudden you've acquired a new brain to work with, to harness for your own doings. So when we worked together we could skill-share and I had the power of Louise. And as you know, with great power comes great responsibility not to misuse that power... which is tempting to do! It meant I could start to have these things in exhibitions to make serious works – as serious as my work could be, I guess – opening up avenues to making stuff in three dimensions. I had dabbled in this before with little sculptures and, to a lesser extent, with the toys that I made with companies like Kidrobot, taking my work and turning it into something three dimensional. I had-made a few things before with other people, with expanded polystyrene and resin, things like that.

So I was able to further explore the third dimension in a different medium. Felt has a charm of its own and my work seemed to suit it. In a strange kind of way, when I work in more solid material it's almost too solid, the lines are too clean, the nature of it is too perfectly sculpted, whereas with the felt I think one of the qualities I like about that material is that it goes out of shape. You can squeeze it a little and it will remember, like memory foam, it can be dented and punctured, you can see where your hand has pressed against it. It's not geometrically super clean. Much like my linework isn't smooth, it's not symmetrical, there are no straight lines. Everything's handmade, everything's a little bobbly and wobbly. The felt reproduces that really nicely.

The frustration I have working in 3D is that my work is line based. I draw lines. There's something this side of the line and something that side of the line and that's it. But with an object you can move around it. I can't dictate exactly how the viewer is going to see it. So it's nice to have those seams and those shapes that are cut which still have that quality I have in my linework. I've had to learn to adapt, to a degree, in going 3D. It's not a one-to-one reproduction. The idea of the work has to translate and then it becomes something different. My sensibilities of working are reproduced in the object. It isn't a 3D version of a 2D drawing, it's something else.

Tickler
Collaboration with
Jon Burgerman
Made for Jon's show "I Can't Sit Still"
700 mm x 330 mm
Editon of two.
Mixed-fibre felt, card, wire and polyester fibre filling.

Luke
Collaboration with
Jon Burgerman
Made for Jon's show "I Can't Sit Still"
580 mm x 500 mm
Edition of two.
Mixed-fibre felt, card, wire, and polyester fibre filling.

Sprouthead
Collaboration with
Jon Burgerman
Made for Jon's show "I Can't Sit Still"
600 mm x 250 mm
Edition of three.
Mixed-fibre felt, card, wire and polyester fibre filling.

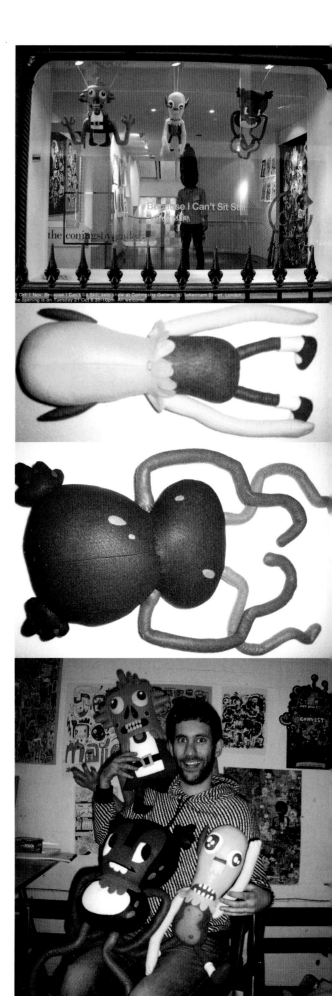

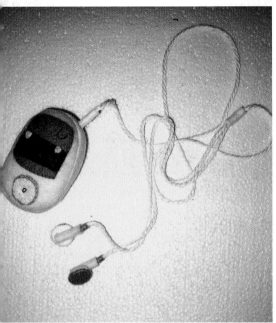

**Enchanter of
Mushrooms, Lover of No
One**
Collaboration with
Jon Burgerman
700 mm x 450 mm
Made for Jon's show
"Brain Drain", Winchester.
Mixed-fibre felt,
embroidery thread, card
and polyester fibre filling.

**Three-Eyed, Two-Faced
Rabbit**
Collaboration with
Jon Burgerman
550 mm x 350 mm
Made for Jon's show
"Brain Drain", Winchester.
Mixed-fibre felt,
embroidery thread, card
and polyester fibre filling.

**Aubodo Burger**
Collaboration with
Jon Burgerman
800 mm x 500 mm
Made for Jon's show
"Fast Food",
Sergeant Paper, Paris.
Mixed-fibre felt,
embroidery thread,
card, and polyester fibre
filling.

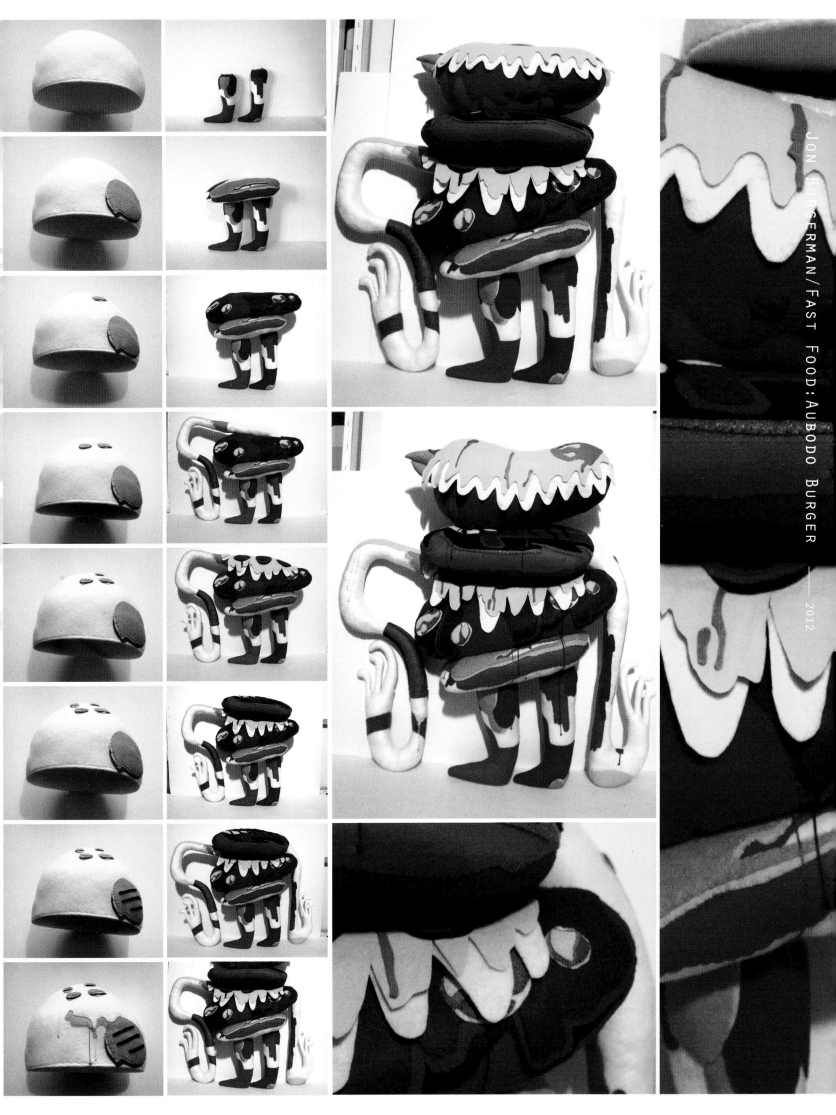

You have an idea of what you want to make and you get to a certain point in the process and the idea gets superseded by the progress of the thing you set out to make. This is what I find in my paintings and drawings. I start out with a concept and then through making it, that thing develops and begins to take on a life of its own. So with Louise, I supply her flat drawings and instructions, "this could look like this and the hand could rotate like that..." and then she will scribble on it and send it back saying "this could be attached like this and this might be a good idea there". I'm always very keen for her to ignore my suggestions and come up with better things because I don't know her material as well as she does, so there may be better solutions or something more fun to do with the material. Through that process the thing becomes something in its own right. By its nature, it becomes 3D and you begin to forget about the original plans and start tweaking and finalising, concentrating on the thing that it actually is.

Much like when people have children, they have wonderful ideas about how their kids are going to do this and that, and when the kid actually arrives and starts evolving its own personality and its own thoughts about what it wants to do, you realise that the kid's not going to be an artist like their dad, they actually want to become a maths teacher. And you can encourage them down that route or start resenting them, not calling them on their birthdays... Anyway, I don't know if that analogy really works, but the creations begin to take on their own lives and it's about supporting it and pushing it and trying to make it the best version of the thing that it now is.

**Aubodo Burger**
Collaboration with
Jon Burgerman
800 mm x 500 mm
Made for Jon's show "Fast Food", Sergeant Paper, Paris.
Mixed-fibre felt, embroidery thread, card, and polyester fibre filling.

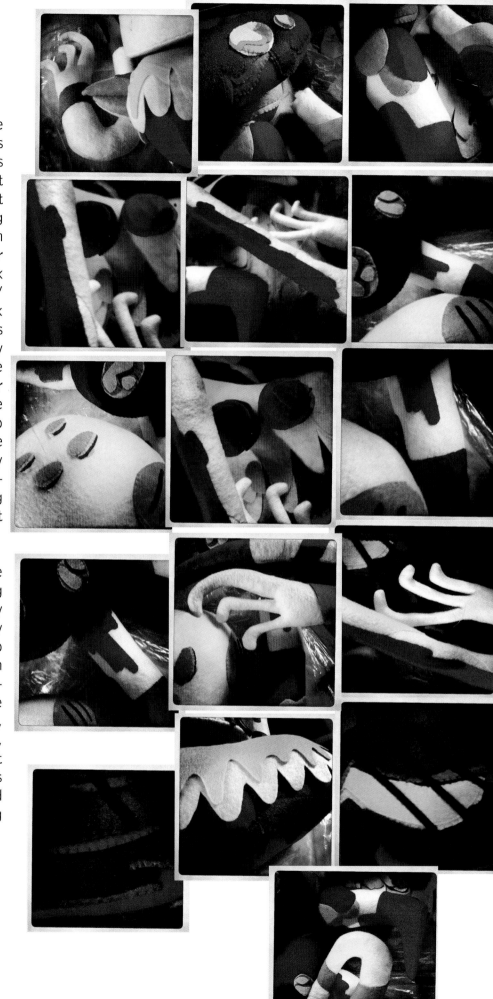

JON BURGERMAN / FAST FOOD : AUBODO BURGER —— 2012

"My American Summer"
Seven pieces made in
Collaboration with Jon
Burgerman for his show
at Giant Robot NYC
2009.

An illustrator is given a brief, draw a pig on a trampoline, and if they don't draw that pig on a trampoline they've failed the brief, whereas this is an art collaboration - or that's how I see it. The idea might start off, let's create this object of a three-eyed rabbit, this is how I think it looks in 2D but let's work out how it could look in 3D. What will happen with it? Does it stand up like this? Should the head be like that? What colours? How are we going to do the tail? Should it be stitched on top, should it be flat? Shall we paint on the fabric? And then it starts to change. The materials play their part in defining it. Why am I not making it out of marble? Why am I not making it out of custard? Why felt? Why stitch these details in this way.

I think that even if you don't know it at the time we make little micro decisions along the way about all these aspects that build up to making the piece. That's what artists do. And that's why you want to work with people that you trust to make decisions. You're not standing over someone saying 'stitch it like that' or 'cut it like this'. So without necessarily knowing it, Louise is making decisions about how this bit curves more than that bit.

It's got to be pleasing for both of us, or we wouldn't work together again. There is also an issue of ownership of it as well, because you're making it for the love of making it, that's why most people make stuff. If you sell the pieces and they go on to earn money in another way that's all well and good but it's certainly not why I set out to make these things. Who would buy a three-eyed rabbit with two faces? It'll scare people under the guise of being a soft cuddly toy.

Showing my work in 3D has allowed people to see another side to it. It opens the doors for more. You don't really know what you can do till you try something and it either works or it doesn't, then you know more for next time. Each project has been an experiment for the next one. For both of us, hopefully. I would like to think that working with me has given Louise ideas for other stuff she would do with or without me. Maybe she hadn't considered making something in the way that we make something together. And that will help inform future collaborations for her, or for her own work.

**Mickey**
Collaboration with Jon Burgerman
450 mm x 270 mm
Mickey wears white vest top, faded blue denim jeans. Red baseball shoes, sweatband and red neckscarf. Sunglasses.
Mixed fibres, felt, card, embroidery thread, plastic and polyester fibre filling.

**Grrf**
Collaboration with Jon Burgerman
320 mm x 200 mm
Grrf wears diamond-patterned hand knitted tunic.
Mixed fibres, felt, card, and polyester fibre filling.

**Brott**
Collaboration with Jon Burgerman
320 mm x 170 mm
Brott wears yellow vest top, cropped grey sweatpants, belt and vintage buckle and a fake leather flight jacket with brown trim.
Mixed fibres, felt, card, and polyester fibre filling.

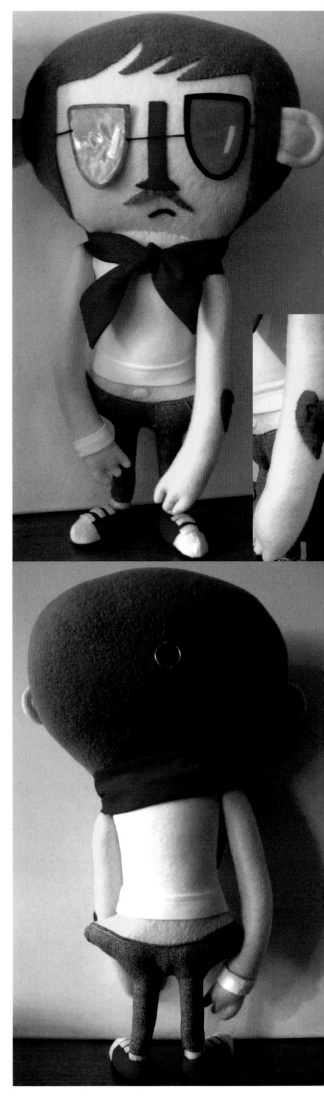

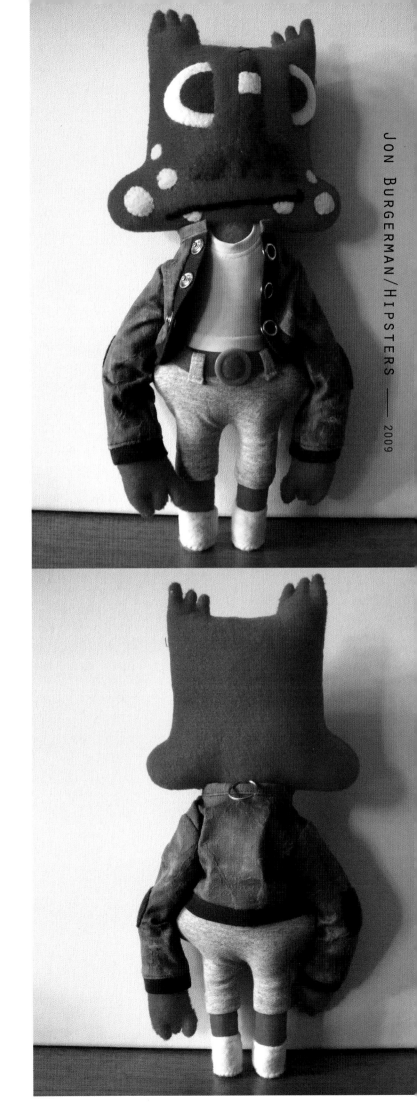

The Aubudo Burger is like the prog rock opera of our collaboration so far. Really trying to push it, over the top, the thread, the stitching, make that more of a feature. I was trying to make it as painty as possible, make it gooey, even though it's dry and soft. I tried to suggest things with the material, to see how that would work. And it was super colourful. Louise was open to that, to ideas about what could be done. She works very fast as well. I like to work fast. It's exciting to see quick results when you're working on stuff together.

We haven't done it yet but we were thinking of me painting on the fabric, sending it back to her and Louise being able to cut it up and so there's a closer relation with the brushstrokes and mark making on top of the object. I'm not sure whether it will work at all. To further blur the boundaries of flat 2D drawing, painting, which is where I'm coming from, and her making things with textiles, which is where she comes from, trying to smudge that boundary even further. I have lots and lots of ideas but now that she's a superstar it's difficult to get hold of her. I have to speak to her through Jonathan and see if she's available. No, I'm joking, that's what we were playing around with at the beginning of the year and that's what I'd like to do. I'd like to get felt, or other fabrics, printed up and painted on and then give them to her to reassemble. That's what I would like.

I'm really pleased to have worked with Louise, I hope we can keep working together. I'm always excited to see what she's making. It would be completely selfish and ridiculous to not want her to work with other people. I was very humbled actually, Pete Fowler was on the radio talking about the music video that he and Louise made. He mentioned that the collaboration between the two of us was something that he saw, that gave him the idea to talk to Louise about working together. So that's incredibly flattering. I'm a big fan of Pete's work. They made a music video, that's brilliant!

I am very pleased that Louise has now had her own show ("Hey! Who's This Guy?"). The collaborations are excellent but she totally should do her own things as well, it's great seeing her work with Jonathan and what she's done for her show is fantastic. So, the more the merrier, really. As long as she doesn't forget about me!

Joshua
Collaboration with
Jon Burgerman
320 mm x 180 mm
Joshua wears pink top
with two-button detail at
neckline and white piping.
Mixed fibres, felt, card,
and polyester fibre filling.

Randel
Collaboration with Jon Burgerman
450 mm x 180 mm
Randel wears black and white
slashed-neck t-shirt, narrow-
legged indigo denim jeans, red
baseball shoes and a blue jacket
with red sleeves (varsity style).
Mixed fibres, felt, card, and
polyester fibre filling.

Hammel
Collaboration with
Jon Burgerman
320 mm x 170 mm
Hammel wears white
t-shirt with pink detail and
appliqued felt letter. Faded
blue denim jeans, knitted
blue acrylic cardigan.
Mixed fibres, felt, card,
and polyester fibre filling.

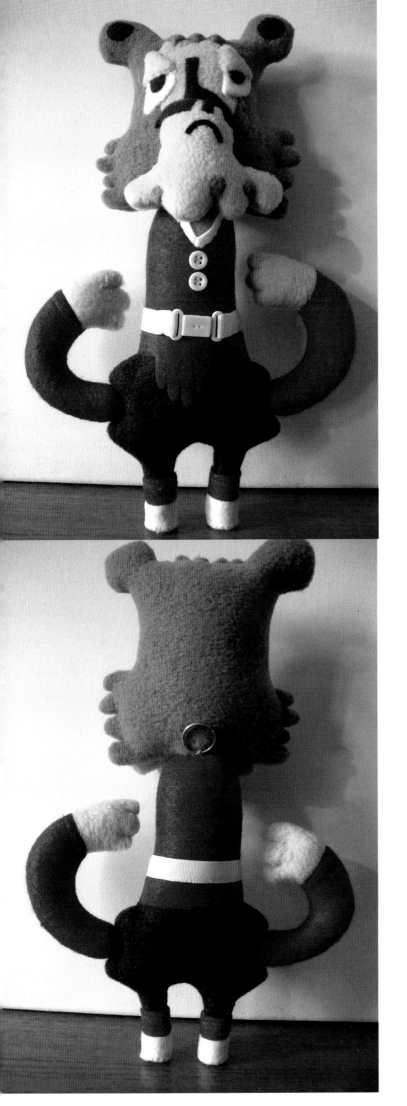

**K8ty**
collaboration with Jon Burgerman
450 mm x 200 mm
K8ty wears pink headband, white
vest top, ribbon belt with vintage
buckle. Short denim skirt, leg
warmers and pink-heeled boots.
Vintage button necklace and
plastic bracelets and bangles.
Mixed fibres, felt, card, plastic,
and polyester fibre filling.

"Lossy Botany Lab",
15 pieces made in
collaboration with
Jon Burgerman for
Heliumcowboy Gallery,
Hamburg, Germany.

Far left / 1

**Aubergine Genie**

Collaboration with Jon Burgerman

170 mm x 120 mm

Made for Jon's show "Lossy Botany Lab", Hamburg, Germany.

Mixed-fibre felt, embroidery thread, card, and polyester fibre filling.

Far left / 2

**Aubergine with Maggot**

250 mm x 180 mm

Mixed-fibre felt, embroidery thread, card, and polyester fibre filling.

Far left / 3

**Wild Onion**

Collaboration with Jon Burgerman

150 mm x 100 mm

Mixed-fibre felt, embroidery thread, card, and polyester fibre filling.

Far left / 4

**Chilli Baby**

200 mm x 60 mm

Edition of two.

Mixed-fibre felt, embroidery thread, card, and polyester fibre filling.

Far left / 5

**The Last Pear in the World**

150 mm x 120 mm

Mixed-fibre felt, embroidery thread, card, and polyester fibre filling.

Far left / 6

**Spotted Lemon**

120 mm x 100 mm

Mixed-fibre felt, embroidery thread, card, and polyester fibre filling.

Far left / 7

**Pea Pods (Sad, Sad, Happy)**

120 mm x 70 mm

Edition of three.

Mixed-fibre felt, embroidery thread, card, and polyester fibre filling.

Left

**Helmot Cirsium (Woodland Mushroom)**

550 mm x 200 mm

Mixed-fibre felt, embroidery thread, card, terracotta plant pot and polyester fibre filling.

Right

**Doodlichos Aipen (Charinky)**

770 mm x 450 mm

Mixed-fibre felt, embroidery thread, card, terracotta plant pot and polyester fibre filling.

1, 2

3

4

5

6

7

Far left
**Headlenium Armarummy
(Bitter Sneezeweed)**
Collaboration with
Jon Burgerman
600 mm x 260 mm
Mixed-fibre felt,
embroidery thread, card,
terracotta plant pot and
polyester fibre filling.

Left
**Laciniaria Punctata
(Lion Root)**
Collaboration with
Jon Burgerman
800 mm x 270 mm
Mixed-fibre felt,
embroidery thread, card,
wire, terracotta plant pot
and polyester fibre filling.

Right
**Bignoniodes Snapla
(Diggut Biter)**
Collaboration with
Jon Burgerman
350 mm x 200 mm
Mixed-fibre felt,
embroidery thread, card,
terracotta plant pot and
polyester fibre filling.

Piccalilicus and
the Magical Cardy of
Wonder and
Wonderment
400 mm x 170 mm
Collaboration with
Jon Burgerman
Made for Art Basel, Miami.

Piccalilicus wears a
diagonal, patterned knitted
cardigan, and woollen
pink and blue patterned
legwarmers, with pink
shoes. He also has his own
boombox.
Mixed fibres, wool, felt,
card, and polyester fibre
filling.

**Fawkward**
Collaboration with
Jon Burgerman
250 mm x 180 mm
Mixed fibres, felt, card,
embroidery thread and
polyester fibre filling.

**Pickle Pig**
Collaboration with
Jon Burgerman
230 mm x 400 mm
Edition of four.
Mixed fibres, felt, card,
embroidery thread and
polyester fibre filling.

The fuliginous sidekick of Inspector Cumulus. His pleasant demeanour (and slight nutty flavour with vanilla undertones) has made him a very well respected figure on the police force.

**Charlie Pipe Smoke**
150 mm x 220 mm
Edition of three.
Felt pipe with removable 'smoke' cloud.
Mixed-fibre felt, velcro, embroidery thread and polyester fibre filling.

Choux Choux likes
Haberdashery and
Elektroclash.

**Choux Choux**
200 mm x 160 mm
Winner of the Momiji
Couture Competition,
shown at Royal Tea, Los
Angeles, USA.
Silk, mixed-fibre fleece and
felt, embroidery thread,
vintage buttons and beads,
ribbons, card and polyester
fibre filling.

Hello Louise

Thank you so much for creating Choux Choux
and entering our Couture Contest. We had
over 100 entries and the love, skill and
creativity shown in each one was amazing.

"Stunning. The dress could have been
made by Preen. The hair and
button detailing is incredible."
Pip McCormac
The Sunday Times, Style Magazine

"Professional. Gorgeous. Love her
little heart."
Barbara Hulanicki

We are delighted to tell you that Choux Choux
was judged to be the Winner of the contest —
so congratulations! As you know we've sent
the Top 20 dolls to LA where they'll be on
display at Royal/T until January 18 and no
doubt having lots fun!

The winner, runners-up and highly
commended entries will be announced on the
Momiji website on Sunday 20 December, so be
sure to check it out for a full run down of the
Top 20.

**Clayton**
150 mm x 300 mm
Edition of two.
Vintage tweed, mixed-fibre felt, plastic safety eyes, satin ribbon and polyester fibre filling.

Clem has a furry hat (a present from a Russian aunt), a knitted tank top and an allotment. He also makes an exemplary cup of tea.

**Clem**
610 mm x 200 mm
Clem wears a patterned, knitted v-neck tank top and a furry Russian-style hat with matching boots.
Mixed fibres, fake fur, fleece, felt, plastic safety eyes and polyester fibre filling.

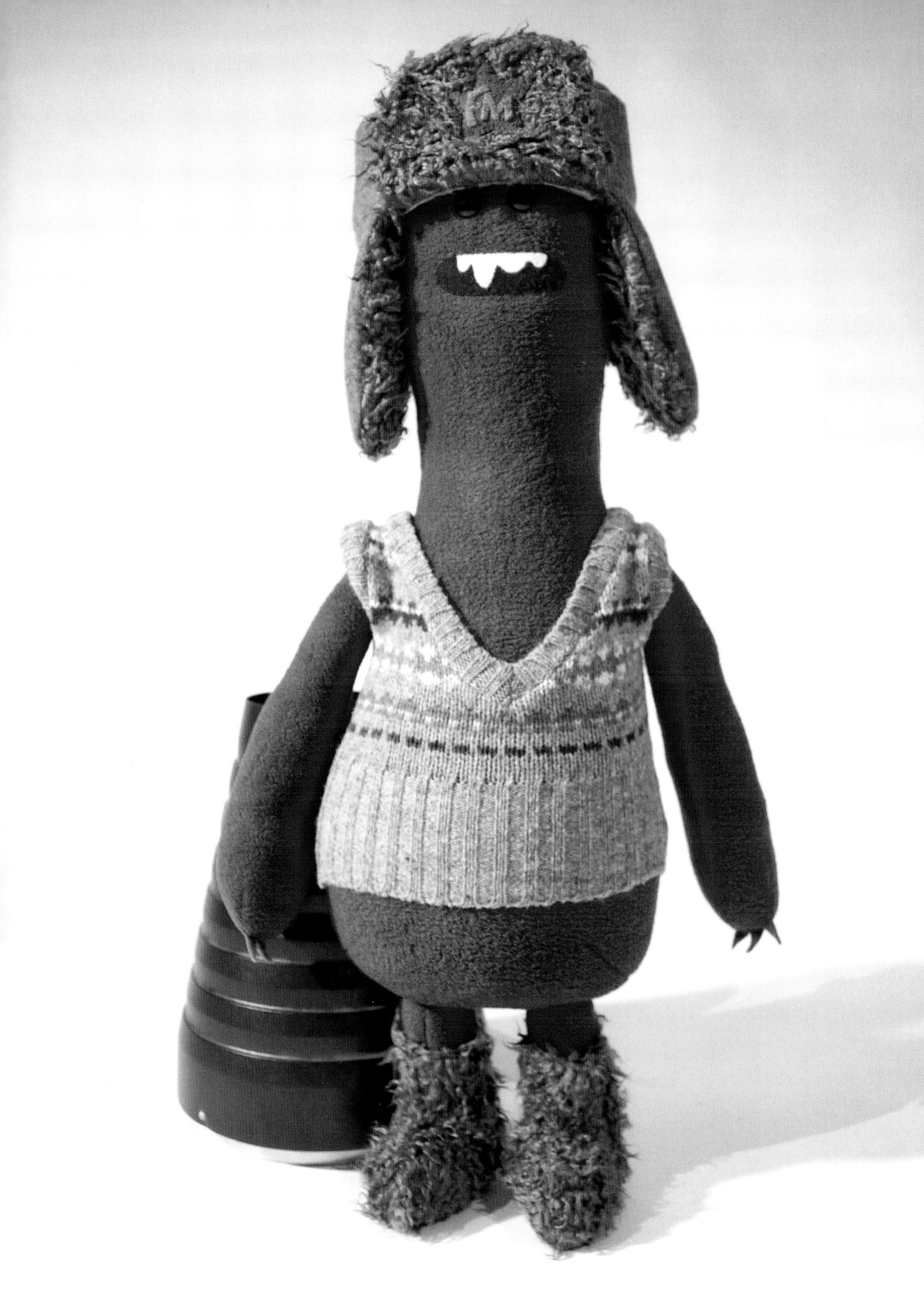


CLEM —— 2010

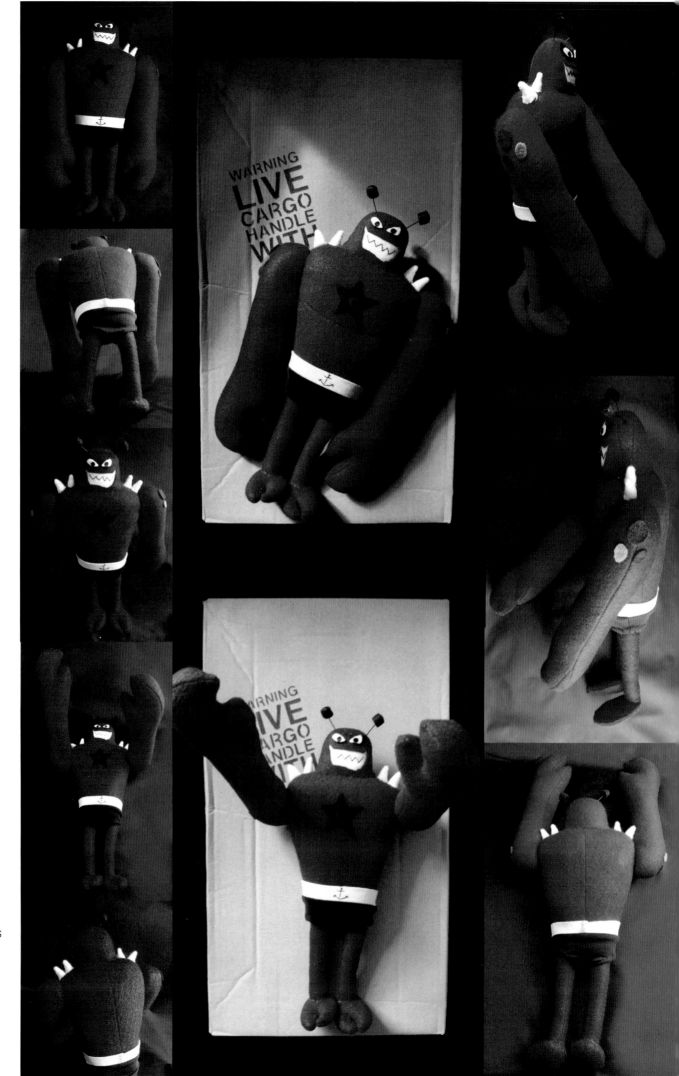

**Crabula**
Designed by Craig Conlan
300 mm x 190 mm
Made as a present.
Crabula wears black pants
with white trim and
anchor embroidery.
Mixed-fibre felt, cotton
lycra, polyester fibre
filling, wire and
embroidery thread.

Myopic Yeti. Voted
"Himalayan Pipe Smoker
of the Year, 2010".

Demetri
500 mm x 320 mm
Made for Pictoplasma's
"Missing Link", Berlin,
Germany.

Demetri wears indigo
denim jeans with double
turn-up and leather belt.
He smokes a pipe.
Mixed fibres, fake fur, felt,
plastic safety eyes, wire,
card and polyester fibre
filling.

Dwight owns and operates his own auto-repair business. He likes monster trucks and "purdy ladies".

**Dwight Klugg**
620 mm x 350 mm
Dwight wears FM trucker cap and black padded body warmer with red trim and embroidered patch.
Mixed fibres, fleece, felt, plastic safety eyes, polyester wadding and polyester fibre filling.

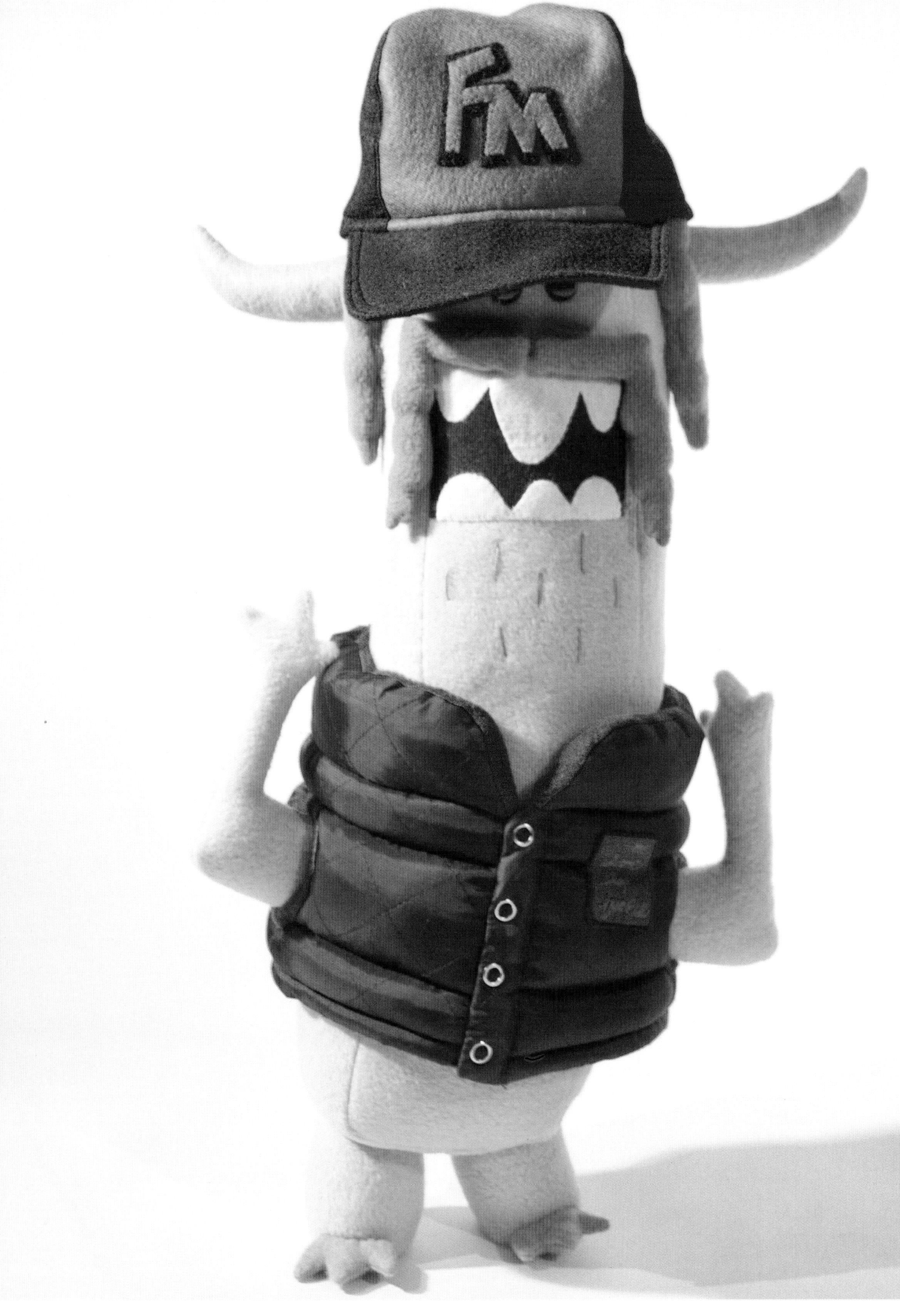


DWIGHT KLUGG —— 2010

Artist, poet, novelist and "nocturnal romantic". Edwin's band, The Decadent Prosimians, split acrimoniously after differences arising over styling mousse in 2005. Since the split Edwin has concentrated on his literary career. He can often be found in his local graveyard communing with restless spirits and the old lady who walks her Yorkshire terrier past his favourite bench every morning.
He enjoys necromancy, Scrabble and tinned aubergines intended for the harvest festival.

**Edwin Crepuscule Flenk**
900 mm x 330 mm
Made for a Halloween Show, Kidrobot, London.

Edwin wears skinny black jeans with turn-ups, white cotton button-down collared shirt, wide cuffs with vintage button cuff links and ribbon bow at neck, and a double-breasted black pea coat with welt pockets and single back vent. He smokes a cigarette.
Mixed fibres, fake fur, felt, plastic safety eyes, wire, card and polyester fibre filling.

Elspeth Frond is one of the world's leading horned models. She rose to prominence after winning America's Next Top Monster and has since modelled for the likes of Alexander McScream, Louis Screechon and Jean-Paul Gruntier.

**Elspeth Frond**
710 mm x 160 mm
Elspeth wears a black, silk organza dress with layered circle skirt and neck frill, black high-heeled knee-length boots with cuff.
Undergarments:
lace pants.
Mixed fibres, fleece, felt, beads and polyester fibre filling.

Elspeth Frond
710 mm x 160 mm

After seeing the success of his brother the Peacock Wrangler's peacock wrangling business, the Flamingo Wrangler started wrangling Flamingos with a similar ferocity.
You go, Flamingo Wrangler!

**Flamingo Wrangler**
950 mm x 330 mm
Mixed fibres, fleece, felt, plastic safety eyes and polyester fibre filling.

# PETE FOWLER

I first came across McFelty, aka FM, aka, Louise Evans, I think through Jon Burgerman, through the collaboration of her helping him make his soft stuff. I saw that and thought 'Wow! This is amazing.' I followed her on Twitter, and then the Clinic video came up and I asked if she fancied making some puppets. I don't think she had made hand puppets before, so that was my 'in', really, being a bit cheeky. Being a bit of a cheeky scamp.

Clinic is a band I always loved. To be asked by a band, you've always loved, to do something for them is a really big deal. It was like going back to what I did with Super Furry Animals. They wanted animation, but they had almost no money for it. So I thought there was no way there was going to be animation, how can I make this video and have loads of fun making it and not stress about it?

I was watching things on YouTube, I am a big fan of Sid and Marty Kroft ("HR Pufnstuf", "Sigmund the Sea Monster" and all that), and thought the whole puppet thing...that would be brilliant, I wonder if Louise would be into this? Amazingly, she was, and it went from there really. There was very little money involved, but Louise is someone I really respect and love, and her agreeing to do it for cost, really, was amazing. I was incredibly grateful for her involvement. She made that. She made that video, I think. I had the ridiculously misguided idea of thinking "oh yeah, I can make puppets." No, I can't make puppets...and I was going to have to spend a couple of years to get to that point. So I was eternally grateful that she got involved and did some amazing work.

I designed all the Illustrator files. I started with drawings, and asked Louise "is this possible, can you make these?" I didn't want to compromise my ideas for the puppets but I knew there were budgetary limitations and time limitations and all these things to be factored in. So I started off with the sketches. I showed her and she said "Yeah, I can do that." And I went on to the colour Illustrator artwork. She took what I did and just took it somewhere else, in a brilliant way.

I think when there's money involved with projects you can start calling the shots, but when there's not a lot of money involved in projects...and I've been on the other end of that...I understand you have things in your head of how you want it to look, but unless you're paying for it, there's only so far you can call the shots. It's a shared creative thing.

Louise brought them to life—and then some—and just kind of went off on it. She was brilliant to work with, we had a very nice dialogue going on between us. I could say to her, "these are my plans, and if you think there is anything that needs changing, or you think you could improve on, from your expertise of making, of working in the medium, go for it." I wanted to give her room to have fun. That was my whole ethos for the project. I didn't want to be stressed out with it. There was hardly any money for anyone involved, so I wanted her to have fun.

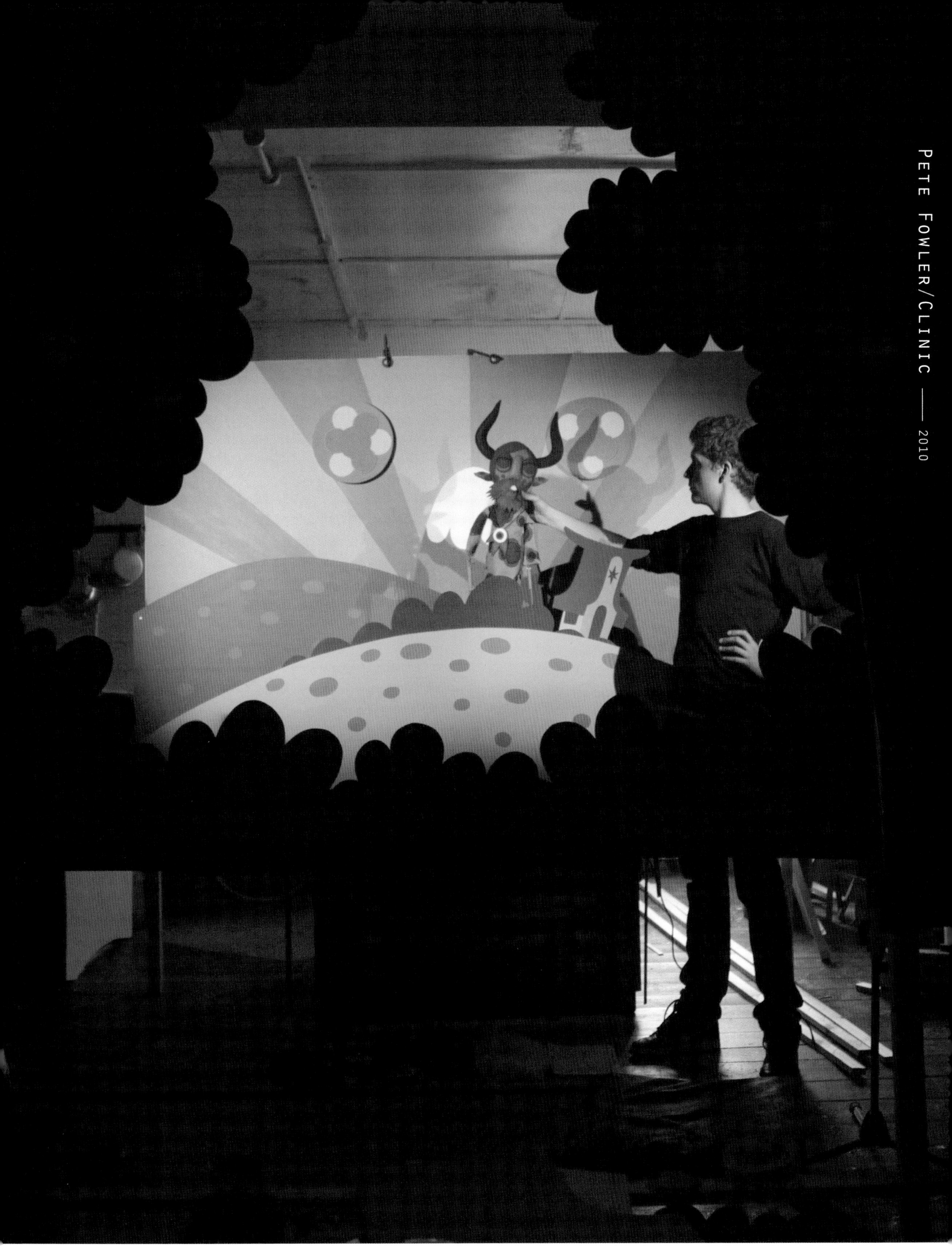

Felt Mistress: Creature Couture

I've had prototypes made of potential soft toys over the years and they were not really that great. Louise is clearly incredibly proficient and confident in what she does, she clearly thinks in fabric and stitching... she really visualises things. This is by no means derogatory, but they had a hand-made quality about them, but were really well done.

The whole concept of the video was almost like a kids' show, but made by adults, sort of a little bit weird, a little bit hippy, commune. It was a little bit odd and these puppets were created to explain what a vision quest is, to explain what a visionary journey is, to spiritually take you to a higher state to add something to your community, to its knowledge, wisdom, whatever... so I kind of wanted it to have that feel, but I didn't really tell Louise. I didn't brief her in that way because I knew her work, and it did have that really beautiful hand-made vibe. She doesn't have a factory to make these things, they are all custom-made, from the heart. And that's where I've always perceived Louise's stuff is. She has genuine passion (and passion is an over-used word) but she has genuine passion for what she does and I felt that was something I really wanted, and wanted to touch on with the video.

When the puppets arrived, I thought 'oh my God, here's the box', and I was totally blown away. I supplied all the artwork in vector files, in Illustrator files and very flat. That was all I could give her really, that's how I do things, with drawings and colour Illustrator data, and she just breathed life into them, like she does with all her pieces.

The Elder
Collaboration with
Pete Fowler
500 mm x 400 mm
Made for the music video
"I'm Aware", by Clinic.
Mixed-fibre felt, embroidery
thread, card and polyester
fibre filling.

Felt Mistress: Creature Couture

Like anyone that has a flair and a skill, and a totally immersive knowledge of the materials they use, they just think in that material. That's what I was hoping to tap into and I was hoping I'd get from Louise. But it was beyond my expectations. I thought "Wow! These are incredible, she's put the same level of attention and detail and love into these as she does with any of her pieces." That's what I think is wonderful about Louise, I don't think I've ever seen a piece where I've thought "she's just knocked that out". She doesn't knock things out.

I can say the same for Jonathan (Edwards), what an incredible couple. Jonathan's work is just endlessly inspiring, as is Louise's. I love all the writing they do for the characters, it's just this fully formed world that they have created. For me, to be able to tap into that and get a favour from her in the form of the Clinic video, it's almost like an 'I'm not worthy' moment.

You see, there's a whole bunch of artists, that I look at, I follow their work, and they are inspirations to me... Louise is really up there. I'll see people replying to Louise on Twitter and think 'What's going on?! What has she made now?!' I feel I'm missing out on something if I don't keep a magnifying glass on her timeline to see what she's doing. It's always fantastic work. I think the best compliment you can give or make to someone is "Your work is you. Your self and your work are the same, it's a projection of yourself." Louise does that to a tee, absolutely, with no slacking.

I'd like to think that we are all like that, in any circles of artwork and artists that you have, there's a lovely group of friends that inspire each other and unknowingly, perhaps, push

Guitarist
Collaboration with
Pete Fowler
500 mm x 400 mm
Made for the music video
"I'm Aware", by Clinic.
Mixed-fibre felt, embroidery
thread, card and polyester
fibre filling.

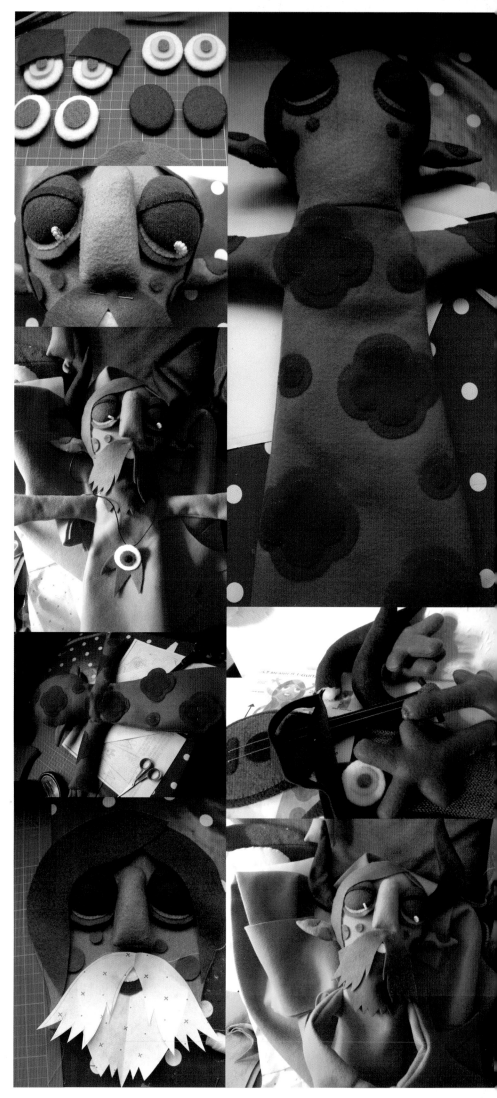

each other. Not in a competitive way (maybe it is a little competitive) but in the nicest possible way. Jonathan and Louise's work always inspires me. If I'm ever feeling down, or at a bit of a crossroads with work, or just having one of those days where I feel 'I'm rubbish', I look at people's work on the Internet and think 'I've got to pull my socks up'. But seeing Louise's work never makes me feel like 'God, my work is crap' – it's just inspiring. It's like 'Wow!' it's an incredible way of working, a way of... I think it's interesting seeing the way that people think in their work. I don't think I've ever seen a single drawing... I don't even know if Louise draws. That's not important. She thinks in the medium she uses incredibly well.

## The Stuffs

Felt Mistress was, again, hugely instrumental in making that show what it is. It was a bit of a journey because the puppets we made for Clinic were quite simple, you put a finger in the head, and a thumb in one arm. None of the puppets in the Clinic video spoke, none of them had operating mouths, whereas "The Stuffs" is all about dialogue, it's all about writing and all that goes with that. The way Louise responded to those very fundamental parts of the puppet that make it what it is... the arms must be operated and the mouth needs to be articulated... was fantastic. The work she put into the two key and other two characters was fantastic. It breathed life into the writers' work, and, again, breathed life into my, very flat, artwork.

Cult Member
Collaboration with
Pete Fowler
500 mm x 400 mm
Made for the music video
"I'm Aware", by Clinic.
Mixed-fibre felt, embroidery
thread, card and polyester
fibre filling.

I've been doing toys for ages and I've got really used to how sculptors and model makers interpret your design, and I give them very technical drawings...front...three-quarters front...side, and so on, it depends how complex the character is. But when it comes to making things out of felt and fabric and fleece and hair and fur and all sorts, I can't think in that area. And again, after my experience of the Clinic characters, "The Stuffs" puppets, when they arrived, completely blew me away. Nothing really prepared me for how much of a huge leap there was from my 2D flat designs to what Louise delivered. She literally did breathe life into those characters. The Dawson brothers that we have writing the show are fantastic, really really talented writers but the real conduit we have for everything that goes into that show are the puppets. I don't even think of them as puppets anymore. I see them as those characters in the same way as you see Kermit, in the same way you see Fozzie Bear, it's the same thing. It's like they are no longer puppets, they're these people. I think with Louise's work, in general, her work becomes the characters she makes, they become real selves. You don't think of them (well I don't think of them) as made out of the materials they are. They are just amazing characters, with personalities. The non-puppet stuff, I can take care of that. Having a puppeteer, a vocal artist developing the voice, there were a lot of things that went on afterwards but her making the puppets informed the whole thing. Absolutely. Without a doubt.

I feel like a very small person in that chain. I designed them, but without Louise, I don't think they would have been as funny, as expressive, as believable as characters. They are alive, they aren't just fabric. That's the best thing you can do as an artist...breathe life into the character, breathe a pumping heart into the raw materials... this thing is alive. It's got courage, it's got love, it's got blood, sweat and beers. Blood, sweat and tea, I think. Blood, sweat and tweed. So I do feel very humbled and very honoured for Louise to even reply to my emails and tweets. I really do think that. Fantastic talent. I don't think anyone touches, at all really, what she does.

She's got the skills, but that's not all you need to do it. It's her love of it and the characters and what she brings along with those skills, that's the important thing. Anyone can learn skills, but it's the things that can't be taught that are really important...the things that the creative person naturally brings to the raw materials, be it paint, be it cardboard, be it plastic toys, be it felt, fleece, fur and tweed.

Cosmic Owl
Collaboration with
Pete Fowler
500 mm x 400 mm
Made for the music video
"I'm Aware", by Clinic.
Mixed-fibre felt,
embroidery thread, card
and polyester fibre filling.

PETE FOWLER/CLINIC ——— 2010

Pete on set with Clinic
puppets, 2010.

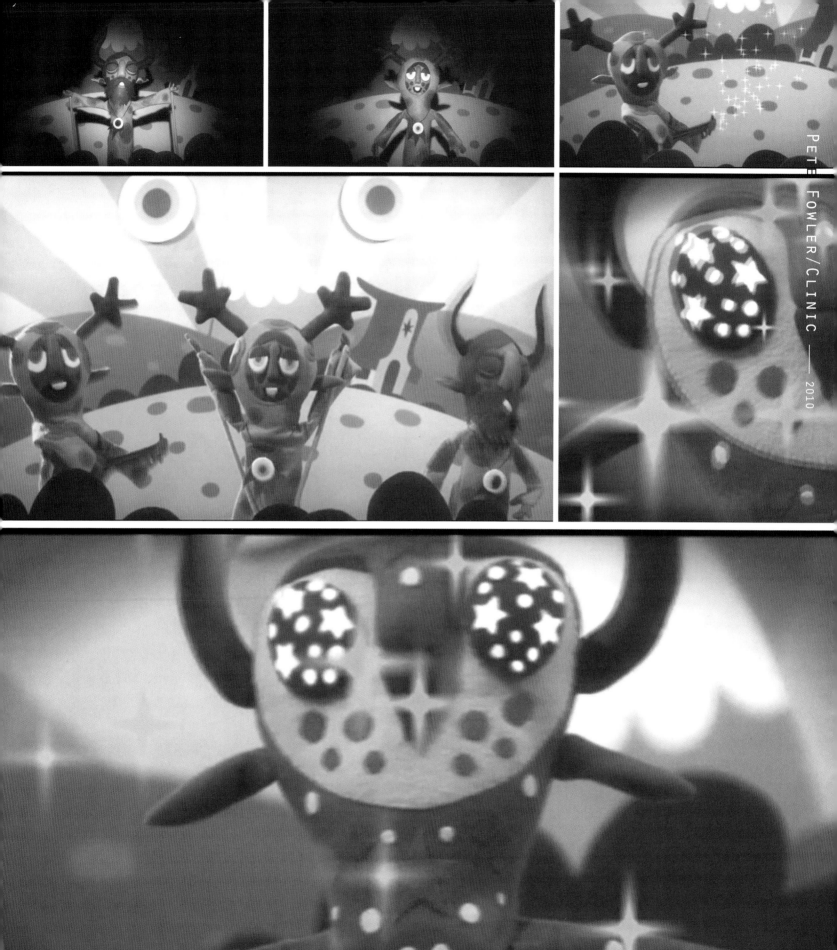

**Codey**
Collaboration with
Pete Fowler
750 mm x 270 mm
Made for the puppet show
"The Stuffs", shown both
online and on Cartoon
Network.

Codey wears indigo
denim jeans with turn-ups,
blue striped long-sleeved
t-shirt, hand printed neck-
scarf, baseball shoes and
spotted trucker cap.
Mixed fibres, felt, foam,
plastic safety eyes, wire,
card and polyester fibre
filling.

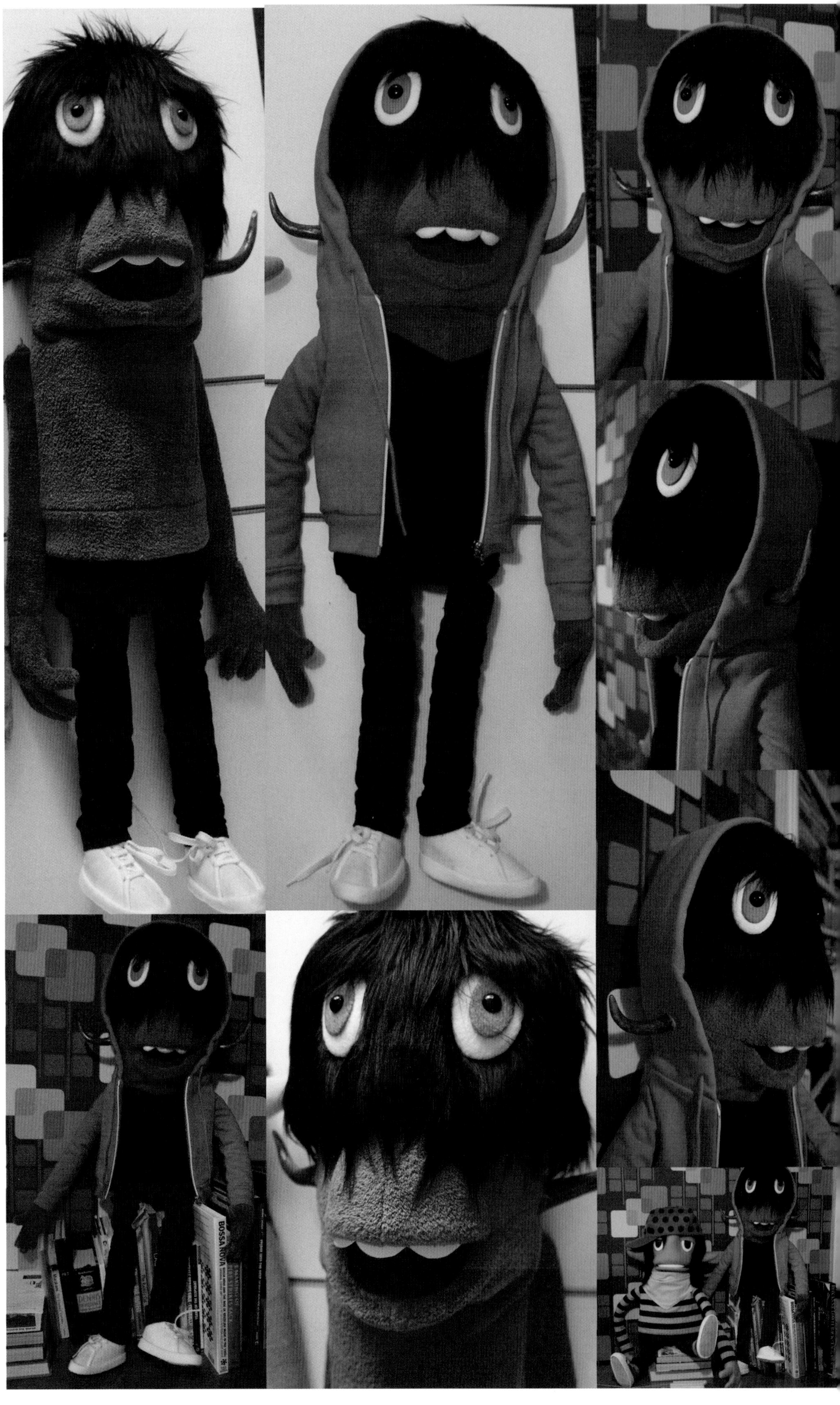

**Trendy Boy**
Collaboration with
Pete Fowler
800 mm x 270 mm
Made for the puppet show
"The Stuffs", shown both
online and on Cartoon
Network.

TB wears brown cord
trousers, white plimsoles,
black v-neck t-shirt and
orange hoody with pin
badges.
Mixed fibres, felt, foam,
plastic safety eyes, wire,
horn, card and polyester
fibre filling.

**Dooder McTavish**
Collaboration with
Pete Fowler
800 mm x 270 mm
Made for the puppet show
"The Stuffs", shown both
online and on Cartoon
Network.

Dooder wears cut-off
faded denim shorts with
frayed hems, plaited
leather belt, slip-on blue
boat shoes, cotton hawai-
ian shirt (never buttoned
up) and a shark's tooth
necklace.
Mixed fibres, felt, foam,
plastic safety eyes, wire,
card and polyester fibre
filling.

**Rogue Girl**
Collaboration with
Pete Fowler
800 mm x 270 mm
Made for the puppet show
"The Stuffs", shown both
online and on Cartoon
Network.

RG wears shot pink/purple
A-line sleeveless dress
with RG felt appliqued
logo, striped knee-high
socks and two-tone
lace-up dance shoes, a
heart-shaped crystal ring,
diamante bracelet and an
orange watch. RG also
wears a brace.
Mixed fibres, felt, foam,
plastic safety eyes, wire,
card and polyester fibre
filling.

Fradley has so many records he can no longer get out of his flat. He files his socks alphabetically and by genre.

**Fradley Benford**
780 mm x 370 mm
Fradley wears a skinny knitted grey and orange striped polo-neck, blue denim skinny jeans with yellow topstitching, neon lace-up high-tops, thick black round-framed glasses and large blue and orange headphones.
Mixed fibres, fake fur, felt, plastic safety eyes, card, wire and polyester fibre filling.

Frang Tootle is considered the originator of the "Croak Folk" genre. His seminal debut album "Songs of Pain and Discomfort" is still influencing slightly aggrieved and misanthropic song writers to this day.

Frang Tootle
750 mm x 300 mm
Frang wears cream cable-knit jumper, mustard jumbo cord flared trousers, black heeled pointy boots. He carries his acoustic guitar.
Mixed fibres, fake fur, felt, plastic safety eyes, wire, card, embroidery thread and polyester fibre filling.

Frimpton can often be found in the snug of drinking establishments in various Cornish harbours. He likes to reminisce at length about his days travelling the oceans, negotiating with sea monsters and pirates, and his current career as painter of seascapes and mermaids.

**Frimpton Wallis**
410 mm x 300 mm
Frimpton wears chunky knit fisherman-style jumper, denim work jeans and carries a corn-cob pipe.
Mixed fibres, fake fur, felt, plastic safety eyes, wire, card and polyester fibre filling.

**Frootling**
250 mm x 200 mm
Frootling wears thick black
round-framed glasses.
Mixed fibres, fake fur, felt,
plastic safety eyes, card,
wire and polyester fibre
filling.

**Fuegondo**
Custom for Dudebox
Launch Show, Village
Underground, London
260 mm x 250 mm
Vinyl toy custom with felt
covering.
Felt, embroidery thread,
polyester fibre filling, card
and plastic safety eyes.

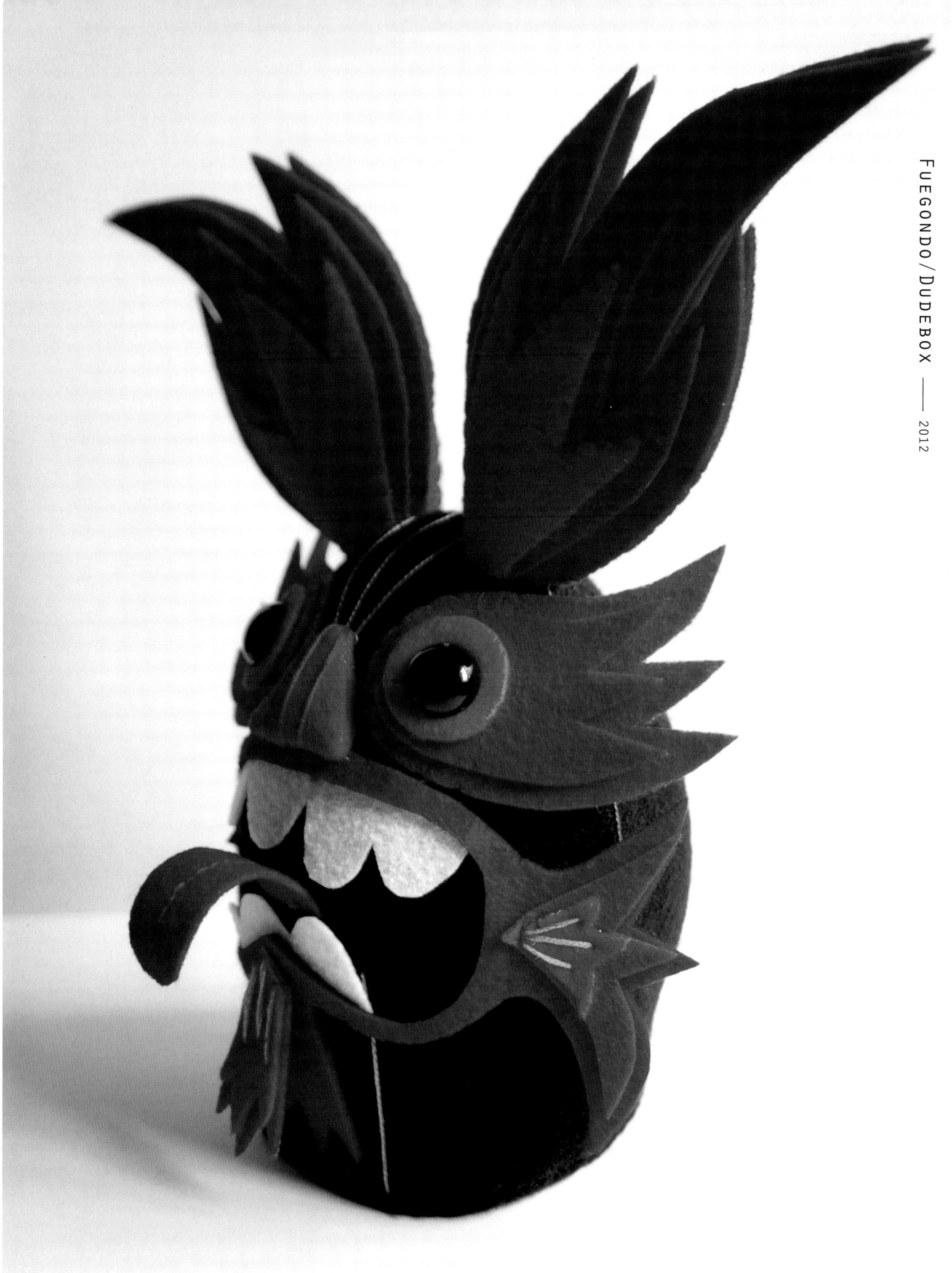

FUEGONDO / DUDEBOX —— 2012

The Furry Mayhem consists of Flink Strothers (Lead guitar, vocals), Groobo Tubbs (Bass guitar, backing vocals) and Thrubb (Drums, backing howls, grunts).

The Furry Mayhem are widely considered to be the true progenitors of the Furry Metal genre. They formed in the early noughties after meeting at the legendary rock club Heebie Geebies and were soon signed to FM Records. Their debut album, We Are The Furry Mayhem, made them household names all over the world and even their roadie, Wilko Roby, has become a celebrity in his own right.

Flink is married to leading model, Elspeth Frond, Groobo has opened his own chain of crazy golf courses and Thrubb was recently a contestant in the popular TV series "I'm A Celebrity", but was sadly disqualified after eating three hammocks, two trees and one of the cameras.

**The Furry Mayhem**
Made for "Tales From The Sock Drawer" Show, touring UK Art Centres.

Mixed fibres, fake fur, felt, plastic safety eyes, wire, card and polyester fibre filling.

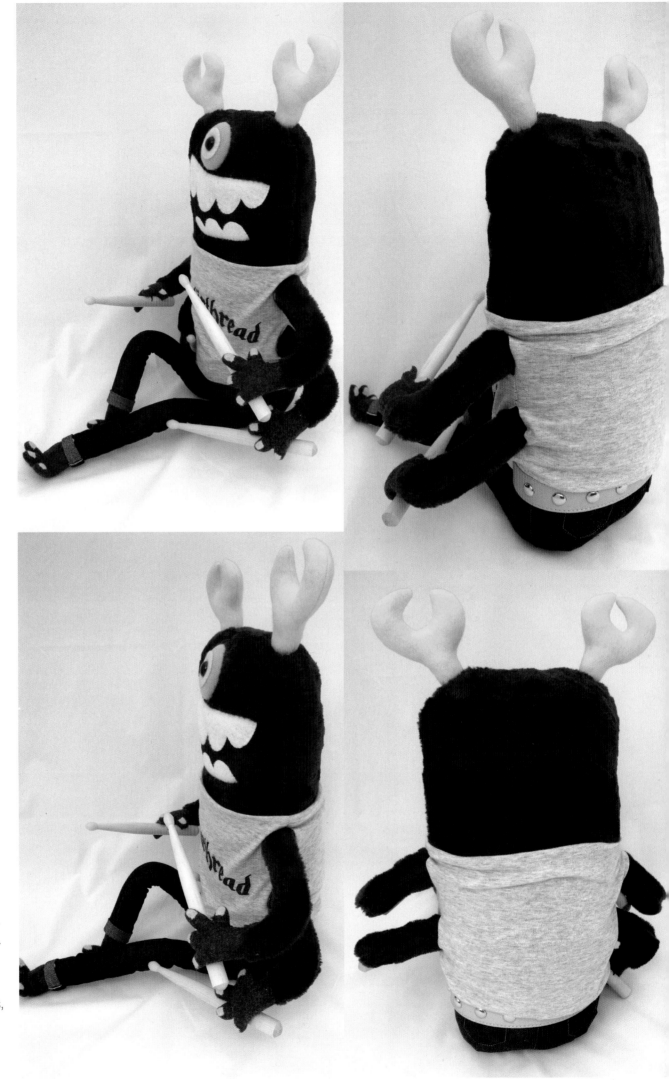

**Thrubb**
650 mm x 260 mm
Thrubb wears skinny-legged black jeans with turn-ups, yellow leather belt, and grey marl sleeveless "Motörthread" t-shirt. He carries his wooden drum sticks.
Mixed fibres, wood, fake fur, felt, plastic safety eyes, wire, card and polyester fibre filling.

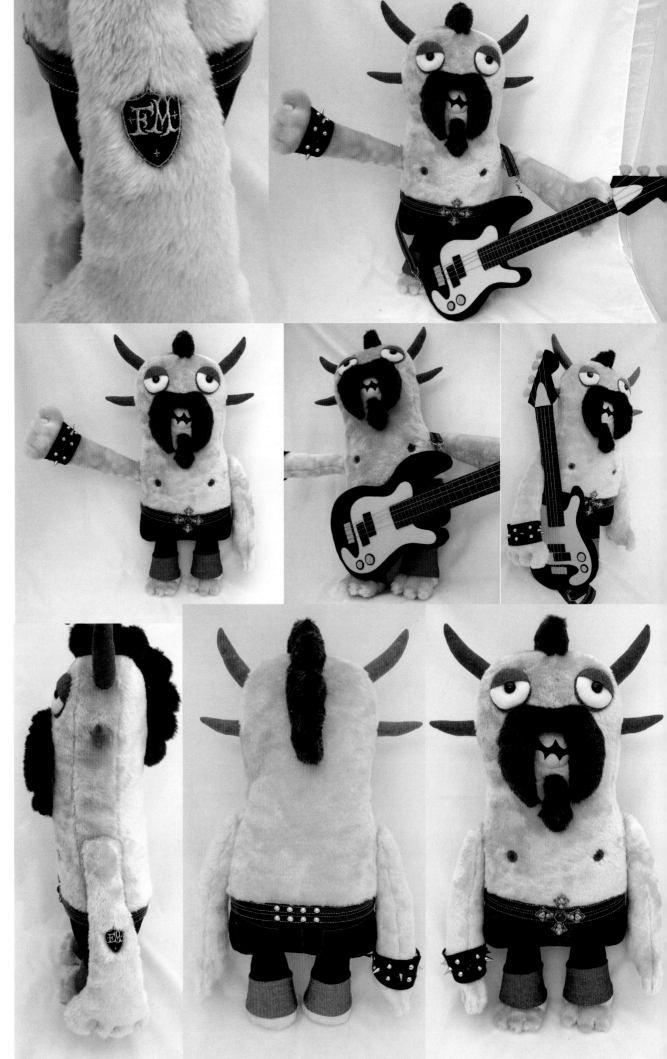

**Groobo Tubbs**
600 mm x 360 mm
Groobo wears black denim jeans with double turn-ups. Leather belt with cross-shaped buckle and studded wrist bands. He carries his black and yellow bass guitar.
Mixed fibres, fake fur, felt, plastic safety eyes, wire, card and polyester fibre filling.

**Flink Strothers**
700 mm x 280 mm
Flink wears black denim skinny jeans with turn-ups, yellow and back sleeveless t-shirt, studded leather belt and wrist bands, a plectrum neckace and black high-top baseball boots. He carries his black flying V guitar.
Mixed fibres, fake fur, felt, plastic safety eyes, wire, card and polyester fibre filling.

**Geraint**
800mm x 220mm
Prototype puppet
Geraint wears short-sleeve checked cotton shirt with button down collar, indigo straight-legged jeans with turn up. Black belt and aviator sunglasses.
Mixed fibres, fake fur, felt, wire, card and foam and polyester fibre filling.

**Bishops 'O**
Collaboration with
Ben Newman
260 mm x 200 mm
Made for the "Ghosts Of
Gone Birds" show, London.
Mixed-fibre felt,
embroidery thread, plastic
safety eyes, card, and
polyester fibre filling.

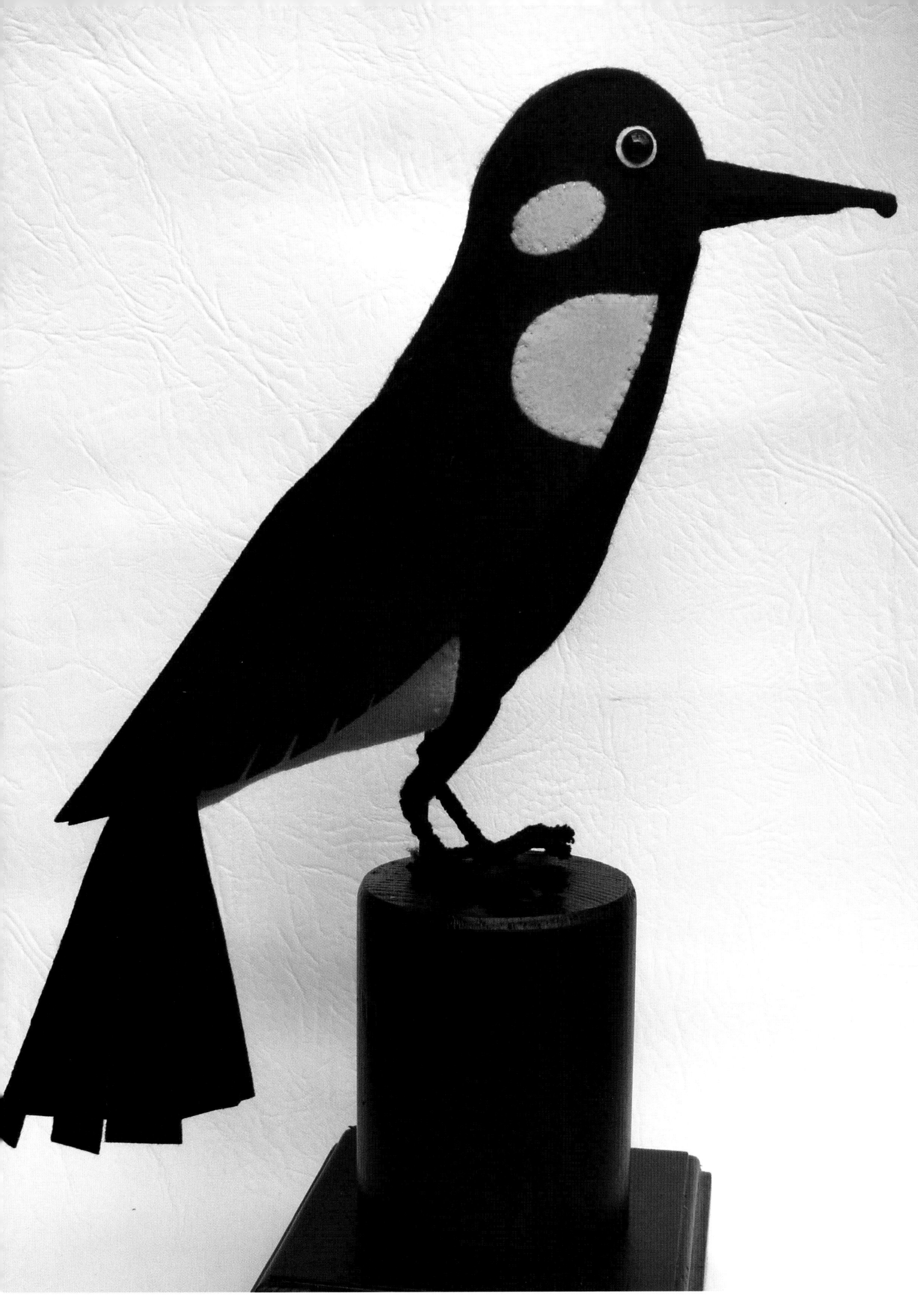

Ghosts of Gone Birds: Bishops 'O (Ben Newman) — 2011

Giant Hoopoe
350 mm x 200 mm
Made for the "Ghosts Of
Gone Birds" show, London.
Mixed-fibre felt,
embroidery thread, plastic
safety eyes, card, and
polyester fibre filling.

**Goth Panda (renamed Patchy by owner)**
450 mm x 230 mm
Made as a present for Louise's goddaughter. Panda wears black sleeveless A-line dress with white lace trim and matching bow hair clip.
Mixed fibres, brushed and plain felt, plastic safety eyes, wire, card and polyester fibre filling.

**Bernard**
450 mm x 230 mm
Made as a present for Louise's godson. Bernard wears hand knitted, round-neck arran tank top, shirt with embroidered collar and checkered bow tie.
Mixed fibres, brushed and plain felt, plastic safety eyes, wire, card and polyester fibre filling.

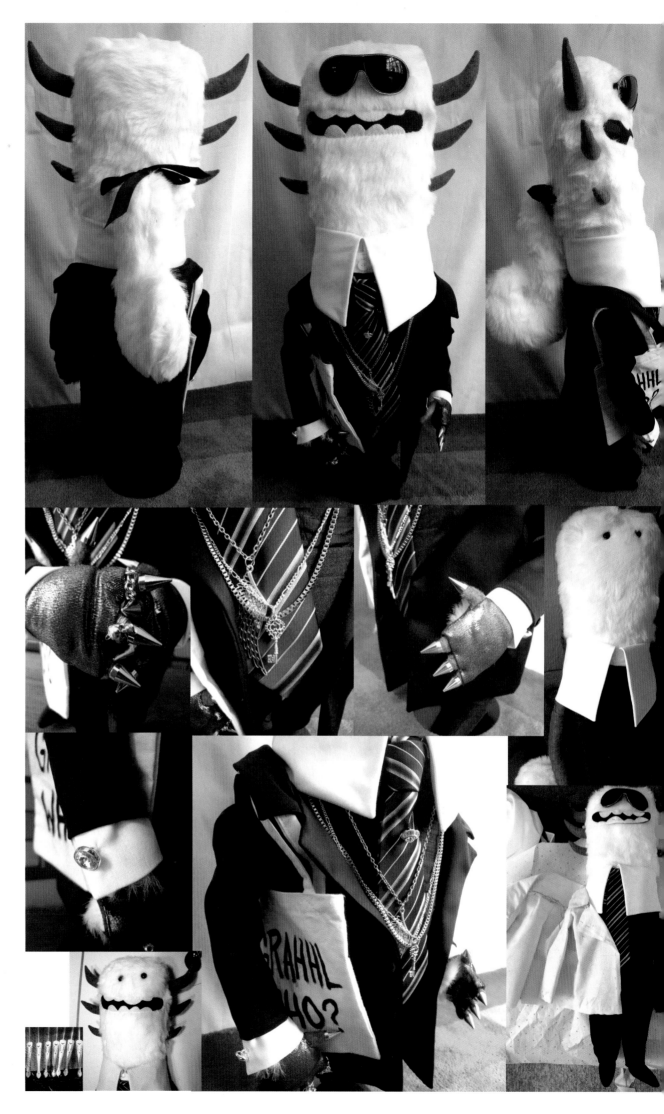

A leading light in the creature couture world, Grahhl became creative director at The House of Shnarrll after a long career dressing some of the world's most glamorous beasts.

Grahhl Lagerfurr
780 mm x 370 mm
Grahhl wears black three-button suit with narrow lapels, welt pockets, single back vent and narrow-legged trousers. Black silk shirt with white deep collar, large cuffs with diamante button cuff links and a silver and black striped satin tie with diamante button tie pin. He has long metallic silver stud claws and silver fingerless gloves. Black pointy shoes and black sunglasses. Adorned with numerous silver necklace chains and pendants including a decorative key. He also carries a "Grahhl Who?" canvas tote bag and has a black satin ribbon bow on his pony tail.
Mixed fibres, fake fur, felt, card, wire and polyester fibre filling.

**Grûber**
260 mm x 200 mm
Magazine tutorial
commissioned by
Mollie Makes
magazine.
Mixed-fibre felt,
embroidery thread,
plastic safety eyes,
vintage buckle, ribbon
and polyester fibre
filling.

# Headspace Gallery, Japan

During May and June 2011, Louise and Jonathan were Artists in Residence at the Headspace Gallery in Nara, and the headline guests at the annual Headspace Art and Music Festival in Osaka.

They were based in Nara, often travelling to Osaka and Kyoto. For ten days they also stayed in the Kayamori house, which is up in the mountains in Sakurai. This had amazing views and wildlife, including terrifying Mukade. They often heard wild boars crunching the bamboo behind the house.

Their month in Japan was spent working towards the Headspace "Monster" event at Cafe Absinthe in Osaka. This was the art and music event that they were headlining. Working with Osaka-based fashion designer, Kyoko Amano, Jonathan was asked to create creature designs inspired by Osaka's distinctive Sun Tower. His illustrations were then used to create a kimono fabric, designed by Tamotsu Shimada. Louise made a doll (Fenella Snark, a monster catwalk model) for the collaboration with Kyoko. Louise used the special fabric to dress Fenella Snark and Kyoko dressed a human model in the same fabric.

The photographs of the model were displayed at the Headspace event. The decoration of the doors and DJ booths during the event were illustrations by Jonathan. The event MC was Diane Orrett, with music from bands downstairs and DJs upstairs. Jonathan spent the night doing some live painting, one on his own and another smaller collaboration with Osaka artist, Hemneko. Other artists exhibiting their work that night included: Boss Hiko, Ben McDonough, and David Bateman.

**Left**
Kimono fabric designed by Tamotsu Shimada. The image is by Jonathan Edwards, based on Tower of the Sun, Osaka. Created exclusively for the Headspace event and used to dress a model.

**Right**
Model styled by Kyoko Amano Make-up by Hario Kiyomitsu Photographed by Kozo Ono.

Made during artist residency at Headspace Gallery, Japan and shown at Head Space Arts And Music Festival, Osaka, Japan.

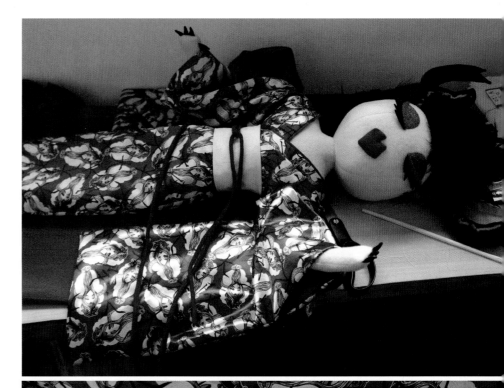

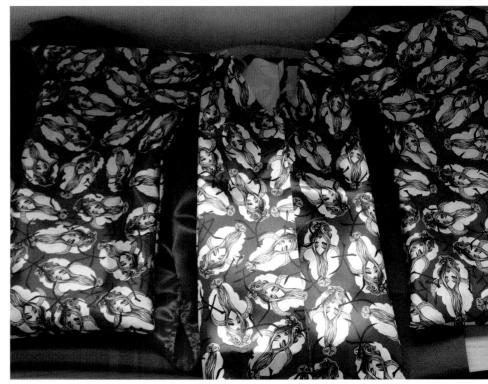

Barnaby is a western rockstar who's made it big in Japan. He is currently the face of the leading brand of facial shampoo – "Super-Clean Furry Beast".

**Barnaby Grangle**
700 mm x 350 mm
Made during artist residency at Headspace Gallery, Japan and shown at Head Space Arts And Music Festival, Osaka, Japan.

Barnaby wears narrow-legged black jeans with turn-up, studded belt and red high top base-ball shoes. He carries his black and red electric guitar.
Mixed fibres, fake fur, felt, plastic safety eyes, and polyester fibre filling.

HEAD SPACE ARTS AND MUSIC FESTIVAL, OSAKA, JAPAN/BARNABY GRANGLE — 2011

Hubert is a university professor and visiting lecturer at Yokai Institute, Nara. He is responsible for setting up Japan's first bar billiards league. He is the brother of Wilbur Grumph.

**Left**

**Tippy Head Mascot**
Edition of two
90 mm x 100 mm
Made as gifts for Japanese Team Tippy members Aiko & Noriko
Fake fur, felt, plastic safety eyes, wire, card, cord and polyester fibre filling.

**Right**

**Hubert Grumph**
580 mm x 380 mm
Made during artist residency at Headspace Gallery, Japan and shown at Head Space Arts And Music Festival, Osaka, Japan.

Hubert wears beige knitted polo-neck jumper, dark green needle-cord trousers, vintage tweed three-buttoned sports jacket with welt pockets, elbow patches and single back vent. Thick angular black-framed glasses. He smokes a pipe.
Mixed fibres, wool tweed, fake fur, felt, plastic safety eyes, wire, card and polyester fibre filling.

Gilbert first came to Japan five years ago as foreign correspondent for the International Yokai Times. His editor likes to keep him as far away from the head office as possible. Sorry, Osaka!

**Gilbert Twang**
780 mm x 350 mm
Made during artist residency at Headspace Gallery, Japan and shown at Head Space Arts And Music Festival, Osaka, Japan.

Gilbert wears black half-rimmed glasses, skinny faded grey denim jeans, black leather belt, checked cotton shirt with button-down collar, black satin tie and grey slip-on shoes. He carries a vintage grey tweed bag with black felt shoulder strap and smokes a cigarette. Mixed fibres, fake fur, felt, plastic safety eyes, and polyester fibre filling.

Photographer and doughnut connoisseur. Learnt Japanese from a Kappa so speaks with a slight "amphibious" accent. Niece of Uli Snooks and granddaughter of Lady Margaret Fribbington-Snooks.

**Pooky Snooks**
530 mm x 300 mm
Made during Artist Residency at Headspace Gallery, Japan and shown at Head Space Arts And Music Festival, Osaka, Japan.

Pooky wears vintage Welsh tweed trapeze-line cape with high mandarin collar and frog fastenings. She carries her felt Leica. Mixed fibres, fake fur, felt, plastic safety eyes, and polyester fibre filling.

Popular horned model and sister of Tabitha Snark, Fenella is enjoying great success in Japan, where she endorses the leading brand of horn dusting powder, "Yokai Glimmer Powder".

**Fenella Snark**
710 mm x 300 mm
Made during artist residency at Headspace Gallery, Japan and shown at Head Space Arts And Music Festival, Osaka, Japan.

Fenella wears a long-sleeved printed kimono with red trim and a black satin Obi. Fabric pattern illustration by Jonathan Edwards. Print designed by Tomatsu Shimada. Fenella also has a living ponytail with hidden cats' eyes.
Mixed fibres, fake fur, felt, plastic safety eyes, wire, card and polyester fibre filling.

Amateur painter/poet Albert arrived accidentally in Japan after going for a nap in a crate. He makes a living giving Ukulele lessons to Yokai.

**Albert Krang**
580 mm x 320 mm
Made during artist residency at Headspace Gallery, Japan and shown at Head Space Arts And Music Festival, Osaka, Japan.

Albert wears a hand knitted welsh wool arran jumper, black denim jeans with turn-ups and thick black-framed glasses. Mixed fibres, wool tweed, fake fur, felt, plastic safety eyes, wire, card and polyester fibre filling.

ALBERT KRANG
AMATEUR PAINTER/POET/UKULELE TUTOR

Dwink arrived in Japan as part of the UK Undergrowth Exchange Scheme and can be found living in the woodlands surrounding the Kayamori House. His evenings are spent drinking home-made sake and playing poker with a group of local Mukade. He has no intention of going home to his native Yorkshire.
There is a Japanese Kappa living in a council house in Keighley waiting for a plane ticket that will never arrive.

Left
**Tammy**
500 mm x 300 mm
Made during artist residency at Headspace Gallery, Japan and shown at Head Space Arts And Music Festival, Osaka, Japan.

Tammy wears striped chunky roll-neck jumper and washed out denim jeans with turn-ups.
Mixed fibres, wool, fake fur, felt, plastic safety eyes, wire, card and polyester fibre filling.

Right
**Dwink**
500 mm x 240 mm
Made during artist residency at Headspace Gallery, Japan and shown at Head Space Arts And Music Festival, Osaka, Japan.

Dwink wears a printed cotton cravat and a yellow diver's watch.
Mixed fibres, fake fur, felt, plastic safety eyes, and polyester fibre filling.

Tupsy (Winkles) is the sister of Tippy. Currently teaching English in Japan as part of the JET scheme.

**Tupsy Winkles**
480 mm x 180 mm
Made during artist residency at Headspace Gallery, Japan and shown at Head Space Arts And Music Festival, Osaka, Japan.

Tupsy wears a bow of embroidered Kimono fabric.
Mixed fibres, fake fur, felt, plastic safety eyes, and polyester fibre filling.

# JON KNOX

I had seen Felt Mistress's work online via several different art/design blogs. The detail was unlike anything I'd ever seen in plush, and I was an instant fan. I was impressed by the amount of layering in her work and its sculptural quality. It's quite rare in the world of plush design. I had made plush toys previously, but I wasn't capable of producing the amount of detail I wanted. I'd been a fan of her work for a while and had been wanting to collaborate with her, so I emailed her to see if she was interested in collaborating on some pieces for a solo gallery show I was doing in Chicago. A gallery show was a good opportunity to do something on a larger scale that would be seen in person by a lot of people. Later that week we were already discussing ideas.

The final pieces far exceeded my expectations. Because she's an expert craftswoman, we didn't have many limitations and were able to make exactly what we envisioned. The characters' clothes were of the same quality you'd buy for yourself in a boutique, and their facial structure was very close to how I would sculpt them with clay. When they arrived in the mail, I couldn't stop showing them off. People were fawning over them at the show.

Collaborating with other artists always forces you to reflect on your own aesthetic and the way you work. It's natural to develop habits that you aren't always conscious of, and therefore you can neglect opportunities to improve your work. With the Felt Mistress collaboration in particular, it made me consider more closely the way clothes were constructed. I normally sculpt my characters in clay before casting them in resin, so I was able to get a better idea of how clothes would fit and drape on a fictional character, which is quite a challenge when working with clay.

Louise's work thrives because of her ability to execute the finest detail — it's why people love and relate to it, and it's the reason she works well with others. She is a pioneer in her field, and her work is a constant inspiration to challenge the limitations of your medium.

Pepper, Dillon and
Jeffrey
Collaboration with Jon
Knox for Jon's show "Teen
Dream", Chicago, USA.

**Pepper**
Collaboration with
Jon Knox
620 mm x 260 mm
Pepper wears white cotton
vest top, faded grey denim
shorts with double turn-
ups, turquoise trainers
and white thick-framed
sunglasses.
Mixed fibres, felt, fleece,
embroidery thread, card,
and polyester fibre filling.

**Dillon**
Collaboration with
Jon Knox
620 mm x 280 mm
Dillon wears grey and
purple striped polo-neck,
blue denim straight-legged
jeans and purple trainers.
Mixed fibres, felt, fleece,
embroidery thread, card,
and polyester fibre filling.

**Jeffrey**
Collaboration with
Jon Knox
650 mm x 240 mm
Jeffrey wears black and
white striped t-shirt, black
narrow-legged jeans, blue
trainers and black thick
framed glasses.
Mixed fibres, felt, fleece,
embroidery thread, card,
and polyester fibre filling.

Herzog is a experimental film maker from East Berlin. He feels under-dressed without a tie and wears his trademark high-waisted jeans to conceal a gunshot scar. He plays it down by referring to it as "merely a flesh wound".

**Herzog**
740 mm x 320 mm
Herzog wears high-waisted denim jeans, yellow belt and yellow and grey-striped tie.
Fake fur, Mixed fibres, felt, plastic safety eyes, and polyester fibre filling.

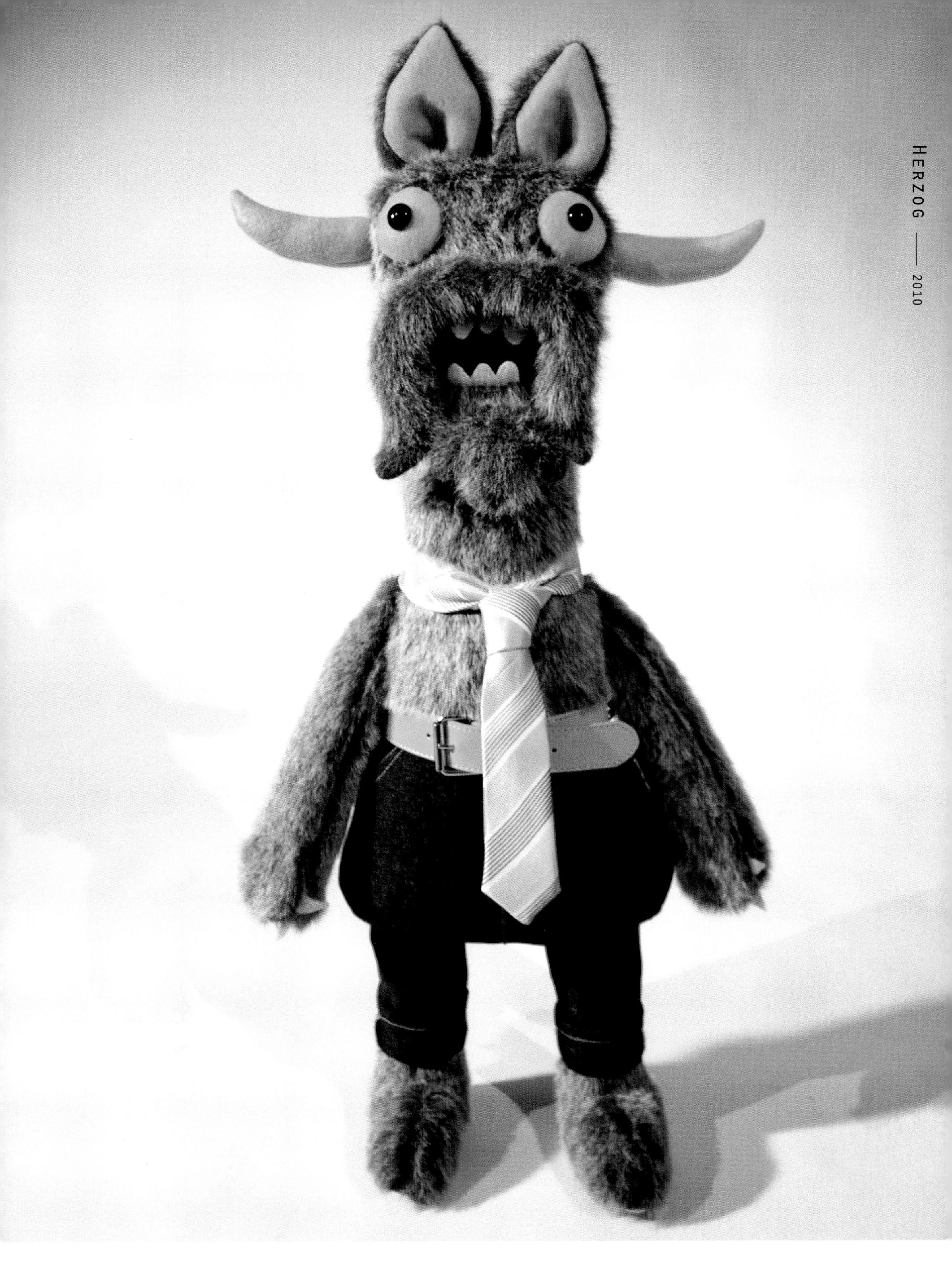

Herzog — 2010

# JASON KIRK
# KIRK ORIGINALS

It was through Twitter I came across Felt Mistress' work. We started following each other. As a matter of course, whenever anyone follows us on Twitter I always have a look and see what they do and find out about their products, and I simply liked what they did and sent Louise a little message. She said that all her new characters wore glasses and that was the beginning of a very simple and easy collaboration. I love really interesting collaborations. There's a lot of stuff that's completely commercial and kind of transparent in the way that it works and I'm not a big fan of that. Unless both parties have really got something to bring to the other one I don't see the point in it, I find it a bit cynical.

Felt Mistress is fantastic, the monsters are gorgeous, they've got so much character. Jonathan is a brilliant, brilliant illustrator, so to get involved with both of them is an absolute pleasure. I know how keen they were on our glasses so that was lovely, very gratifying. We love what they do and our glasses go with their characters.

We want people to think differently about eyewear. Most people don't have that positive approach and that's what we are trying to instill. We are trying to make people feel good about their glasses. We try to find people of a like mind to collaborate with, on something quirky, something with a sense of humour, something that doesn't take itself too seriously but still has a sense of quality, style, design, character, which is what Felt Mistress presents for us.

The characters are amazing, really interesting. Anton is pretty cool! But they're all great, their faces say so much. The attention to detail, the styling, the colouring, everything is really, really cool. I'm very pleased to be involved with them.

# HEY!
# WHO'S
# THIS
# GUY?

## NOBROW
## SHOP

Exhibition/installation
at Nobrow Shop
39, Great Eastern St
London, EC2
May 2012.

**JAKe Doll**
250 mm x 100 mm
Made as a birthday
present. JAKe wears a
zip-up hoody with felt
applique letters, denim
jeans, red t-shirt, white
trainers and messenger
bag.
An attachable beard
was a slightly later
addition.
Mixed fibres, polyester
fibre filling, embroidery
thread and cardboard.

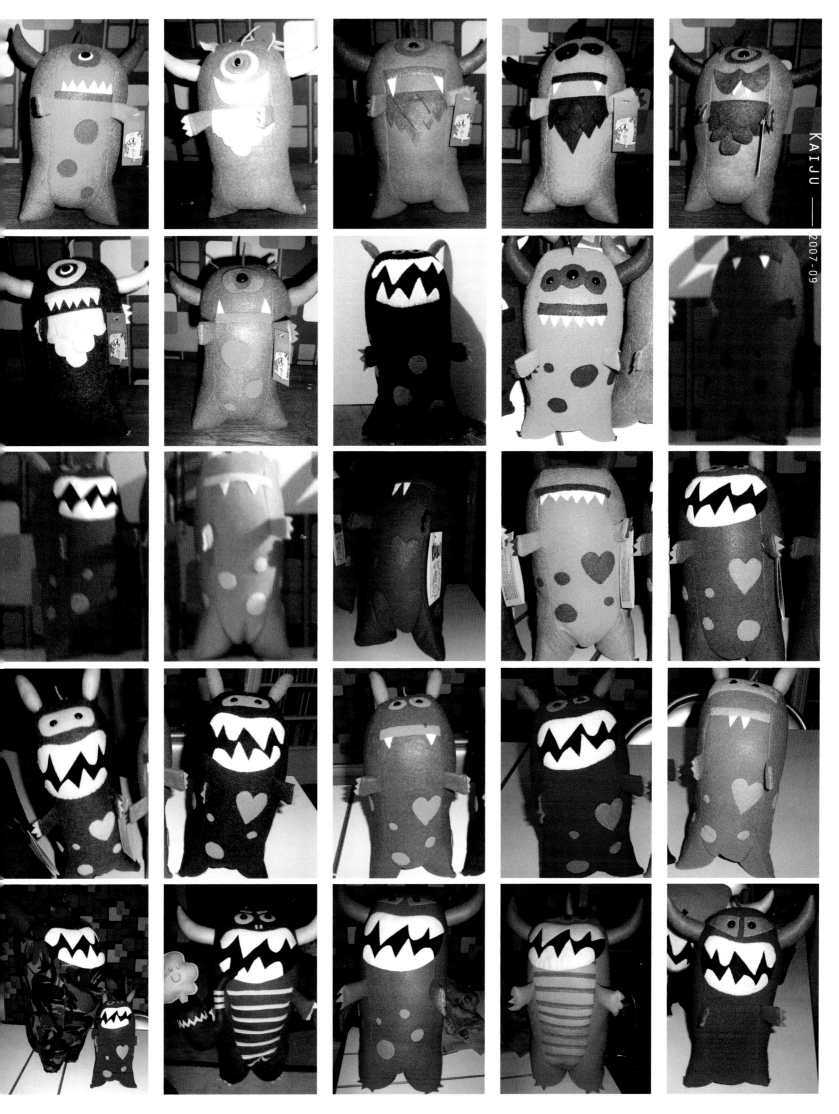

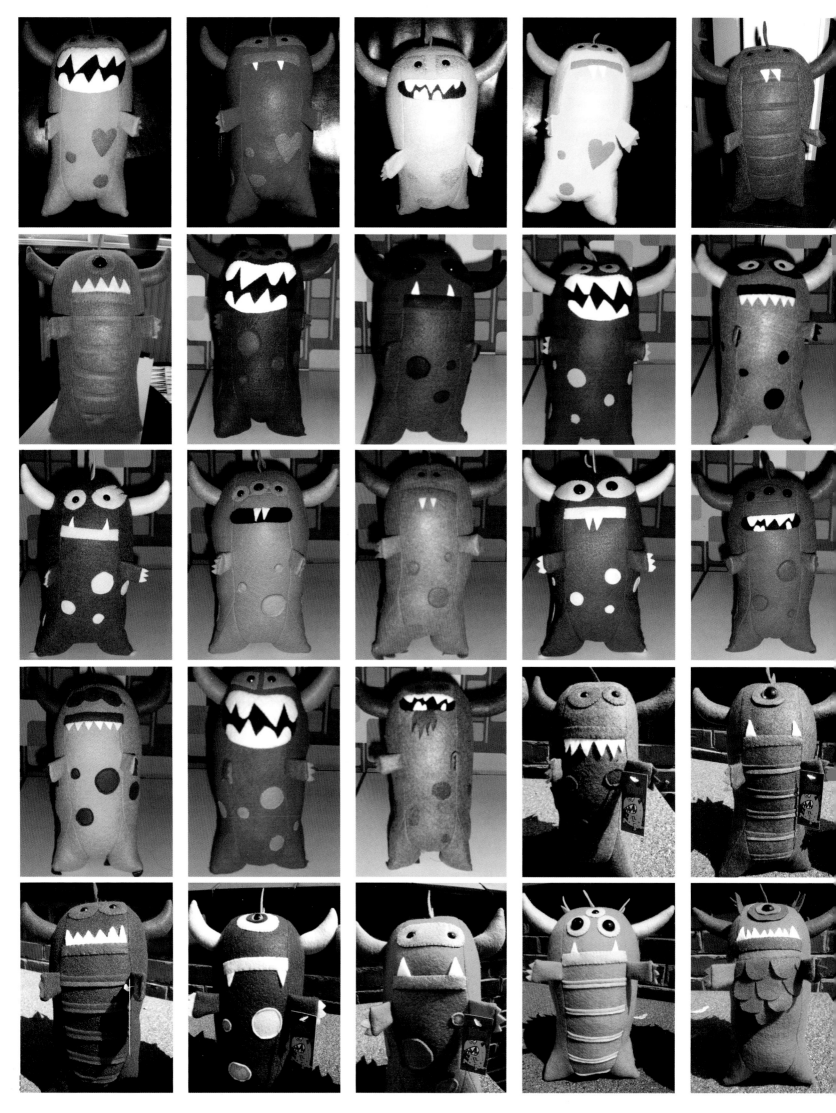

# Kaiju
## 2007 - 2009
310 mm x 160 mm
Edition of 200.
Kaijus were mainly made in mixed-fibre felt with plastic safety eyes and polyester fibre filling, but a few (approximately 12) were made in vintage tweed. Every one was different in surface detail. The number of eyes varied from one to three. Skin patterns included spots, stripes, or scales and some came with a felt heart. These were mostly sold through shops.

Left / 1
**Large Kaiju**
580 mm x 300 mm
Edition of four
Made to display at trade shows and shops. All four are different with unique colourways and details.

2
**Lucha Libre Kaiju**
310 mm x 160 mm
Black polyester fleece with mexican wrestler -style details.

3
**Christmas Pudding Kaiju**
310 mm x 160 mm
This was the 100th Kaiju. Made with dripping brandy sauce and holly leaf details.

4
**KISS Kaiju**
310 mm x 160 mm
KISS-style facial details and long Gene Simmons-style tongue. Metal square studs on chest.

Right / top
**Inky Goodness Kaijus**
310 mm x 160 mm
Special variants for Inky Goodness. Black polyester fleece with orange details.

Right / bottom
**Kaiju West**
310 mm x 160 mm
Special Edition; the 150th Kaiju. Details based on the Kanye West/ Kaws album artwork. Prince of Wales-check mixed-fibre suiting, with mixed-fibre felt.

Kipston is a nervous soul but still considers himself a gentleman droog.

**Kipston**
440 mm x 250 mm
Kipston wears a black bowler hat, and a black skinny tie.
Mixed fibres, distressed fake fur, felt, plastic safety eyes and polyester fibre filling.

Lady Garrrgghh Garrrgghhh! rose to prominence in the infamous monster clubs situated in the labyrinthine network of tunnels beneath New York City. Inspired by previous glamonster icons such as David Growlie and Furry Mercury, Gaarrgghhh Garrgghhhh has taken the creature world by storm with a combination of killer tunes (literally!), outrageous outfits and an ability to breathe fire (during a recent performance she inadvertently toasted the entire front row of her audience)!

Her recent tour of Japan saw her break all previous audience records. The Japanese Yokai community have taken her to their hearts partly due to her Stag Beetle ancestry (she inherits her shiny black antlers from her grandmother's Stag Beetle side of the family),

### Lady Garrrgghh Garrrgghhh!

1160 mm x 450 mm
Lady G wears fake leather dress with ruff and feather inserts at the neckline and diagonally across the front, exaggerated hip shaping. Gunmetal lace headpiece with studs. Gunmetal lace fingerless gloves and long metal cat claw studs. Knee-high PVC boots with metal toe-tips and chain details. Undergarments include black PVC tape crossed over nipple area, PVC pants and ripped thigh-length fishnet tights. Mixed fibres, felt, fake fur, fake leather, metal, wire, chain, card, lace, wooden doweling, studs, PVC and polyester fibre filling.

LADY GAARRGGHHH GARRGGHHHH
**ANTLER FACE**

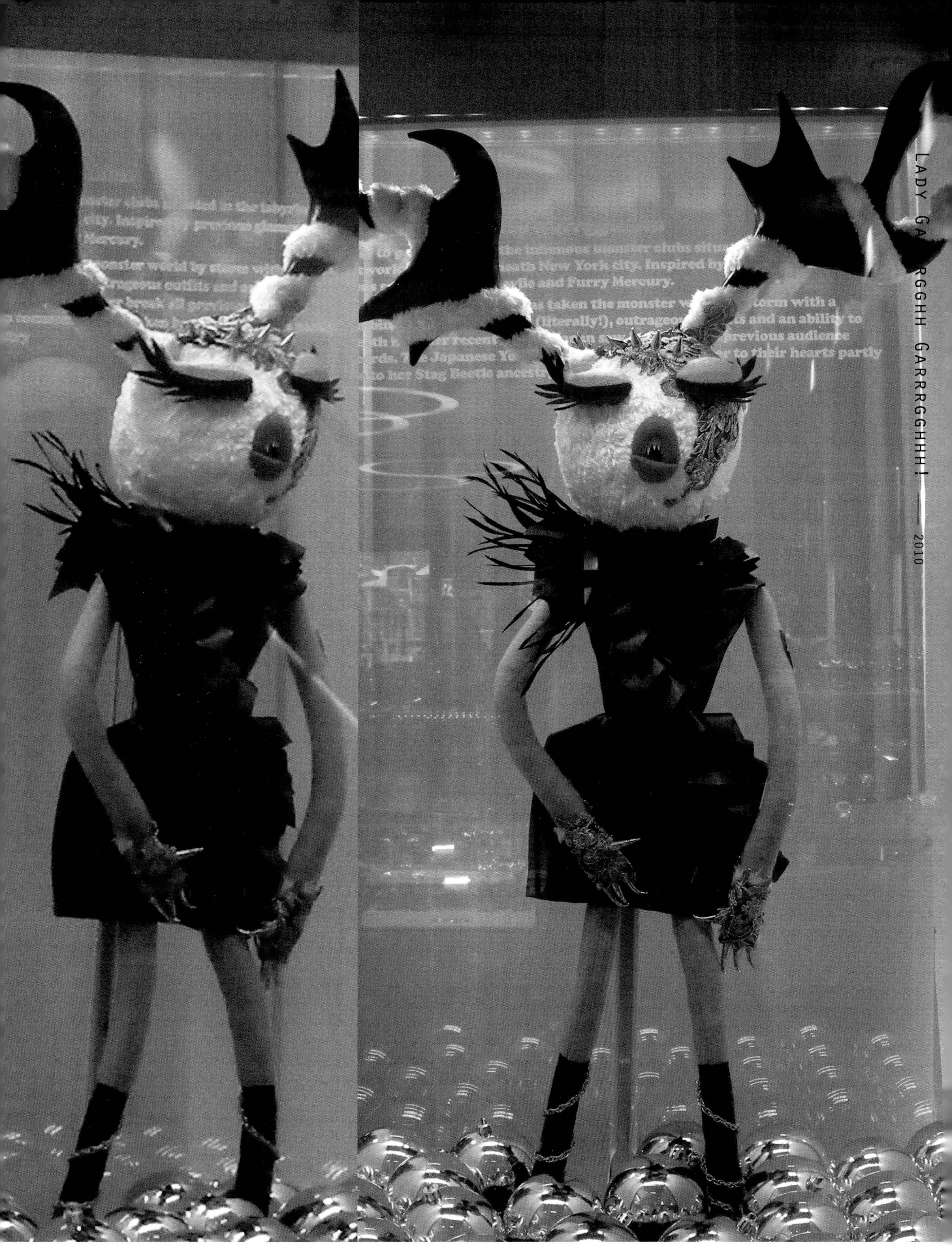

Fashionista Lady Persephone can often be spotted shopping in Selfridges with her "dog" Minkles.

Lady Persephone
Grimm-Fribbington
1000 mm x 300 mm
and Minkles
150 mm x 190 mm
Lady P wears black and white vintage tweed coat dress with circular pockets, fluted sleeves with pleats at sleeve head and a waist belt. Hand-printed FM pink silk scarf tied in a pussycat bow. Fake black leather fingerless gloves with six-button detail. Minkles wears matching coat, leather collar and chain lead.
Mixed fibres, fake fur, felt, plastic safety eyes, card, wire and polyester fibre filling.

**Mack**
330 mm x 170 mm
Designed by Joe List,
made as a gift to Joe to
celebrate The Annotated
Weekender's birthday.
Mixed-fibre felt,
embroidery thread, plastic
safety eyes, and polyester
fibre filling.

**The Mad Hatter**
800 x 500 mm
Made for the "Go Ask Alice" show at Paul Cumes Gallery, Santa Barbara.

MH wears white cotton shirt with oversized cuffs and vintage button cufflinks, red polkadot cravat, double-breasted tweed suit with welt pockets, single back vent, and trousers with creases and slight flare, blue socks and brown pointy heeled boots, brown top hat with curved crown, ribbon and feather. He carries a china cup of tea.
Mixed fibres, felt, plastic safety eyes, wire, card and polyester fibre filling.

**Madonarrrgghh**
750 mm x 300 mm
Private commission.

Madonarrrgghh wears
metallic fake leather
conical bra, lace-up corset.
Fishnet tights, knee-length
fake leather boots and pvc
fingerless gloves.
Mixed fibres, fake leather,
PVC, fake fur, felt, wire,
card and polyester fibre
filling.

**Marceline
"Drain The Red"
1300mm x 350mm**

Made for the Cartoon
Network Adventure Time
anniversary show at
Gallery Nucleus, Alhambra,
California.

Marceline wears red and
black Mixed-fibre slash
neck skinny knit jumper,
skinny legged indigo denim
jeans and deep red pointy
calf length boots.
She carries her axe bass,
wearing an FM plectrum
necklace around her
neck and a "Nocturnal
Romantic" Edwin pin
badge on her guitar strap.
Mixed fibres, felt, fake fur,
metal clasps and rings,
embroidery thread,
polyester fibre filling, wire,
card and wood.

MARCELINE "DRAIN THE RED"/GALLERY NUCLEUS — 2012

Modster man - One of the sixties' leading 'ace faces', he was often seen hanging around Carnaby Street and even taught a young David Bowie how to whistle. Fact.

Ms Modster - Spotted during the sixties hanging around with Twiggy, Scratchy and Flaky. She once bit the bottom off a garment Mary Quant was working on and inadvertently invented the mini-skirt!

## The Modster Couple

### Male
670 mm x 180 mm
He wears a fully-lined three-buttoned grey gabardine suit with three welt pockets, single back vent and narrow leg trousers with crease line. High-collared, button-down gingham shirt with deep cuffs and black skinny tie. Retro bowling shoes with white stripe.
Mixed-fibre felt, card, plastic safety eyes, wire and polyester fibre filling.

### Female
570 mm x 180 mm
She wears polyester black polo-neck, Op Art print poly-cotton shift dress, low waist belt with vintage plastic buckle. Black shoes with double button detail.
Mixed-fibre felt, card, plastic safety eyes, wire and polyester fibre filling.

Benji
260 mm x 200 mm
Designed as a kit for
workshops.
Mixed-fibre felt, fake fur,
embroidery thread, plastic
safety eyes, card, and
polyester fibre filling.

Gustav
200 mm x 260 mm
Designed as a kit for workshops.
Mixed-fibre felt, embroidery
thread, plastic safety eyes, card,
and polyester fibre filling.

Egon
200 mm x 260 mm
Designed as a kit for workshops.
Mixed-fibre felt, embroidery
thread, plastic safety eyes, card,
and polyester fibre filling.

# MONSTER LONDON

## FOYLES BOOKSHOP

**Monster London**
The Gallery at Foyles
Foyles Bookshop
London.

The Mope sits on you in the night and you wake up miserable.

**The Mope**
400 mm x 230 mm
Character designed by John Allison, made as a present for John.
Mixed-fibre felt, fake fur, plastic safety eyes, embroidery thread, card, and polyester fibre filling.

**Mr Smashing**
400 mm x 150 mm
Edition of 20
These and Kaijus were
the first pieces made in
multiples, for shops.
Printed and plain cotton or
vintage wool tweed, mixed-
fibre felt, card, embroidery
thread and polyester fibre
filling.

**Original Mr Smashing**
400 mm x 150 mm
Edition of two
Made as presents for a
friend's children.
Printed and plain cotton,
mixed-fibre felt, card,
embroidery thread and
polyester fibre filling.

**Hollywood Smashing**
250 mm x 150 mm
Made as a present for Woodrow
Phoenix while he was away
working in Los Angeles, hence
the name.
Printed and plain cotton, mixed-
fibre felt, embroidery thread,
card and polyester fibre filling.

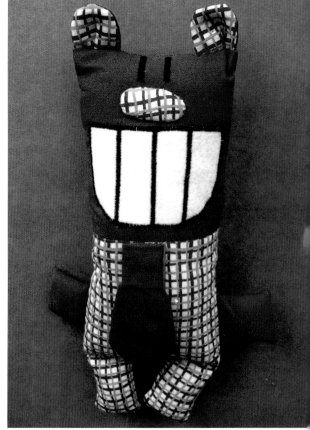

**Client A (Female)**
700 mm x 350 mm
She wears a black, large rever-collared tailored jacket with exaggerated shoulders, welt pockets and single back vent, metallic gunmetal silver sleeveless top, skinny black jeans, fake leather fingerless gloves and knee-high pointy heeled boots. Jewellery includes: Chanel jet-bead belt (worn as necklace) and diamante choker (supplied by client) She has a pet "monster turtle" with diamante collar and chain lead.
Mixed fibres, felt, wire, card and polyester fibre filling.

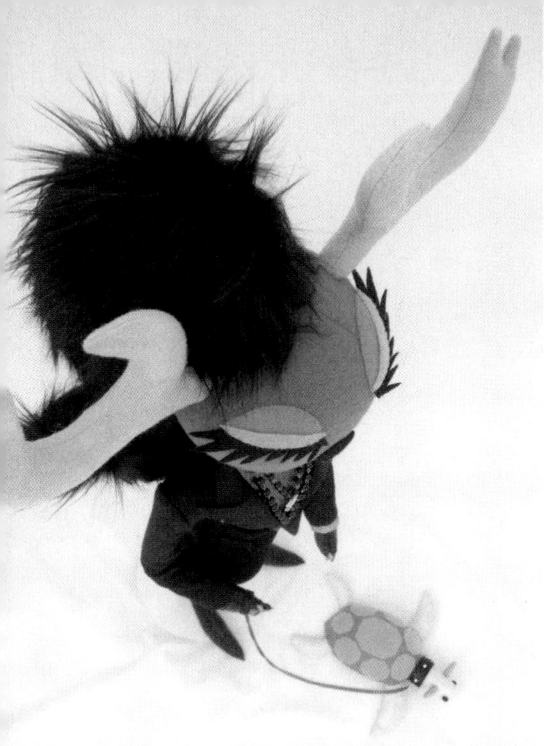

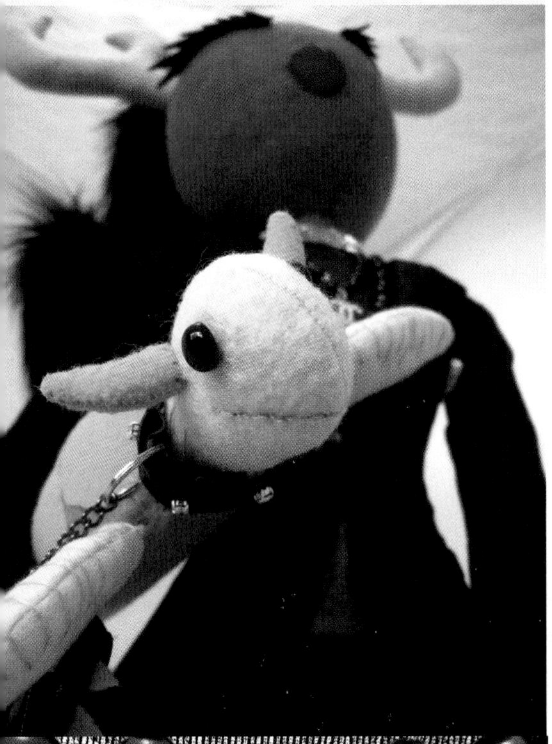

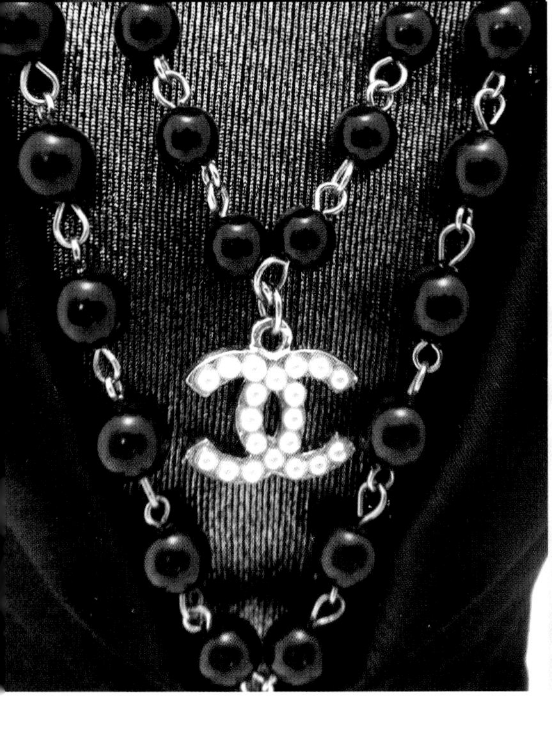

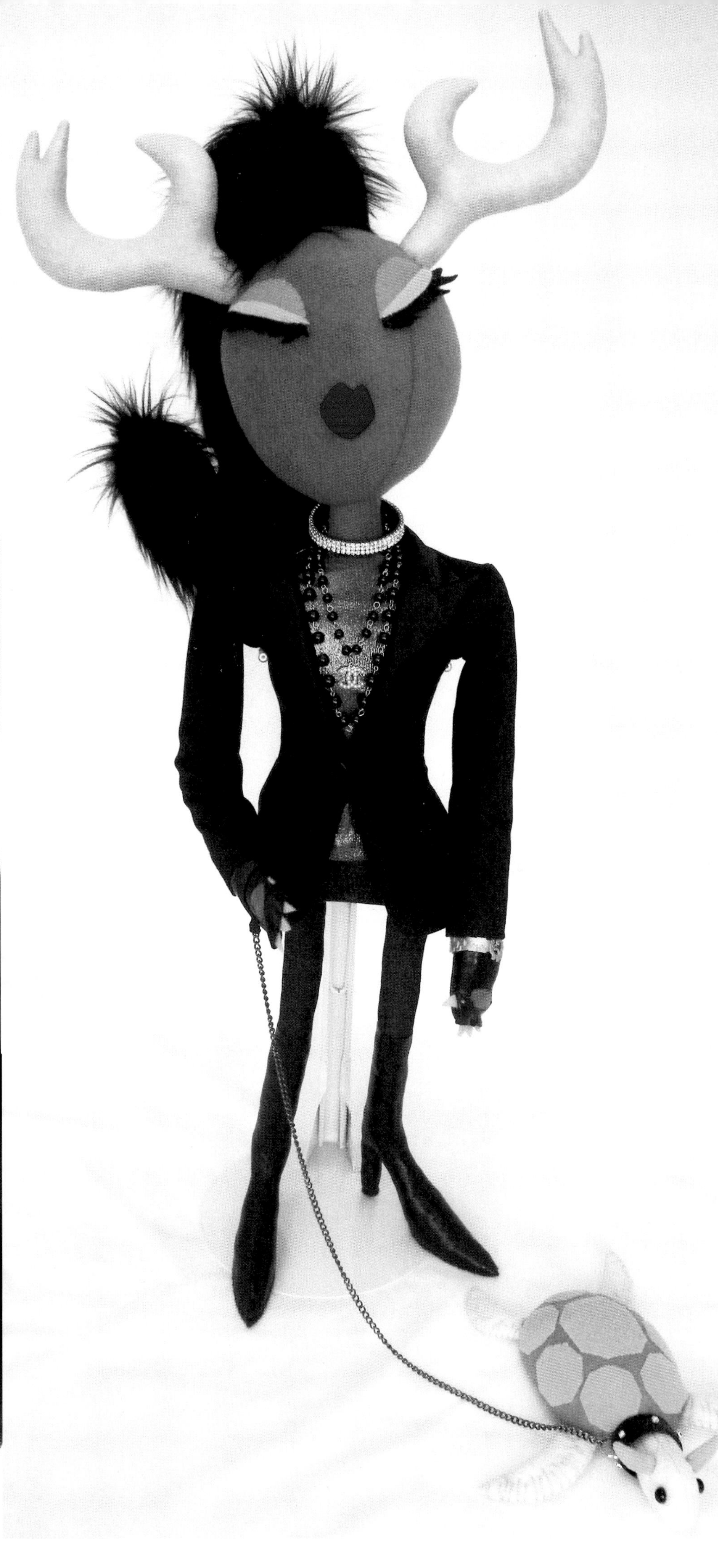

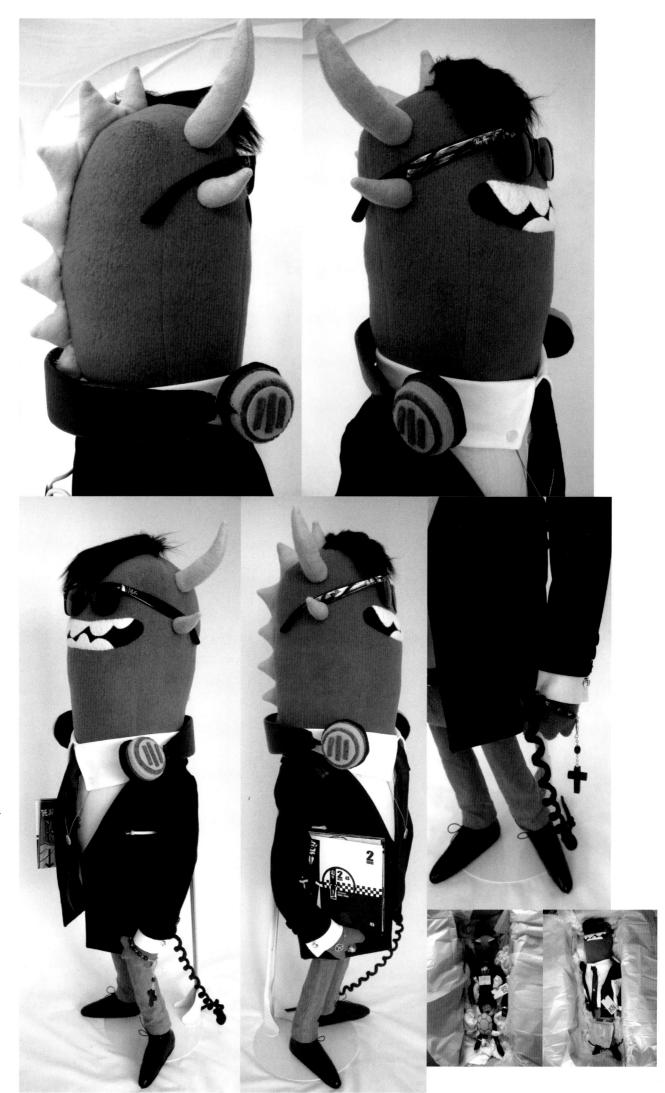

**Client B (Male)**
800 mm x 350 mm
He wears a black three-button suit jacket with welt pockets and single back vent, white cotton shirt with button-down collar and large cuffs worn with diamante button cufflinks. Black Rayban sunglasses (supplied by client), black satin tie, faded grey denim straight-legged jeans and black lace-up shoes. Jewellery includes: rosary beads (worn as bracelet), circular metal pendant necklace, diamante CND bracelet (all supplied by client) and a handmade metallic skull ring with Mickey Mouse ears. He also wears large headphones and carries a selection of handmade record sleeves, designed by Jonathan Edwards and based on the client's favourite records.
Mixed fibres, felt, wire, card and polyester fibre filling.

# BEN NEWMAN

I was taking part in an exhibition in Bristol at the Here Gallery. It was Christmas 2008, and the show was with Stuart Kolakovic and Felt Mistress. It was the first time I had seen Louise's work, and I remember thinking how I would love her to reinterpret my work one day. I knew she often worked with Jon Burgerman, and I didn't know if I could ever be at the point where I could get her to turn my work into these incredible 3D objects but it was a thought that lingered in the back of my mind for some time.

Fast-forward to early 2011, where I was starting to put together a body of work for my first solo exhibition in London which would open in September. As it would be part of the London Design Festival, I wanted to make it extra special so I had started working with my father on wooden interpretations of my designs and I thought it would be great to see if Felt Mistress was available, and whether she would like to collaborate on some pieces for the show. I sent her an email saying how I'd really love to work with her. I wanted to make some of the characters from my book, The Bento Bestiary, into these 3D objects, and Louise said she already owned a copy and would love to be a part of the exhibition.

My part in the process was relatively minimal and straight forward because Louise had the book already, she just blew up the images and made the figures from that. We talked at length on the phone about ideas for the figures but I didn't need to send her a thing. She laboured away and would send me 'work in progress' photos to keep me up to date and whet my appetite. That was the most amazing part, I was quite happy to go 'well, you know what you're doing, so I'm just going to let you do what you do', and luckily, that's exactly how Louise likes working. She likes to be able to have freedom with how she visualises things and I quite enjoy taking a back seat from time to time too.

I was imagining the pieces to be about 50cm high. She sent me these photographs and they were absolutely gigantic! They were just huge. It is amazing how you can give her something quite simple and she'll still make it magnificent.

I can never get my head around her craft(wo)manship and she will never let the artist compromise when she works on a collaboration. I remember when we were working on the 3D Felt Masks for my show in

**Neko Mata**
Collaboration with
Ben Newman
975 mm x 300 mm
Made for Ben's show
"Masks", Nobrow Gallery,
London.
Mixed-fibre felt,
embroidery thread, card,
and polyester fibre filling.

Berlin, I was thinking about all the overlapping lines and just how difficult that would be to sew by hand. I got worried that I'd gone over the top and asked Louise if she wanted me to simplify some of it, and she said "Oh no, don't be silly, it'll be fine." She must have cursed my name for a few days but never let on to me. Every collaboration we've worked on so far has never required me to make any changes, no matter how complicated I make it, she can always make it work. When you're designing things and juggling lots of projects, handing a part of the work to someone else who can reinterpret in 3D to such an incredibly high level is a Godsend and an amazing gift.

**Taimatsu Maru**
Collaboration with
Ben Newman
650 mm x 330 mm
Made for Ben's show
"Masks", Nobrow Gallery,
London.
Mixed-fibre felt,
embroidery thread, card,
and polyester fibre filling.

The thing I enjoy most about our collaborations is that I got to make a new friend whom I trust implicitly and who never lets me sweat the small stuff. I happily relinquish all control of that side of the project to her and then sit around excitedly waiting to see the final results which always leave me floored.

I never feel any apprehension about seeing the final product with her. It's a good relationship and I think Louise likes that set-up with the artists she works with creatively. She's a professional! Big time.

Dateotoko Fishu San
collaboration with
Ben Newman
1400 mm x 360 mm
Made for Ben's show
"Masks", Nobrow Gallery,
London.
Mixed-fibre felt,
embroidery thread, card,
and polyester fibre filling.

"Masks",
Collaboration with
Ben Newman
Pictoplasma, Berlin.

MASKS

**Goom**
Collaboration with
Ben Newman
580 mm x 400 mm
Made for Ben's show
"Masks", Pictoplasma,
Berlin.
Mixed-fibre felt,
embroidery thread, card,
plastic safety eyes and
polyester fibre filling.

Inugami
Collaboration with
Ben Newman
580 mm x 270 mm
Made for Ben's show
"Masks", Pictoplasma,
Berlin
Mixed-fibre felt,
embroidery thread, card,
plastic safety eyes and
polyester fibre filling.

**Tigraaarrr**
Collaboration with
Ben Newman
580 mm x 450 mm
Made for Ben's show
"Masks", Pictoplasma,
Berlin.
Mixed-fibre felt,
embroidery thread, card,
plastic safety eyes and
polyester fibre filling.

# BEN NEWMAN

Felt Mistress made three of my Mask designs for my Pictoplasma show in Berlin. My work is regularly seen on paper or a screen, but one of the key parts of the show, that Louise and I were talking about, was how we wanted to hang these masks as if they were floating freely in the room. We wanted the audience to be able to interact with the Felt Mistress masks so people could stand behind them and 'wear' the masks for photographs. When we put the show on in Berlin, these felt masks were a real crowd pleaser, it was interactive and fun. It created a really strong positive reaction from the audience and I think they were one of the most photographed things in the show.

Louise took my designs and was not only able to develop them, but evolved them into something more, something that exists in the real world. I think that is one of the big effects that she has had on my work. It feels more interactive. It exists. It is a beautiful object.

That's the special thing that I enjoy most about working with the Felt Mistress.
I never need to worry about anything, I just get to be excited about the results, and she brings my illustrations across that barrier from the page into the physical real world. I cannot wait to see what we collaborate on next.

Top
Ben Newman with Tippy,
Pictoplasma, Berlin.

Right
Masks show,
Berlin-Weekly.com Gallery Space,
Berlin.

# NOBROW

## ALEX SPIRO/SAM ARTHUR

ALEX SPIRO (AS) We commissioned Hilda specially for the release of Luke Pearson's **Hilda and the Midnight Giant**, and we take her to all the comic fairs and conventions. She even has her own suitcase that we carry her in.

SAM ARTHUR (SA) Occasionally her feet fall off (they're actually on little poles, they're not stitched). It feels quite dark putting her feet back on!

AS The only place we didn't take her was Brooklyn. She's been to Angouleme, and all the signings…it's been great.

Obviously it was a great honour for us for Felt Mistress to have a show in our space. We had stopped having shows in the gallery, but when Louise said that she was interested in doing something, we thought, well, if we were going to have one last show, it should definitely be her.

Felt Mistress was always someone we had wanted and we had always spoken from the very beginning about her having a show with Jonathan here. It had never come to fruition because of the timing when we decided to scale down the gallery, and so we were really pleased that there was a reason to do it and we were very honoured to have her there.

Hilda
Collaboration with
Luke Pearson
750 mm x 260 mm
Commissioned by Nobrow.
Mixed-fibre felt,
embroidery thread, card,
plastic safety eyes, wood,
and polyester fibre filling.

**Hilda**
Collaboration with
Luke Pearson
750 mm x 260 mm
Commissioned by Nobrow.
Mixed-fibre felt,
embroidery thread, card,
plastic safety eyes, wood,
and polyester fibre filling.

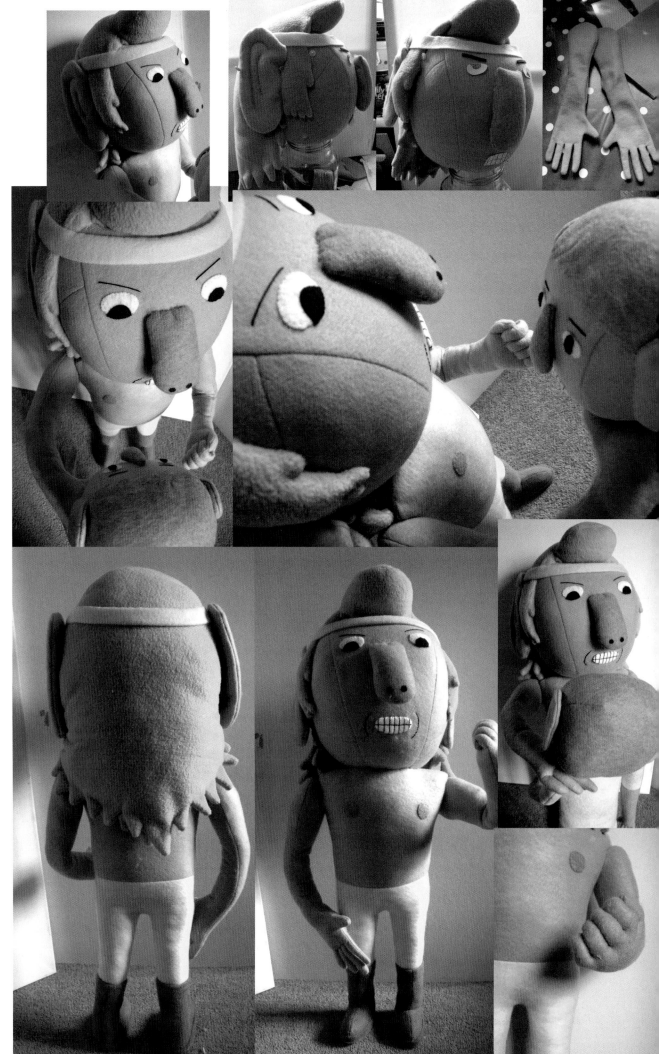

**Thug Life**
Collaboration with
Jon Boam
800 mm x 270 mm
Commissioned by Nobrow
for the Jon Boam/Matthew
The Horse show "Doom
3.0".
Mixed fibres, fleece, felt,
wire, card and polyester
fibre filling.

**Thug Life**
Collaboration with
Jon Boam
800 mm x 270 mm
Commissioned by Nobrow
for the Jon Boam/Matthew
The Horse show "Doom
3.0".
Mixed fibres, fleece, felt,
wire, card and polyester
fibre filling.

# Nobrow

AS I had seen a post about Felt Mistress on Creative Review, I'd also seen her work for Start, a fashion shop, just around the corner, and Sam and I thought it was pretty impressive stuff. I remember we were just walking around and saw her window at Start and thought 'that's amazing, who did that?'.

We were looking for ways of having 3D physical manifestations of the illustrations we were publishing for the artists we were working with, of the characters they (our illustrators) were producing. So when we realised Felt Mistress was collaborating with Jonathan on his pieces, we asked her if she would be up for trying to do something.

SA We had the whole magazine of stuff to choose from, but those Karine Bernadou characters really stood out because they were beautifully simple and very colourful. So we thought immediately those would be the best ones. We didn't know if it was doable or not. We sent Louise the picture and said "do you think you can do anything with these?" And she said 'Yeah!'

Top
**Family Games**
Original illustration by
Karine Bernadou from
**Nobrow 3: Topsy Turvy.**

Right
**Father/Daughter**
Designed by Karine Bernadou
460 mm x 200 mm
Made for Nobrow
Exhibited at "Pick Me Up"
Somerset House, London
Mixed fibres, felt, embroidery
thread and polyester fibre filling.

SA Two or three weeks later, we got a parcel and it was amazing. The picture was so flat, so graphic, and yet she managed to embody the drawing completely and do a 3D version of something for which there was no 3D information. There were no turnaround drawings, or anything. It really works, it really looks like Karine Bernardou.

AS Karine Bernardou wants them! She wanted them straightaway. She was kind of gob-smacked really, she didn't really know what to say, she was just 'Omigod, this is so cool...' It was really nice to do that.

SA The whole thing about Nobrow magazine was everyone gets involved in doing something, because they are interested and want to do it. Louise did that work because she was passionate about it. Based on that we have ended up commissioning her several times. That's because we're also so impressed by her enthusiasm for what she does, it's amazing.

AS It's her ability to make these things come to life. And it is worth mentioning it was for the first Pick Me Up show at Somerset House (May 2010). We had spoken to Louise and said we would give out her card at the event and publicise her involvement. It was great for us because we were able to display these beautiful things in our space, which we did a lot of work on, we handprinted wallpaper, lots of touches. But adding that 3D element made the whole thing come together.

SA We got a lot of comments about them. A lot of people asking about them and loads of people wanted to buy them. We weren't selling them.

Dog/Mother
Designed by Karine Bernadou
690 mm x 210 mm
Made for Nobrow
Exhibited at "Pick Me Up"
Somerset House, London.
Mixed fibres, felt, embroidery
thread and polyester fibre filling.

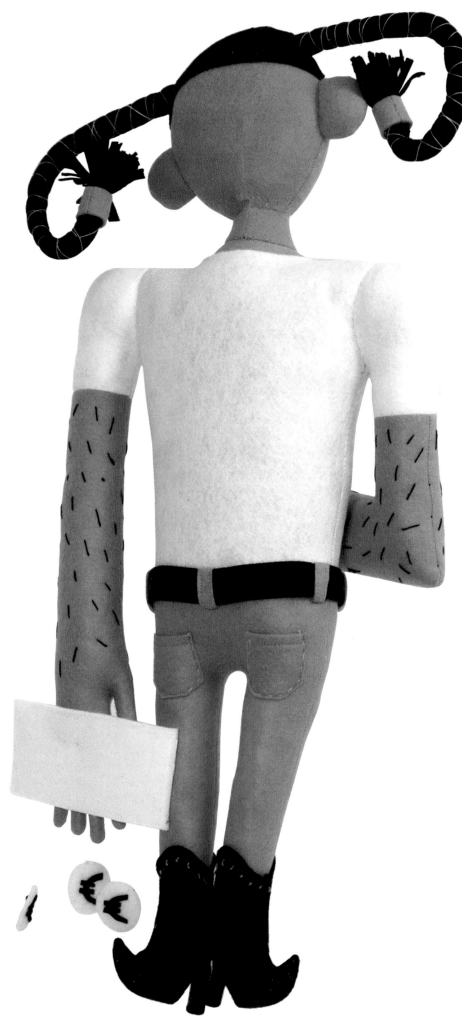

AS I think it was good for both of us. From then on, whatever projects we were doing, we would ask Louise if she wanted to get involved. Obviously, with the stuff we did in the gallery, we could sell the pieces for her, and we would pay her for working on them. We started the working relationship like that.

SA You give something to her, she comes back with it really quite fast, and when you look at the craftpersonship involved in it, it's just immense. It's like a language for her that she just speaks. It feels like it comes quite naturally to her but you know there is a lot of training there.

Daughter/Father
Designed by Karine
Bernadou
710 mm x 310 mm
Made for Nobrow
Exhibited at "Pick Me
Up" Somerset House,
London.
Mixed fibres, felt,
embroidery thread and
polyester fibre filling.

You have wauted your entire life to see a teeny tiny ant fighting crime in a pair of giant robot pants.

**Pants Ant**
290 mm x 210 mm
collaboration with
Woodrow Phoenix
Edition of two.
Mixed-fibre felt, wire,
cardboard, polyester fibre
filling and embroidery
thread.

The Peacock Wrangler is the UK's premier wrangler of peacocks. You got peacocks need wrangling? Just call for the Peacock Wrangler.

**The Peacock Wrangler**
950 mm x 330 mm
Mixed fibres, fleece, felt, plastic safety eyes and polyester fibre filling.

We've made sculptural work in the past and also puppets but this is the first time that we combined the two. Floyd has always been a favourite character of ours so we jumped at the chance to make our own version. We wanted to riff on Floyd's built-in Beatles influence and we also referenced Yellow Submarine animator Heinz Edelmann and the 60s poster art of Milton Glaser.

**Pepperdelica**
950 mm x 300 mm
Made for the Jim Henson tribute show "The Lovers, The Dreamers and Me", Gallery Nucleus, Alhambra, California.

Pepperdelica wears purple trousers, cowboy boots, a military Sgt. Pepper-style jacket with frog fastenings and a peaked cap. He carries his left-handed bass guitar.
Mixed-fibre felt, foam, wire, embroidery thread, card and polyester fibre filling.

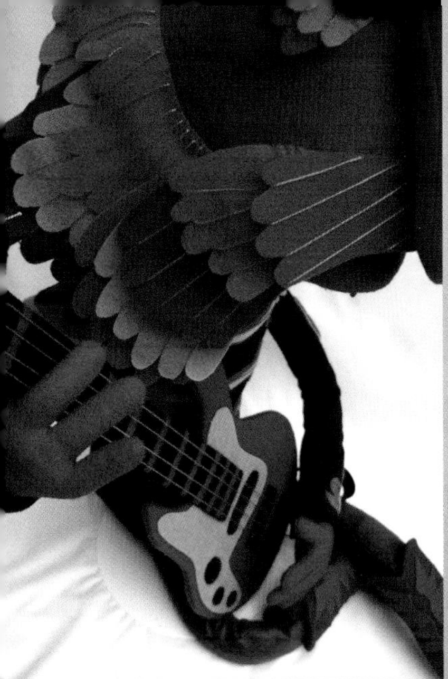

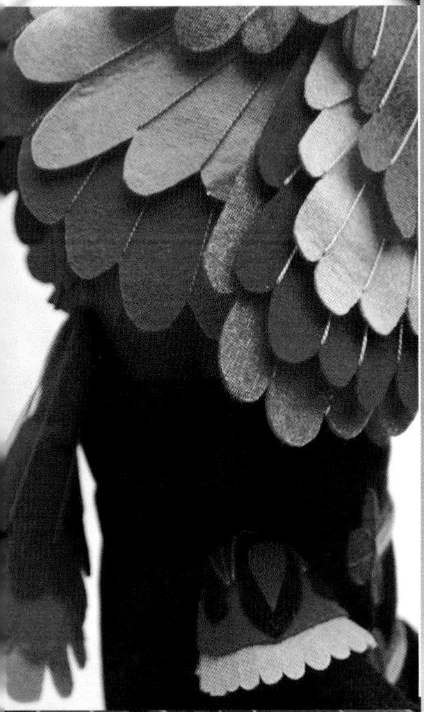

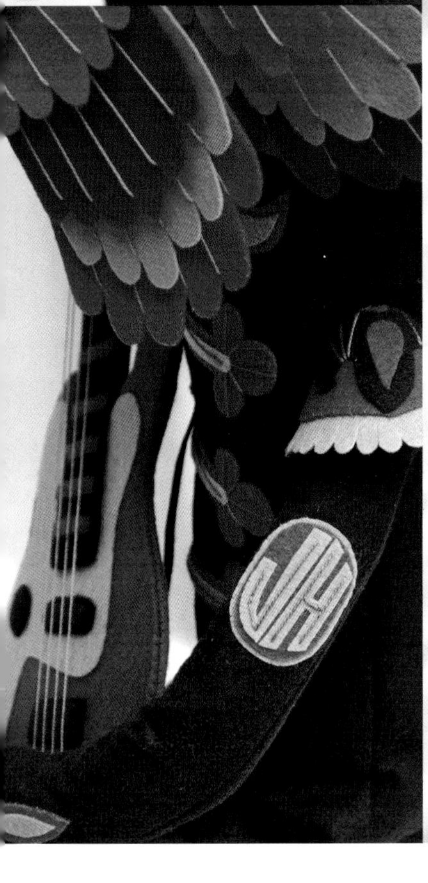

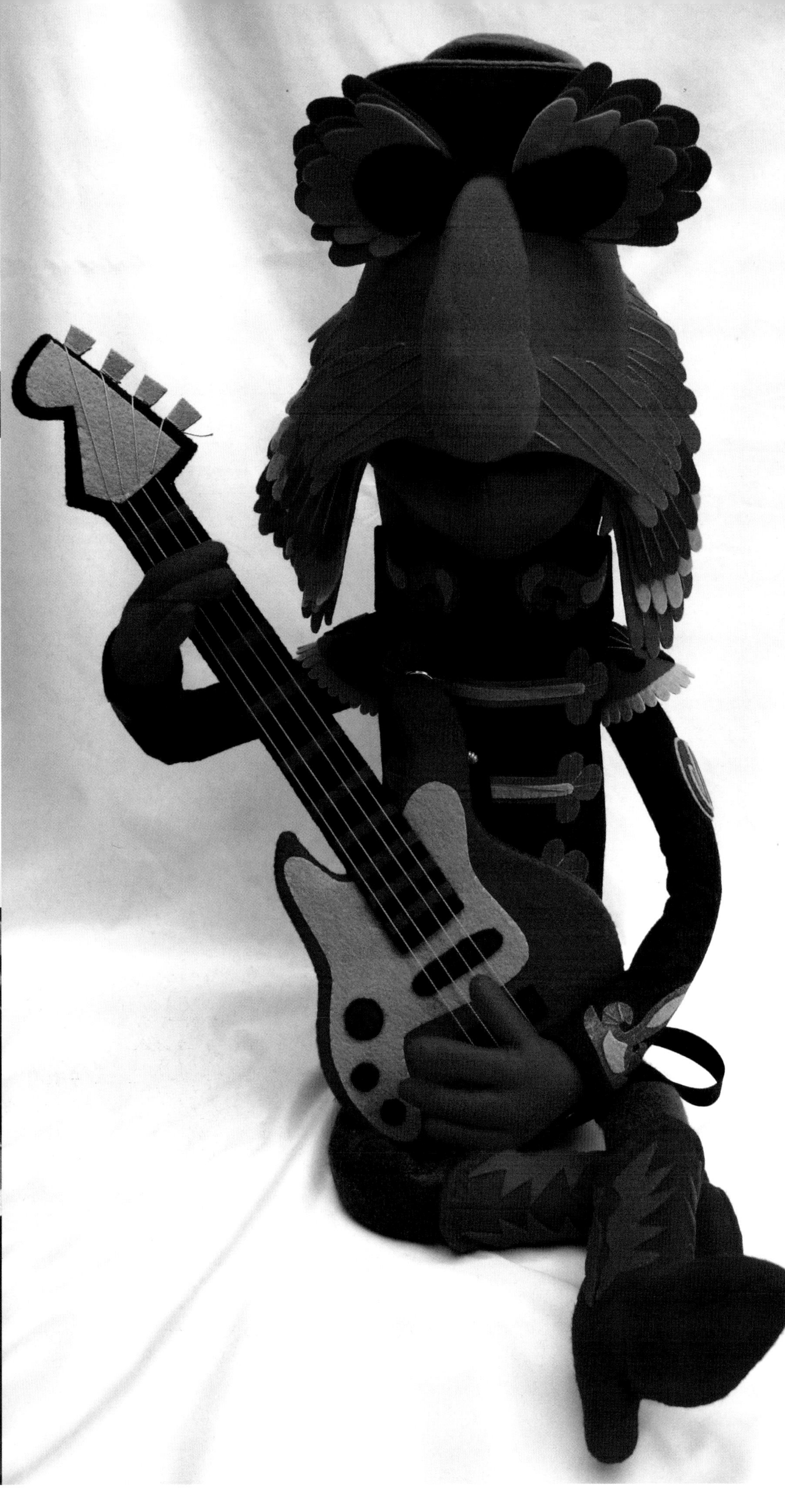

PEPPERDELICA — 2011

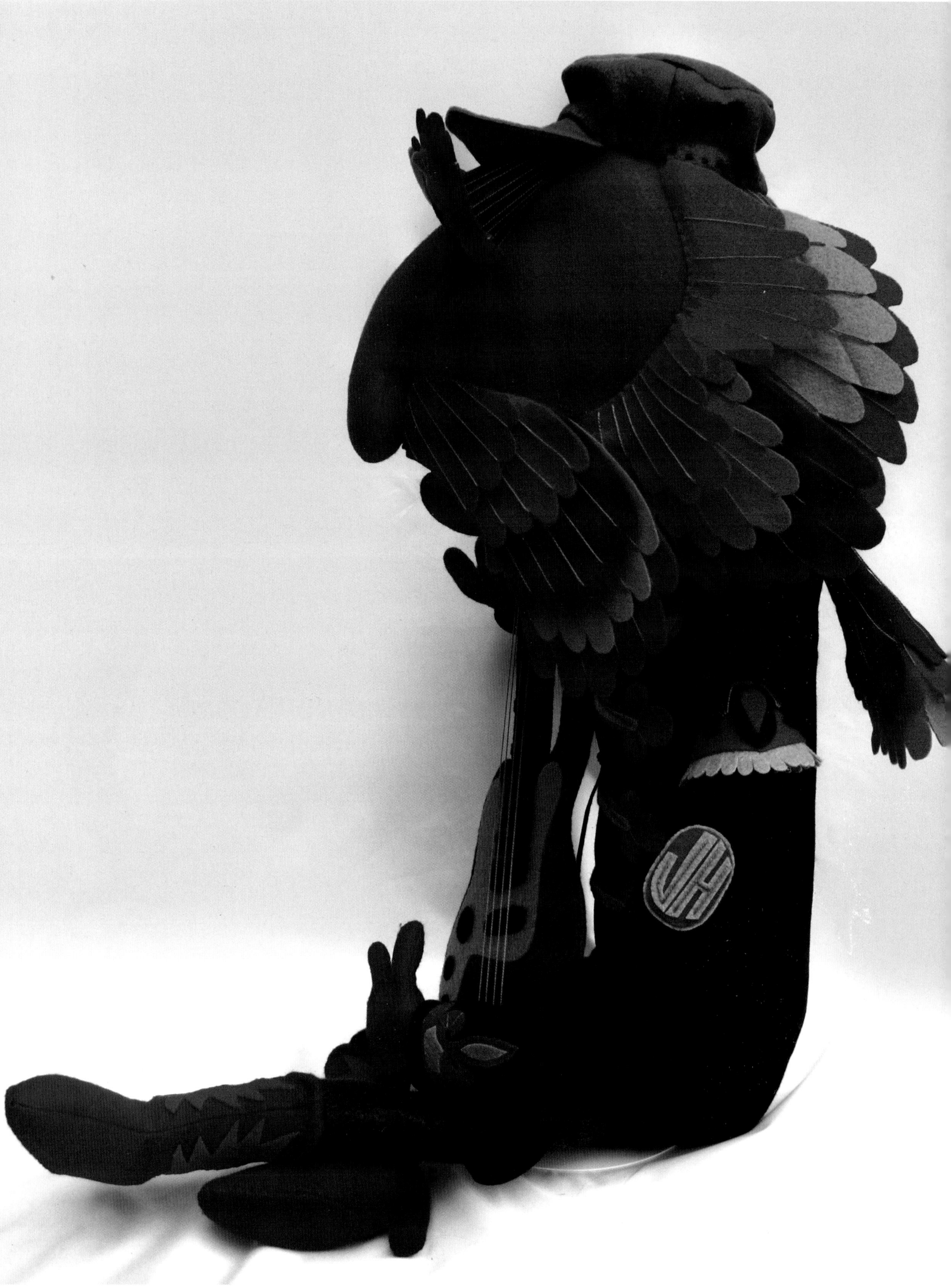
JH

**Pincushion Man**
140mm x 100mm
Olive green polkadot
cotton head with felt
fez. The base is a
wooden sake box.
Cotton, felt, plastic
safety eyes, embroidery
thread, polyester fibre
filling, card and wood.

Professor Skeffington is a professor in Nautical Activities and an avid connoisseur of Aquatic Jazz (Thelonius Monkfish, Eric Dolphin, etc).

**Professor Skeffington**
750 mm x 330 mm
Edition of 30
Polyester fibre fleece, Mixed-fibre felt, plastic safety eyes, and polyester fibre filling.

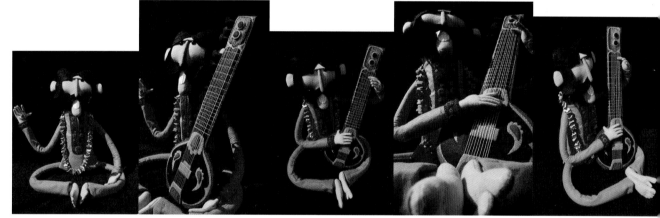

**Rishikesh George**
George Harrison, made for "All Together Now" The Beatles tribute show at Gallery Nucleus, Alhambra, California
1200 mm x 360 mm
Sitar 690mm x 260mm

George wears a short, orange, embroidered kurta with matching loose-fitting trousers and has flower garlands around his neck. His right hand has an appliquéd eye detail.
Felt, plastic safety eyes, embroidery thread, card and polyester fibre filling.

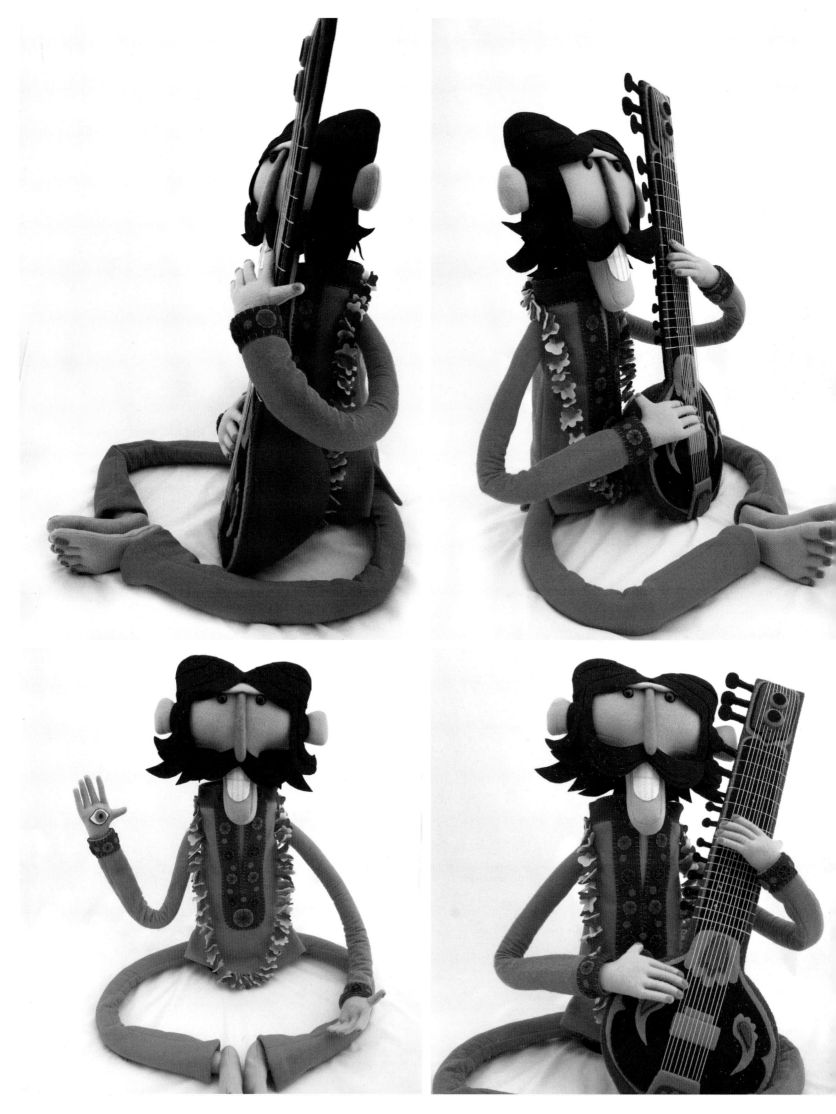

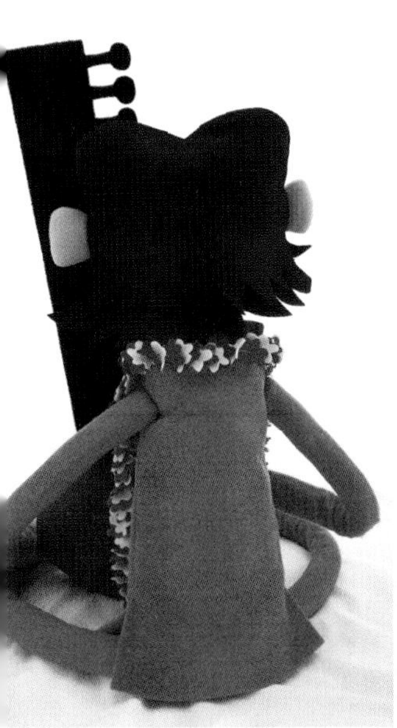

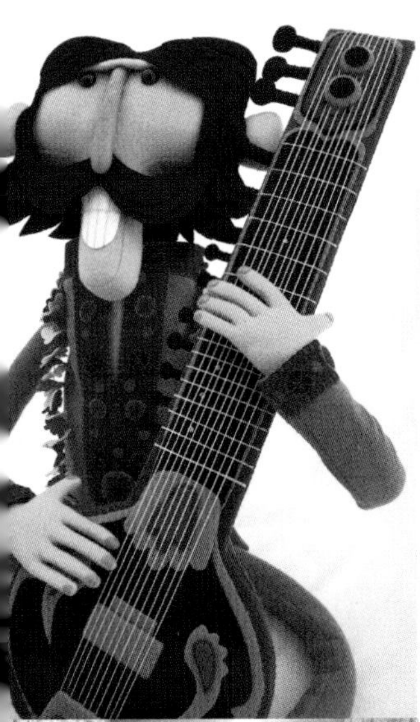

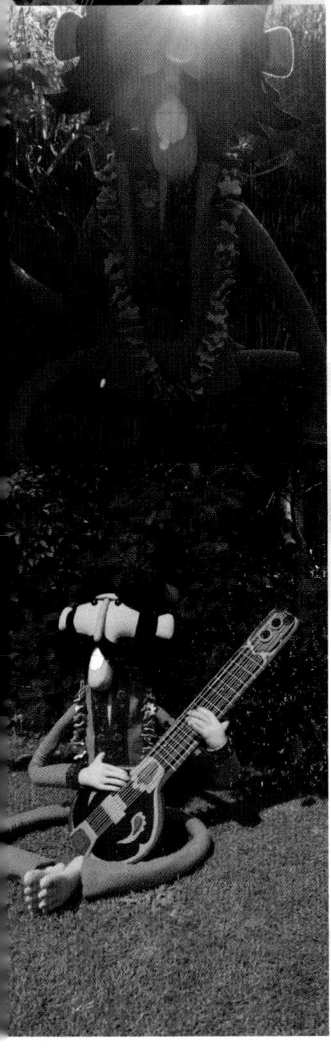

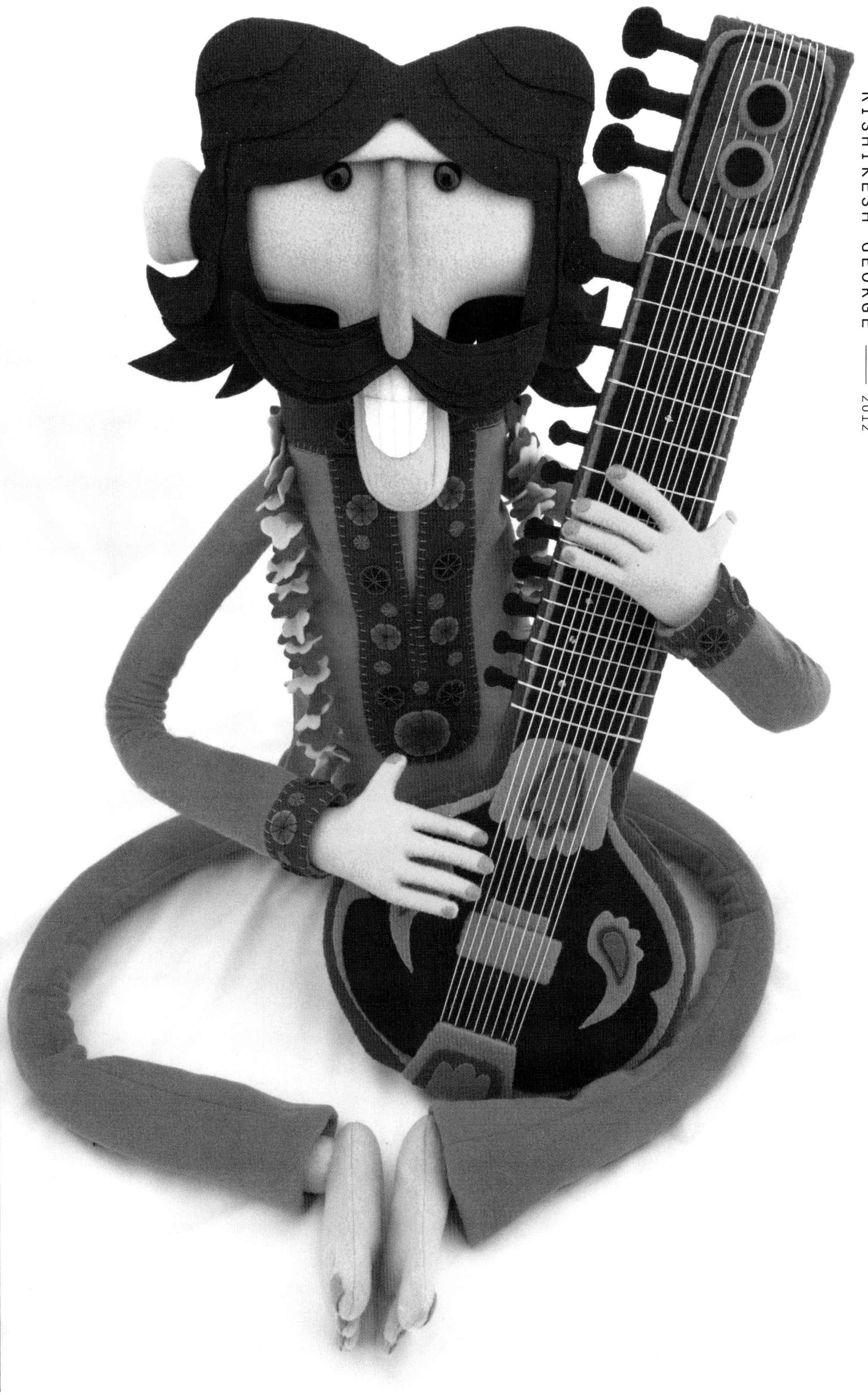

Rishikesh George —— 2012

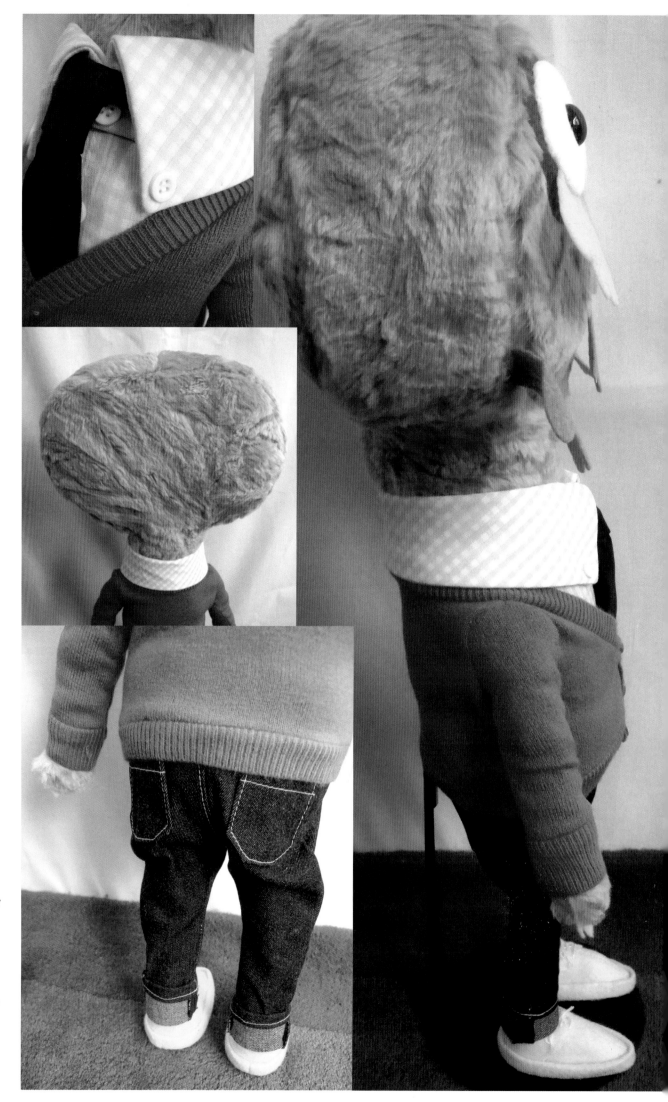

After aquatically traversing the globe for many years, Rudy finally climbed out of the Riddarfjarden and made Stockholm his home. He enjoys sushi, skinny jeans and the music of Sparks.

Rudy Froops
530 mm x 280 mm
Rudy wears yellow cotton gingham button-down collared shirt, black skinny tie, pink knitted cardigan, narrow legged indigo denim jeans with turn-ups and yellow lace-up pointy shoes.
Mixed fibres, fake fur, felt, plastic safety eyes, card, wire and polyester fibre filling.

A fresh kid with a penchant for neon kicks and a love of crate digging, Scrimpton divides his time between DJing at the legendary EBGB's and running his own record label, Fleeps Bleeps.

**Scrimpton Fleeps**
650 mm x 350 mm
Scrimpton wears a yellow vest top with monster badge. Narrow-legged indigo denim jeans, rainbow stripe snake belt, orange and lime green trucker cap, high-top trainers, white framed wayfarer-style glasses, big orange headphones and pink satchel-style back pack.
Mixed fibres, fake fur, felt, plastic safety eyes, wire, card, metal and polyester fibre filling.

Scrimpton Fleeps
650 mm x 350 mm

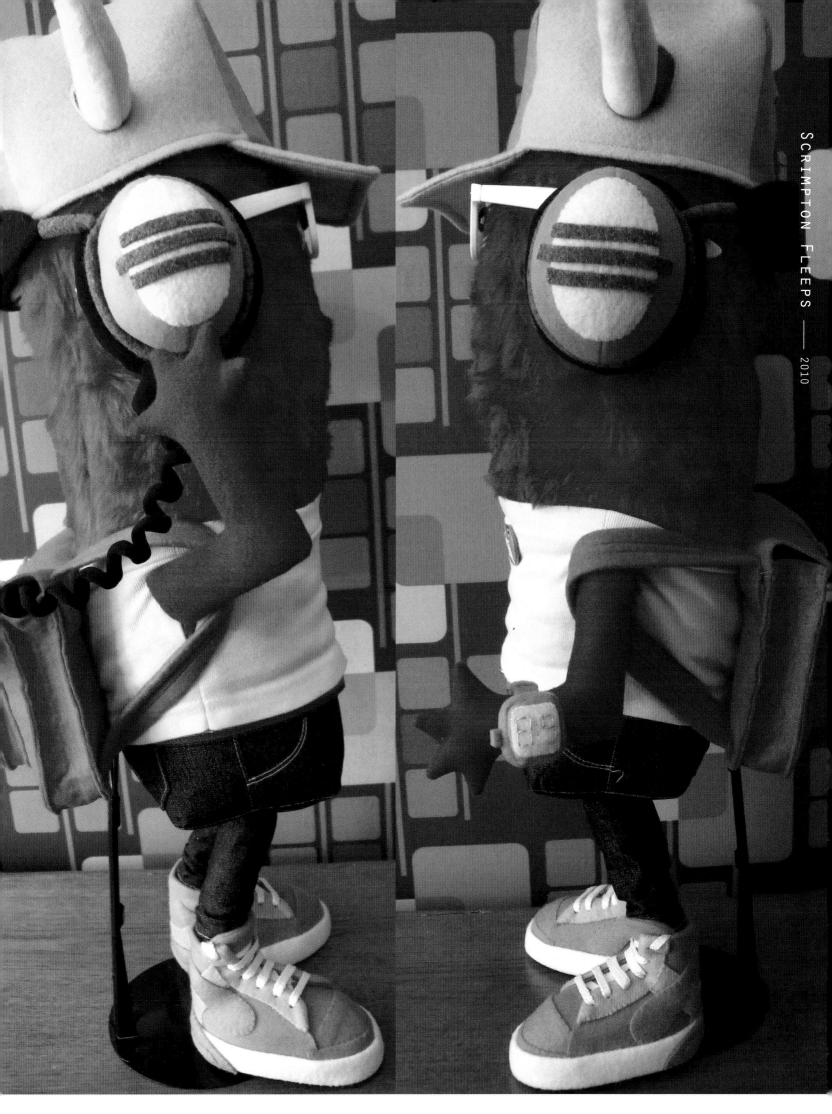

Sebastian, a French dude with an encyclopedic knowledge of 1980s Electronica, runs the Paris Synth Exchange. He claims he can identify a Roland D-50 by smell alone.

Sebastien
800 mm x 220 mm
Puppet
Sebastien wears white thick-framed sunglasses, skinny jeans with turn-ups, black and white stripey skinny-knit jumper and a black and white checked fringed scarf.
Mixed fibres, fake fur, felt, plastic safety eyes, wire, card and polyester fibre filling.

# SELFRIDGES

Selfridges' theme for Christmas 2010 was 'play'. Jonathan and Louise were delighted to be asked to design a doll's house-themed window display, to be featured in one of their Oxford Street windows over the course of their Christmas campaign. Jonathan produced a sketch of exactly the type of doll's house that the Felt Mistress characters were likely to inhabit and once it was approved, Louise ran with it. The illustrations were printed onto MDF and the house was constructed by Selfridges' excellent prop team. While Louise was making all the characters, Jonathan designed accessories for the interiors of all the rooms. They wanted the doll's house to be full of funny little details that would perhaps go unnoticed at first glance, so that there would be surprises to be discovered on second and third visits.

Other Felt Mistress one-off characters were displayed in a second window on Oxford Street and sold in Selfridges' concept store, The Wonder Room.

Felt Mistress available in the Play Shop on G

L to R:
Tabitha Snark
**Uli Snooks & Rondo**
Wilbur Grumph
Scrimpton Fleeps
Graahl Lagerfurr
Elspeth Frond
Lady Garrrgghh Garrrgghhh!

Next page/Left
Kipston
**Snapper Duval**
Brunhilde
Herzog
Next page/Right
Chet Krink
Andre Krunkle
Jean-Paul Schmunkle
Wilko Roby

**Snapper Duvall**

Dapper snapper, Snapper Duvall, can be seen all over the world and at all the best parties with his trusty Leica. He's been described as a cross between Terry Thomas, Terry Richardson and Terry Towelling. No one has ever seen him without his trademark red framed sunglasses.

**Chet Krink**

Chet is a poet and part of an existentialist, beat collective - a bunch of ... Gauche, espresso-sipping, jazz-loving, poem-writing Bea(s)tniks. Che... ne er without his copy of "Growl" by his hero, Allen Grimsberg.

**Elspeth Frond**

Elspeth Frond is one of the worlds ... ed models. She rose to prominence after winning Ame ... yster and ha ... ree mode ... for the likes of Alexander Mc ... en and Jean Paul Grun...

**Serge Gainsbourg**
360 mm x 190 mm
Edition of two
Made as Louise's entry for
the blog "Draw Serge".
Serge wears a black
woollen polo-neck,
charcoal gabardine
trousers, and black shoes.
He smokes a cigarette,
complete with smoke.
Mixed fibres, felt, card,
and polyester fibre filling.

**Señor Gonzalez**
770 mm x 220 mm
Made for "Animals Take Over Berlin", exhibited at various locations in Berlin, Germany.

Señor Gonzalez wears black woollen ribbed polo-neck. Skinny blue jeans with turn-ups. He has three pin badges: Adam Ant, an ant, and 'I heart Berlin'. Mixed-fibre felt and fleece, plastic safety eyes, and polyester fibre filling.

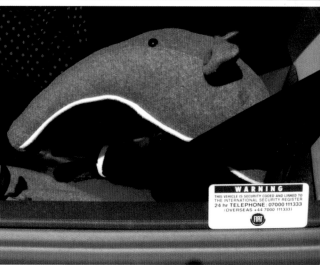

**Skull**
250 mm x 170 mm
Made as a birthday
present for Jonathan.
Fleece, felt , plastic safety
eyes, polyester fibre filling.

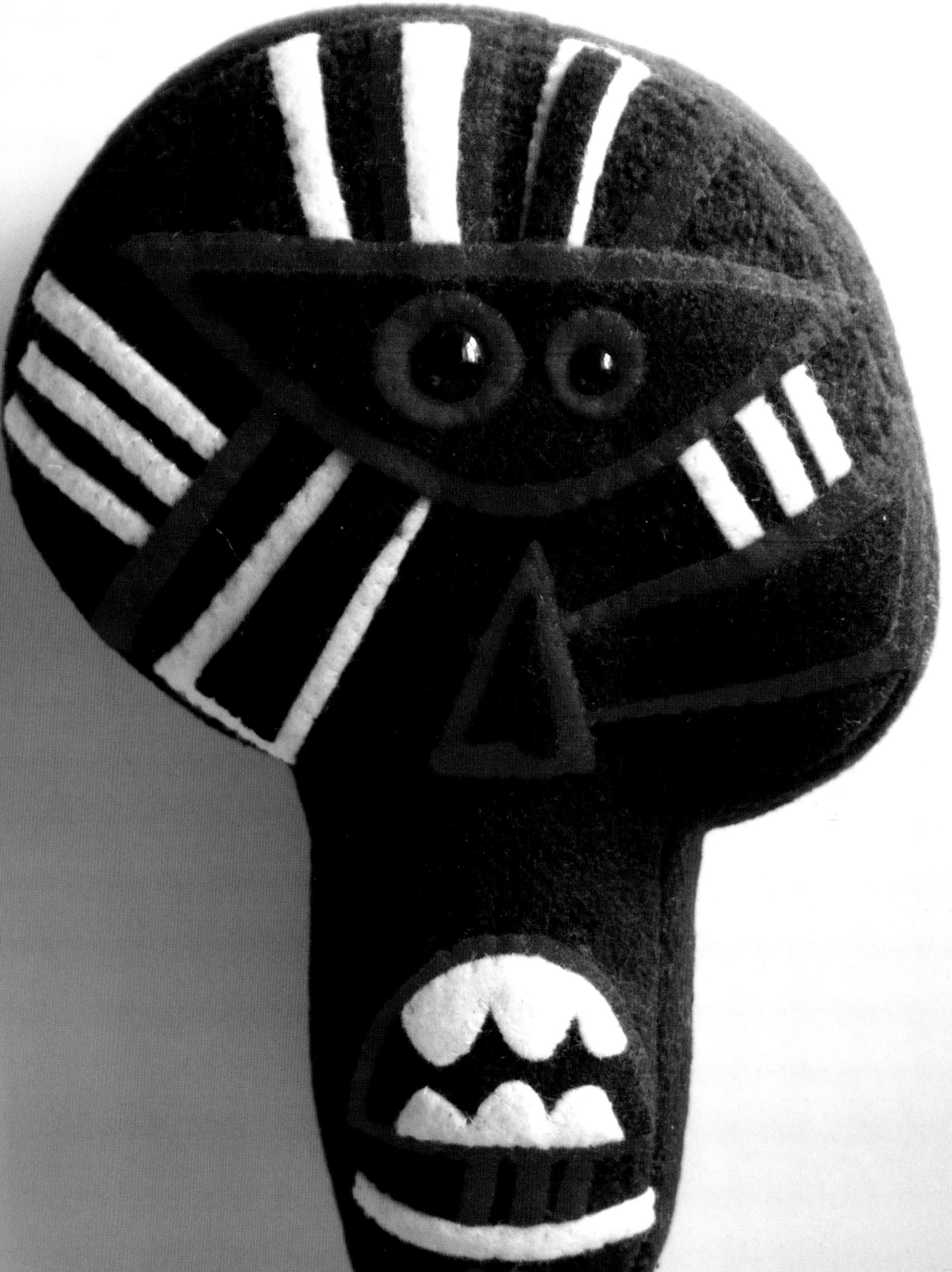

SKULL —— 2009

Dapper snapper, Snapper Duvall, can be seen all over the world and at all the best parties with his trusty Leica. He's been described as a cross between Terry Thomas, Terry Richardson and Terry Towelling. No one has ever seen him without his trademark red-framed sunglasses.

**Snapper Duval**
810cm x 300 mm
Snapper wears short sleeved checked button-down collared shirt with red bow tie. Red-framed aviator-style glasses, skinny indigo blue denim jeans with turn-ups and a red leather belt.
Mixed fibres, fake fur, felt, leather, plastic safety eyes, wire and polyester fibre filling.

**Spyghetti Western**
180 mm x 120 mm
Made for Mad magazine's
Celebration "50 years of
Spy vs Spy Custom Show",
San Diego, California.
Mixed-fibre felt, cotton,
embroidery thread, card,
spray paint, and plastic.

WANTED

WHITE SPY "DEAD OR ALIVE"

# START LONDON

Louise and Jonathan are big fans of The Fall. A brief discussion on Twitter of the fact that Louise was thinking about making felt versions of frontman Mark E Smith and his ex-partner, former Fall guitarist Brix, led to Louise being contacted by Brix herself. Now Brix Smith-Start and owner of a men's and women's wear store in Shoreditch, she liked what she saw of Felt Mistress' work so much that she invited Louise and Jonathan to display their pieces all over her store during London Fashion Week, 2010.

The BBC's 'Culture Show' featured a report on Start London that week and several FM characters made their television debut!

Opposite page, top:

**The Start Group**

L to R:

Dwight

The Modsters

Kipston

The Flamingo Wrangler

Hugh Scruntin

Elspeth Frond

Zeep

Tommy Floom

Lady Jemimarraggh Grunk

Terry

The Peacock Wrangler

Leonard Groyle

Clem

Herzog

Tabitha Snark is an 'It Girl' and an 'It' Girl. Often seen hopping out of taxis with her horned pet, Rolando, in London, Paris and New York, Tabitha is heiress to the Snark fortune and can always be spotted on the front row at all the most prestigious catwalk shows.

Tabitha Snark
770 mm x 420 mm
and Rolando
190 mm x 15mm
Tabitha wears dogtooth check dress with pussycat bow at neckline, gathered skirt, nipped-in at waist with grosgrain ribbon bow and vintage buckle, three-quarter length fluted sleeves with button details, Rick-rack braiding details on sleeve edge, hem and bow. Matching bow hair clip. Undergarments: lace pants.
Rolando wears fake leather studded collar and chain lead.
Mixed fibres, wool tweed, fake fur, felt, plastic safety eyes, wire, card and polyester fibre filling.

TABITHA SNARK — 2010

Terry was born and raised in Salford. His knowledge of the Manchester music scene is second to none and he claims to have attended the Sex Pistols gig at the Free Trade Hall, the first night at the Hacienda and was responsible for Morrissey having to wear a hearing aid. He growls.

**Terry**
500 mm x 350 mm
Terry wears sleeveless "This Nation's Saving Grace - The Fall" t-shirt, studded leather collar and lead. He also has a growl box inside.
Mixed fibres, fake fur, felt, plastic safety eyes, leather studs and polyester fibre filling.

Terry likes long country walks, ties, novelty cookie jars, the music of Herb Alpert and hugging people. He can't pass a bus queue without giving every single person a "bit of a fuss".

**Terry Grunts**
750 mm x 330 mm
Terry wears a silver jaquard tie.
Mixed fibres, fake fur, felt, plastic safety eyes, and polyester fibre filling.

Tippy enjoys travelling the world trying to recruit new members to Team Tippy. He likes the colour orange, tying his own shoelaces, the music of Polysics and chocolate eclairs. He can often be found socialising with his crew: Pedro the squirrel, Grayson the Horse and Mr Neville (the newsagent).

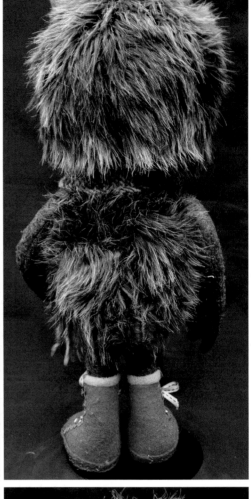

**Tippy Winkles**
480 mm x 180 mm
Made to star on our Christmas cards, now travels with us.

Tippy wears orange lace-up winter boots with rick-rack braiding and ribbon details. He wears a wool knitted scarf with fringed ends but also has two other scarves, a wool tweed scarf and a fleece scarf with appliqued felt pattern.
Mixed-fibre felt, card, plastic safety eyes, wire and polyester fibre filling.

**Tippy Winkles**
480 mm x 180 mm
Tippy wears his skiing
outfit complete with skis,
woollen hat, woollen polo-
neck and body warmer. He
won gold with this outfit in
the Schmancy Winter Plush
Olympics, Seattle.
Mixed-fibre felt, card,
plastic safety eyes, wire
and polyester fibre filling.

**Tippy Winkles**
480 mm x 180 mm
Tippy wears orange
lace-up winter boots with
rick-rack braiding and
ribbon details. He wears a
checked woven wool scarf.

**Pops Winkles**
750 mm x 28mm
Pops wears a checked
woven wool scarf.
Mixed fibres, fake fur, felt,
plastic safety eyes, card,
wire and polyester fibre
filling.

MERRY CHRISTMAS

*Felt Mistress*

x

**Reindeer Tippy**
Customised wooden
Pecanpal by Noferin
350mm x 140mm
Reindeer Tippy wears
blue narrow-leg jeans
with studded leather
belt, knitted grey and
red striped jumper and
red converse (painted
on). He carries a small
camera from the
original toy.
Original wooden toy
base, acrylic paint, felt,
fake fur, plastic safety
eyes, card and polyester
fibre filling.

Tommy is part of a rock duo with his "significant other", Heppy Mixenpix. Think the Mouldy Peaches meets Fraggle Rock. Tommy's weapon of choice is the Rickenbacker 4000 series bass.

**Tommy Floom**
840 mm x 350 mm
Tommy wears blue denim jeans with double turn-up, studded leather belt and key chain. White collar and pink and black satin skinny tie. Red high-top lace-up baseball style boot and bike chain bracelet. Mixed-fibre felt, card, plastic safety eyes, wire and polyester fibre filling.

# TOTEM

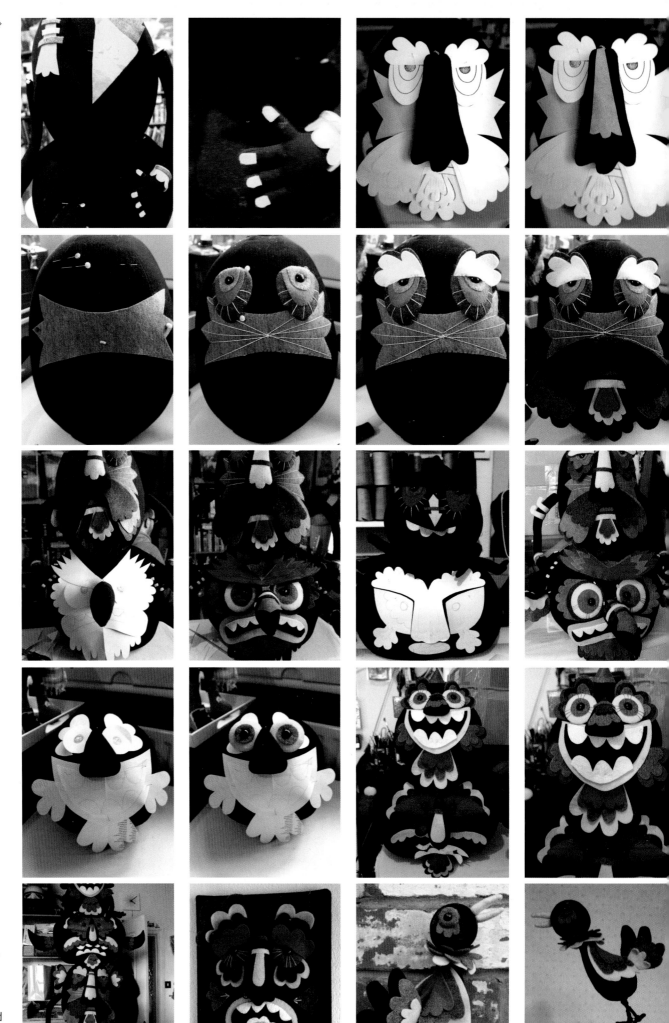

Totem Pole
Made for "Inky Goodness
Totem" show,
Pictoplasma, Berlin.

When stacked/interlocked
the Full Totem measures
1950 mm x 700 mm.

Shaboo
The worrier. Not good with heights, unfortunately. Avid ornithologist.

Rombondo
The grumpiest of the group. Enjoys macrame and strudel.

Right/Top
Shaboo
600 mm x 700 mm
Wool, Mixed fibres, felt, embroidery thread, plastic safety eyes, card, and polyester fibre filling.

Right/Bottom
Rombondo
600 mm x 700 mm
Wool, Mixed fibres, felt, embroidery thread, plastic safety eyes, card, and polyester fibre filling.

Bulbobo
Stoic and good in a crisis.
Enjoys the music of the Pan
Pipes and fried breakfasts.

Looboo
The life and soul of the party.
Enjoys observation decks and
stepladders.

Left
**Bulbobo**
850 mm x 350 mm
Wool, Mixed fibres, felt,
embroidery thread, plastic
safety eyes, card, and
polyester fibre filling.

Right
**Looboo**
650 mm x 330 mm
Wool, Mixed fibres, felt,
embroidery thread, plastic
safety eyes, card, and
polyester fibre filling.

**Travis**
690 mm x 180 mm
Commissioned by an uncle whose niece had lost her dog.
Mixed-fibre fleece and felt card, plastic safety eyes, and polyester fibre filling.

**Tweed Travis**
690 mm x 180 mm
Vintage wool tweed, mixed-fibre felt, card, plastic safety eyes, and polyester fibre filling.

Mum, Dad, Klipsy and Fring. Triumphant winners of "Ask The Furry Family" (thanks mainly to Dad's impressive knowledge of bark).

## Mum Treep

520 mm x 250 mm

Mrs Treep wears vintage wool tweed dress, trimmed in yellow bias binding with lace panel down centre front. Turquoise polka dot cotton apron with large pocket and hand carved wooden spoon.

Mixed fibres, fake fur, vintage tweed, felt, plastic safety eyes, card, wire, wood and polyester fibre filling.

## Dad Treep

600 mm x 330 mm

Mr Treep wears skinny yellow polo-neck, knitted turquoise v-neck jumper and charcoal grey straight-legged trousers. He smokes a pipe.

Mixed fibres, fake fur, felt, plastic safety eyes, card, wire and polyester fibre filling.

## Klipsey Treep

300 mm x 220 mm

Klipsey wears turquoise cotton polkadot dress with bow at neckline. Turquoise knitted bolero-styled cardigan with rick-rack braid edging.

Mixed fibres, fake fur, felt, plastic safety eyes, card, and polyester fibre filling.

## Fring Treep

300 mm x 240 mm

Fring wears a turquoise knitted polo-neck with FM embroidered patch and charcoal grey straight-legged trousers.

Mixed fibres, fake fur, felt, plastic safety eyes, card, and polyester fibre filling.

**Tweedocaster**
Custom Fender
Stratocaster cover.
Made for a friend who
wanted his guitar to look
less "rock'n'roll" and more
"geography teacher".
Vintage herringbone
tweed.

Esteemed cravat-wearing critic, Uli Snooks, is infamous in the UK for being the first person to say "flumps" on live televison. His trusty walking stick (and fellow critic), Rondo, is always at his side but they have never been known to agree on anything.

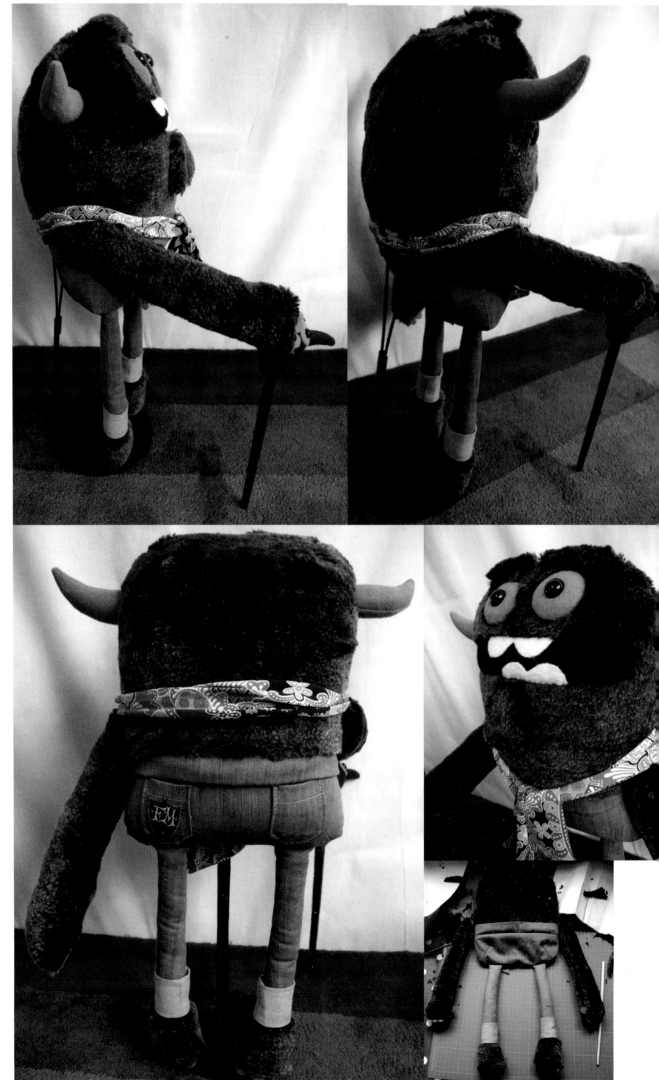

**Uli Snooks & Rondo**
500 mm x 350 mm
Uli wears faded blue denim jeans with double turn-ups, and loosely tied printed rayon cravat. He always carries his walking stick, Rondo.
Mixed fibres, fake fur, felt, plastic safety eyes, card, wire and polyester fibre filling.

Undetermined Wrangler
550 mm x 180 mm
Made as a present.
The Wrangler wears a
skinny-knit, grey and
yellow polo-neck.
Mixed fibres, fake fur, felt,
plastic safety eyes, and
polyester fibre filling.

**Voodoo Tron**
Made for the Inky
Goodness show
"Wonderland",
Vaad Gallery,
Birmingham.

Right
**General Dombolo**
550 mm x 200 mm
Mixed-fibre felt, card,
plastic safety eyes, wire,
embroidery thread and
polyester fibre filling.

Left
**Topo**
900 mm x 480 mm
Mixed-fibre felt, card,
plastic safety eyes, plastic,
wire, embroidery thread
and polyester fibre filling.

Right
**Doblolanomi**
700 mm x 420 mm
Mixed-fibre felt, card,
plastic safety eyes, wire,
embroidery thread and
polyester fibre filling.

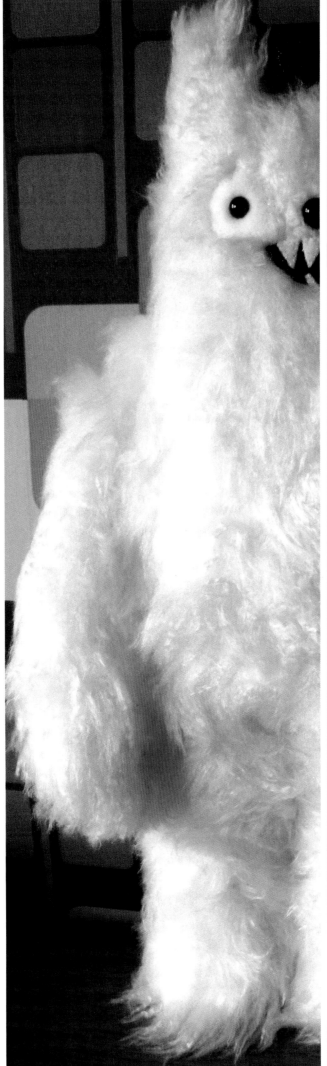
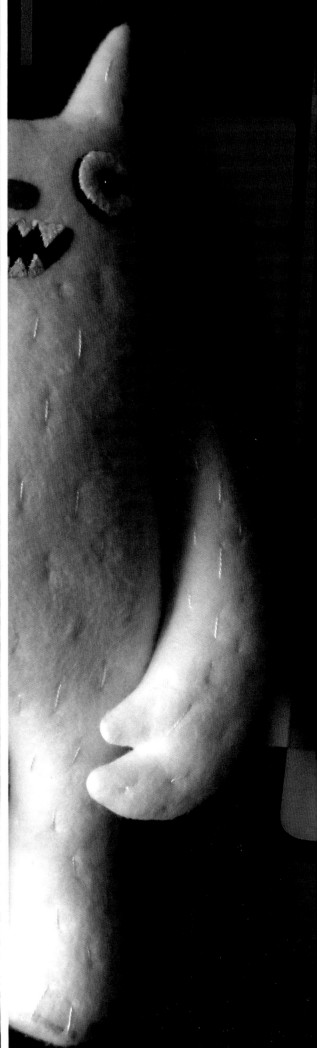

**Wendigo**
440 mm x 230 mm
Edition of two, (one fake
fur, one fleece).
Designed by John Allison,
made as a present for
John.
Mixed-fibre felt, fleece,
fake fur, embroidery
thread, plastic safety eyes,
card, and polyester fibre
filling.

Lecturer at St Grunks' University and the world's leading expert on Frunggology, Wilbur shares a study with Professor Skeffington. Arguments are often had about the merits of Prog Rock over Jazz, and the enduring qualities of corduroy and pipe tobacco.

**Wilbur Grumph**
580 mm x 250 mm
Wilbur wears a fully-lined brown checked three-button sports jacket with elbow patches, purple woollen polo-neck and beige straight-legged corduroy trousers. He also smokes a brown pipe.
Fake fur, Mixed fibres, felt, plastic safety eyes, and polyester fibre filling.

WILBUR GRUMPH — 2010

Legendary roadie Wilko Roby hails from Dudley in the West Midlands. Wilko's reputation soon superseded those of the bands he was working for. On the now legendary Grimble Twins 1979 World Tour, Wilko ate an entire pool table (including cues) "for a bet"!

**Wilko Roby**
750 mm x 450 mm
Wilko wears studded sleeveless denim jacket with embroidered patches including Iron Maiden, Led Zeppelin, AC/DC and FM, with pin badges including AC/DC, Slayer, Saxon, KISS and Metallica. Around his neck is a thick metal chain necklace and a backstage pass for The Grimble Twins. Mixed fibres, fake fur, felt, plastic safety eyes, wire, card and polyester fibre filling.

# USTWO™

## NEIL MCFARLAND (PARIS HAIR)

**Willow**
Collaboration with Neil McFarland (Paris Hair)
300 mm x 750 mm
Made for ustwo™, the makers of the game "Whale Trail", designed by Neil McFarland. Also featured in the video promo for the Gruff Rhys single "Whale Trail", directed by Neil McFarland.
Mixed-fibre felt, embroidery thread, and polyester fibre filling.

Right
Frames from "Whale Trail" video directed by Neil McFarland of ustwo™

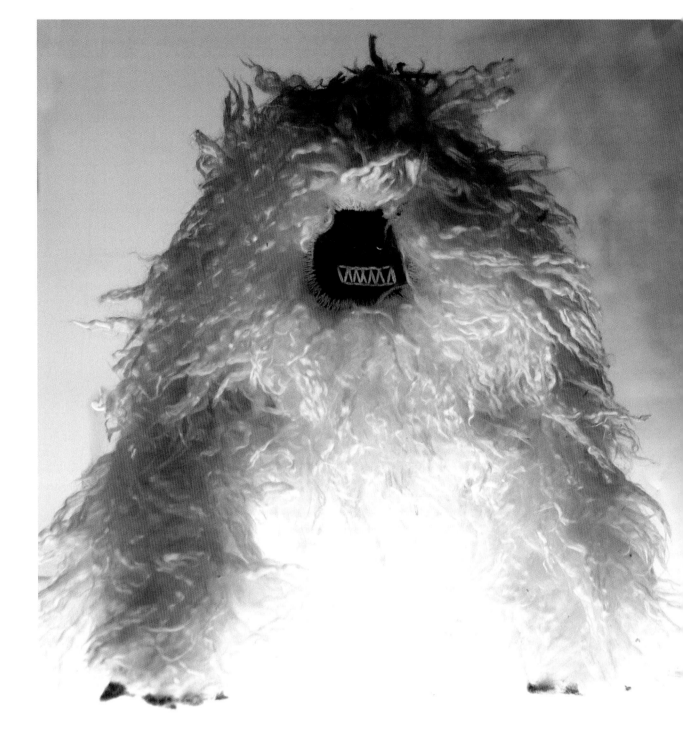

Yeti
200 mm x 120 mm
Made as a present for
JAKe.
Mixed-fibre fake fur and
felt, machine embroidery
and beads. Polyester fibre
filling.

**Zipper Toothed Rabbit**
390 mm x 180 mm
Made as an entry for
Pictoplasma's "Bunny
Mandala" (sadly, it
wasn't used).
Denim, metal zipper,
Mixed-fibre felt,
embroidery thread,
metal washers, with
polyester fibre filling.

**Zultantara**
300 mm x 220 mm
Made for the Rabbids
"Eeerz" Custom Vinyl
Invasion Tour, London
and Paris.
Mixed-fibre felt,
embroidery thread,
card, and polyester
fibre filling.

JONTOFSKI AKA

JONATHAN
EDWARDS

JONATHAN EDWARDS (JE) Louise wanted to do something creative that she could give as a gift. When you know somebody who draws, they often give a card they've made as a gift. One of the first things Louise made was The Incredible Hulk, a present for Darryl Cunningham, and she did The Thing as well. Sometimes she might ask me "What shape shall I do?", but they were completely Louise, those things.

When I did The Squabbling Dandies [Deadline magazine, 1995] I made a clay head for a dandy, and Louise was going to make a marionette. That never happened, but after that I did Simon Creem. We bought a GI Joe, the US version of Action Man, and it was Louise's idea to make that. I thought it was quite ingenious. I don't know where Simon Creem came from, I remember drawing a Jason King-type character that had a leather sphere for a head and lenses for eyes, but the lenses were the tops off two felt-tip pens cut down and sprayed silver, with a black bead in each of them, on a fake leather head. Then she dressed him and made a little black polo-neck jumper for him and a pair of flared jeans and a little medallion out of jewellery findings. That was 1995...96?

WOODROW PHOENIX (WP) Did you think to yourself, "There's something here I can explore?"

JE I don't know why we didn't do more at that time. I suppose because Louise was so busy making a thousand wedding dresses a year or whatever it was! She made Peepee for Simon Gane, Pants Ant and Urbane Gorilla for you. But I don't suppose I was drawing characters so much then. It was in the transition from when I was doing comic strip stuff to doing illustration. I went through a period of drawing what people asked me to draw rather than stuff I wanted to draw. So it wasn't until I did that range of t-shirts for Sportax Extreme Sports Channel in 2007, Louise said 'ooh I could make these'. It was the Kaiju. Instead of them being two flat pieces of felt stitched together and stuffed, they had a gusset, and they were three shapes so they stood up and they were really nice sculptural objects.

When Sportax asked me to do t-shirts originally they wanted illustrations of skateboarders, snowboarders, etc but I suppose if you look at the kind of t-shirts skaters wear, they don't wear t-shirts with other skaters on. So for the next range they wanted to try something different. I said, I've got all these things in my sketchbook, what if we based the shirts on something from there? I think on the first one, I sent them a design with Inspector Cumulus on it. They took him off the repeated pattern and I'm glad they did now. They really liked just the monster thing. I drew more monsters. I did a French fly monster, and Kaiju and Yetis and, you know, that typical type of stuff.

Louise saw the sketches and while I was away for the day at a Birmingham Comicon, she had nothing else to do so she thought 'I'll make a Kaiju'. When I got back there were two made. They were the very first ones, the tweed ones. I think we just refined them very slightly with their shape but they were really nice with the tails and the spines, really nice items. They worked well from all angles, and considering that my drawing of them was two-dimensional, graphic and abstracted and there was no shading, they looked like my drawing – and like my drawing from every angle.

WP What did that do to your brain?

JE It got me thinking on what else we could do. We made larger ones for when I did the Ispo Expo at Munich. They were about 3ft tall to go on the stand, they were commissioned by Sportax so they owned them, I don't know what happened to them. Also on the repeat pattern was Angry Squared, so Louise made him too. Making a cube out of felt is a particularly odd thing to do! He's got quite sharp angles considering he's soft and plush. The horns were stitched into the seams at that point, tapered in at the bottom, we adapted that. Louise stitched each one individually so they had a proper conical shape to them.

At the same time, we did Mr Smashing. That was two pieces sewed together, but she did it in such a way as to get around the flatness. He was jointed on the arms, jointed on the legs. I think we intentionally designed something that could be made easily, Louise wanted something simple that she could make multiples of. So I came up with a few designs, Louise would say 'I can do this', 'I can't do that', it was pretty much 50-50 between the pair of us. The Kaiju were the first things that we ever sold, produced in great quantity, the Here Gallery took some of those.

When I was in Munich at the Expo, Louise phoned me excitedly and said "They've taken five and they want another five!" That was quite a big thing. The main place for Kaiju was Tokyo Jazz Panda in Chester. They sold the majority of the 200 figures that we made. Just one shop in Chester! Professor Skeffington was another one where Louise said she wanted to make a multiple.

WP He's unlike most of your drawings in that his design is very minimal; he's almost just a shape with very little detail.

JE I think the drawing in my sketchbook originally had echoes of Cumulus to him. Of course, we tried to simplify and simplify it. The eyes were in a different position on him originally, his eyes were either side of his head with a mouth in the middle so he looked almost like Admiral Akbar. When Louise was pinning the eyes on she said "I think they look better here actually." And she moved them. It's something that happens a lot. The drawings will look one way but when we're pinning the features on before they are sewn on, they look different if you move the eyes around. Skeffington was made so that there was the least work in him. He looks like he has boots on, he looks like he has a polo-neck but he's just a couple of pieces sewn together.

SNAPPER DUVALL

WP The point at which what I think of as being the classic Felt Mistress thing— a fully realised creature with distinctive personality expressed through its intricately bespoke clothing—came into existence was with the Behemoth-on-Sea politicians. That was an amazing leap into a new dimension. Literally, with dimensionality. I remember how shocked and delighted I was. I had never seen anything like it before and I didn't know where it had come from. Where did it come from?

JE It was quite a jump. On BBC Parliament one morning there was a repeat of the 1982 election and people were on wearing kipper ties, 1970s leftovers considering it was the 1980s, and I began drawing them in my sketchbook. The first one, Hugh Scruntin, was quite a detailed drawing in my sketchbook. Louise saw it and said "I am going to make him." I wasn't expecting her to actually make a suit and a tie for him, the suit was even lined. I just thought he was going to be more like the Kaiju, a bit more basic. More like Skeffington, where you get the impression of clothing but he isn't really clothed.

It's a bit of a blur – we made the three politicians in the space of just over a week. I think of those as being the first proper Felt Mistress items. They were completely different to anything else. We took them to be photographed in Louise's mother's garden because we thought that the background would look like they were standing on the green outside the House of Commons. Her mother's neighbour saw them and asked us about them. Louise's mother told her Louise had made those. And her neighbour said "Oh, whatever for?" I thought we were on to something.

There was nothing to compare them to really, they're nice, we like them, but we didn't feel we had a model we could base them on. They are not vinyl, they don't look like traditional plush toys, so it just felt like something different.

GRAHHHL LAGERFURR

WP So once Louise had made that jump you started to explore tall things, wide things, narrow things, different shapes...

JE I suppose I always go back to that Matt Groening quote "A good character design is someone you can recognise in silhouette." We've always thought that way and of course, when Louise made wedding dresses, a silhouette is a very important thing isn't it? So to have something that's a very identifiable shape, a distinct shape, is something that interests us.

WP Is the drawing the blueprint for the creature or is it something in its own right?

LADY GARRGGHHH GARRGGHHHH

TABITHA SNARK & ROLANDO

JE They are two separate entities, I think the drawing is something in its own right. Something else happens when Louise gets hold of them. Hugh Scruntin is almost an exact replica of the original drawing, the other politicians are as well. But after that point, Louise always added something to the drawings. The pieces we have just done for our Nobrow show ("Hey! Who's This Guy?") came from a sketchbook that I filled with 60 characters. Louise used that sketchbook for inspiration and they have all changed in some way.

Instead of me thinking how can I draw hair that Louise can make, I just draw hair and then Louise thinks of a way to make it that gives that same impression using fabric. I feel like I am providing her with raw material to work from. I have never said to Louise, "make this". Even when she's working with other artists, with Ben Newman or Jon Burgerman, their work is very two-dimensional. Ben has given her turnarounds, Jon just gives her a watercolour sketch and Louise sees a way to turn that into 3D. A shape that looks like the drawing from all angles.

WP This ability of hers to act like a scanner, to take a line and give it volume and depth, that's a skill that almost no one has. It borders on scary! She not only interprets in 3D but accurately understands and translates the essence of a drawing into 3D. So she's not just reproducing something but inhabiting it, manifesting the core idea of it in some way.

JE I feel the same way. I suppose Louise has had so many years of looking at brides, looking at their shapes, tall and thin, short and fat. They want a certain dress and they want to look good and Louise has that ability to wrap someone up in cloth to make them look the way they want. These are the skills that set her work apart from everybody else.

WP What I find unsatisfying about a lot of plush and vinyl figures is that they are not really 3D. They are flat ideas extruded into a solid. They are not a fully realised figure that has a credibility of its own, merely some thing made out of a material. Everything Louise makes has personality and validity. They are not just 2D items that have some extra width to them.

JE It's weird sometimes when I'll be looking around the house, or Louise will be looking through discarded stuff she has made over the years, I can reach into a box and pull out a blue arm and it's undeniably a Jon Burgerman drawing, but it's 3D in felt. And you can tell it's something Pete Fowler or Ben Newman designed. A strange hand, a leg or arm, all imbued with a definite sense of who drew them originally. It's a fantastic thing.

WP Are you happy for her to deviate from your drawings or do you ever feel that you would like her to follow your line as exactly as she follows other artists?

JE While we're making them I am always able to say "How about making this a bit more like…?" For example, when we were making Lester Flent, when Louise was pinning the hair on, I was saying "Can it just be more bulbous to one side, can it peak towards the left side of his head?" There are things I'm suggesting while she's making them, to make them look the way I feel they should look. But I try not to interfere too much. We always have discussions about colours, about the balance of a figure. The way I draw hair is very distinctive, and the way Louise has made the hair, especially on Lester, looks like my drawings, but it's made up of three or four shapes. From a distance it gives a precise impression, so it's back to the [idea of the] silhouette. It's got to look right from the back and the front and the side. It always does. I don't do turnarounds, just a single drawing. And because everything is made in pieces and we are moving things around and making decisions, moving features further backwards or forwards on the head, I think that's when we do the turnarounds. We can actually turn them around. It happens on the figure.

WP What do you call them, these figures? What name would you choose to describe them?

JE It's a hard one. Soft sculptures sounds perhaps too serious. We tend to call them creatures and not monsters. I don't think 'plush' really does them justice. Other people call them dolls, and I suppose they are dolls. It's back to that thing where I don't know who we can compare ourselves to. They look a bit like animation models as well, some of them are puppets, I don't know what we can call them really. That's half the problem!

WP Creating an alternative world populated with characters: this is what you do now.

JE Yes. And we've got a family tree and everybody connects up in some way or other. I have always liked that in popular fiction, people can write a series of films or books, those characters inhabit a certain world so they'll all know each other, they're all walking around the same planet, even if they haven't bumped into each other yet.

WP Do you think the drive to give them names, histories and biographies is part of your narrative comics impulse?

JE I'm sure it is, yeah. I have always created characters even if I haven't made that many stories with them. They've all got a certain personality. I don't think we could ever make a character who was just 'a bear' or 'a robot'. And also, it helps when we are making them, we can see in their eyes or their posture what they should look like. When we were posing the figures at the Nobrow shop yesterday they all had to have a particular stance, a certain look. The guru had to be sitting in a Zen position, and we knew that Amphibina had to have her arms folded and one leg tucked behind the other. So the backstories all help towards the making of them. The stories come naturally, we aren't contriving stories for them, we know who they are as soon as we make them.

I don't know where the names come from. Most are just sounds, I try to use words that feel good together, I like a bit of alliteration, sometimes I see a word written down that I like. Hector didn't have a name when he was a sketch. Louise finished making him and said 'he looks like a Hector' and he was.

WP It feels like there's a monster Yiddish thing happening with them. They're all somewhat Mel Brooks, Jack Davis, there's a kind of 1950s New York, Damon Runyan kind of feeling to them.

JE Yeah, I read a lot of Mad magazine growing up, I suppose all those names sort of snuck in there, didn't they? When I was a child I knew the names of Spiro Agnew or Ralph Nader. I didn't know who they were, but I read names like these when I was reading Mad magazine all the time.

WP Potrzebie, schmaltz, chicken fat, fershlugginer, those nonsensical Harvey Kurtzman-esque words that they like to use for texture...

JE Thinking about it, that probably is a very big influence that I hadn't even noticed. The other big one is P. G. Wodehouse. Gussie Fink-Nottle, Pongo Twistleton, Hildebrand "Tuppy" Glossop, Sir Watkyn Bassett, CBE...

None of the creatures have real names, I suppose one or two are called Terry or Hector but they usually have something about them that marks them out as different from human names.

WP The clothing adds to the sense of them being autonomous creatures with an interior life, doesn't it? Because all the clothes are real and you can take them all off. I haven't tried undressing the Mad Hatter yet but it's just a question of time.

JE Ha ha! Yes, they all come off. Some have got pants on under their trousers that no one will ever see, all the details are there.

WP Have you got to the point of putting things in their inside pockets? Passports or wallets? Bus tickets, sweet wrappers, a pen, a comb?

### Lester & Hester Flent

Founders of London's influential "Furious Rhomboid" gallery. Currently living in a converted wheelie bin just off Brick Lane.

### Amphibina De Lorian

Stylist, blogger, "it girl" and heiress to the De Lorian French Fancies fortune. Her latest venture is a range of gilets for squirrels.

### Anton Trenche

Owner of Lemon Goon records. Signed (amongst others) Hot Mortar, Pale Nancy, Bag For Life and Ian's Dream. If you've heard of them then chances are he doesn't like them.

### Hector Bunford

Keen entomologist and professional grumph. Lives in a 400 year old oak tree with a bay window (in which he can be found all day long waiting to admonish unruly passers-by).

### G'goob

A serene blue dude. He believes inner enlightment can be achieved through the consumption of Tunnock's teacakes and the music of Boney M.

JE No, not yet. I suppose when we've done things for private clients we have added personal details. One person wanted to include his favourite records. I redesigned the sleeve of a Jam record, a Specials record to make them fit into our world. And really, if they're in a cabinet you would only be able to see the top sleeve, but they are all there.

WP Perhaps that's the next stage of the evolution, to keep adding these details that make them more complete. But you haven't done a lot of imagining of the world around them yet.

JE No, not as yet. I suppose I've done bits and pieces. When Louise made Tommy Floom from a drawing I did, I was going to do a strip about a White Stripes kind of band, creatures who are in a group together, and I had an idea for their manager, their drummer would have had seven arms, the city would have roughly been based on New York, the streets would have looked like Mulberry and Spring and Prince but the names would be slightly changed. I've done drawings in my sketchbook of traffic jams of monsters in cars, so it's all there. One day I will do something that incorporates all these things. If I do make a comic based on Tommy, Snapper Duval will be in there, the Furry Mayhem will show up, all the other characters will be the supporting cast.

WP And then you'll be reinterpreting those characters from 3D back into 2D again.

JE That has happened already. There was a very rough sketch of Snapper Duval. Louise made him, and then when I was providing sketches for Selfridges, I redrew him again and it was two stages along. I drew my version of the figure of my drawing.

WP Were you compelled to be accurate to that figure or did you feel free to take liberties with the interpretation to make the most interesting drawing you could?

JE I took liberties with him, actually. His head was bigger, for instance. Like if I draw a person I'm not going to draw a literal version of a person, I'm going to draw my version. So I drew my version of the toy, which is Louise's version of my original drawing.

WP I think that doing these collaborations has affected the way you draw. There's a depth that wasn't there before. Rather than just putting shapes down next to each other on paper you're trying to give a sense of a solid object using a textured line. They are not flat designs anymore. Is that accurate?

JE Perhaps it is. I hadn't thought. Perhaps I see these characters and some of them are over a metre tall, seeing how they look feeds back into the way I draw. If Louise is working with someone else she'll just take their drawings and make the figures and there is no bend. But she'll say to me when I work with her "Can we do this?" or "I'd like to try longer legs" or she'll want a particular shaped head. The drawings change based on the demands of the kind of creatures Louise wants to make. So I suppose it does affect my drawing.

WP Has there ever been a time when you thought "I really don't want to draw that"?

JE No, not that I can think of. I have never drawn a character and said "I hate this but go ahead and make it". And Louise has never said "I don't like this but I'm going to make it". We always reach a common ground.

## 1994

**The Thing/Ben Grimm**
280 mm x 180 mm
Designed by Jack Kirby
Made as a present for
Jonathan Edwards.
Dyed cotton with machine
embroidery, wears blue cotton
lycra pants with black trim.
polyester fibre filling and beads.

**The Incredible Hulk**
250 mm x 170 mm
Designed by Jack Kirby
Made as a present for Darryl
Cunningham.
Wears deep red ripped cotton
lycra pants.
Made from polyester fleece,
polyester fibre filling, fake fur
(Mixed-fibres) and beads.

## 1996

**Simon Creem**
300 mm x 90 mm
Based on the character from
Jonathan Edwards' comic strip
of the same name in Tank Girl
magazine.
Customised 12" action figure
with fake leather head, black
polo-neck jumper (cotton lycra)
flared denim jeans , black boots
(plastic) pendant (metal) and
cigarette holder (made from
paper).

## 1998

**Bongo Lewis, King of Dogs**
210 mm x 170 mm
Edition of five.
Made as Christmas presents.
Mixed-fibre felt, polyester fibre
stuffing and embroidery thread.

## 1999

**Squidboy**
Designed by Drew Webster
300 mm x 120 mm
Made as a present.
Mixed-fibre felt, polyester fibre
filling and embroidery thread.

**Pee Pee**
from Pee Pee Goes Shopping
180mm x 70mm
Designed by and made as a gift
for Simon Gane.
Felt, polyester fibre filling and
embroidery thread.

## 2000

**Pants Ant**
290 mm x 210 mm
Designed by Woodrow Phoenix
A Carney-Phoenix brainchild.
Edition of two.
Mixed-fibre felt, wire, cardboard,
polyester fibre filling and embroidery
thread.

**Urbane Gorilla**
310 mm x 200 mm
Designed by Woodrow Phoenix
A Carney-Phoenix brainchild.
Mixed-fibre felt, plastic from milk
cartons, cardboard, polyester fibre
filling and embroidery thread.

**Eager Beaver**
210 x 160 mm
Designed by Woodrow Phoenix
Another Carney-Phoenix brainchild.
Mixed-fibre felt, polyester fibre filling
and embroidery thread.

**JAKe Doll**
250 mm x 100 mm
Made as a birthday present.
JAKe wears a zip-up hoody with felt
applique letters, denim jeans, red
t-shirt, white trainers and messenger
bag. A slightly later addition was an
attachable beard.
Mixed fibres, polyester fibre filling,
embroidery thread and cardboard.

## 2001

**Hellboy**
280 mm x 170 mm
Designed by Mike Mignola
Made as a present for Will Kane.
Complete with utility belt including
crucifix and rope. His Right Hand
of Doom has one finger too many
(pointed out to me, via Will, by Duncan
Fegredo). My mistake.
Mixed-fibre felt, card, string, embroidery thread and polyester fibre filling.

## 2003

**Crabula**
Designed by Craig Conlan
300 mm x 190 mm
Made as a present.
Crabula wears black pants with white
trim and anchor embroidery.
Mixed-fibre felt, cotton lycra, polyester fibre filling, wire and embroidery
thread.

## 2004

**Yeti**
200 mm x 120 mm
Made as a present for JAKe.
Mixed-fibre fake fur and felt,
machine embroidery and beads.

**Larry & Laurence**
400 mm x 250 mm
Made as presents for friend's
children. Larry now belongs to Betty
and Laurence to Ava.
Printed and plain cotton, Mixed-fibre
felt, embroidery thread and polyester
fibre filling.

**Original Mr Smashing**
400 mm x 150 mm
Edition of two
Made as presents for friend's
children.
Printed and plain cotton, Mixed-fibre
felt, card, embroidery thread and
polyester fibre filling.

**Hollywood Smashing**
250 mm x 150 mm
Made as a present for Woodrow
Phoenix while he was away working
in Burbank, California, hence the name.
Printed and plain cotton, Mixed-fibre
felt, embroidery thread, card and
polyester fibre filling.

## 2005

**Zipper Toothed Rabbit**
390 mm x 180 mm
Made as an entry for Pictoplasma's
"Bunny Mandala" (sadly, it wasn't
used).
Denim, metal zipper, Mixed-fibre felt,
embroidery thread, metal washers,
with polyester fibre filling.

**Lil Bertie**
400 mm x 150 mm
Made as a present for Bertie.
Printed cotton, brushed Mixed-fibre
felt, embroidery thread, plastic safety
eyes and polyester fibre filling.

**Colin** (stripey monster, aka "Bogey")
400 mm x 290 mm
Made as a present for Bertie.
Printed cotton, Mixed-fibre felt, plastic safety eyes, embroidery thread
and polyester fibre filling.

## 2006

**Cactus Pin Cushions**
Edition of 25 (two variations)
150mm x 80mm
Terracotta pot, felt, polyester fibre
filling, glass beads, card and embroidery thread.

## 2007

**Kaiju 2007–2009**
310 mm x 160 mm
Edition of 200
Kaijus were mainly made in Mixed-
fibre felt with plastic safety eyes and
polyester fibre filling, but a few (approximately 12) were made in vintage
tweed. Every one was different in

surface detail. Number of eyes varied
from one to three. Skin patterns
included spots, stripes, or scales and
some came with a felt heart. These
were mostly sold through shops.

**Mr Smashing**
400 mm x 150 mm
Edition of 20
These and Kaijus were the first pieces
made in multiples, for shops.
Printed and plain cotton or vintage
wool tweed, Mixed-fibre felt, card,
embroidery thread and polyester fibre
filling.

**Monsieur Octopus.**
400 mm x 220 mm
Made as a present for a friend's child.
He wears black felt beret and sports
a large moustache.
Polyester fibre fleece, Mixed-fibre
felt, plastic safety eyes amd polyester
fibre filling.

**Charlie Pipe Smoke**
150 mm x 220 mm
Edition of three.
Felt pipe with removable 'smoke'
cloud.
Mixed-fibre felt, velcro, embroidery
thread and polyester fibre filling.

**Bongo Lewis, King of Dogs (large)**
280 mm x 180 mm
Vintage brown wool tweed, embroidery thread and polyester fibre filling.
Wearing a scarf of Mixed-fibre felt.

**Ms Lapin**
Edition of 20
400 x 150 mm
Miss Lapin wears A-line pinafore
dress with buttons at shoulders,
ribbon bow and frill with braid detail
around hemline.
Printed cotton, Mixed-fibre brushed
felt, plastic safety eyes, embroidery,
plastic buttons, thread and polyester
fibre filling.

**Clayton**
150 mm x 300 mm
Edition of two
Vintage tweed, mixed-fibre felt,
plastic safety eyes, satin ribbon and
polyester fibre filling.

## 2008

**Christmas Pudding Kaiju**
310 mm x 160 mm
This was the 100th Kaiju.
Made with dripping brandy sauce and
holly leaf details.
Mixed-fibre felt, platic safety eyes
and polyester fibre filling.

**Lucha Libre Kaiju**
310 mm x 160 mm
Black polyester fleece with mexican
wrestler-style details in Mixed-fibre

felt. Plastic safety eyes and polyest
fibre filling.

**KISS Kaiju**
310 mm x 160 mm
KISS-style facial details and long
Gene Simmons-style tongue. Metal
square studs on chest.
Mixed-fibre felt, plastic safety eyes
and polyester fibre filling.

**Large Kaiju**
580 mm x 300 mm
Edition of four
Made to display at trade shows and
shops. All four are different with
unique colourways and details.
Mixed-fibre felt, plastic safety eyes
and polyester fibre filling.

**Bunko**
260 mm x 300 mm
Edition of fifteen.
Black body and contrasting horns w
details in either orange, yellow, red
or green.
Polyester fleece with Mixed-fibre
felt details, plastic safety eyes and
polyester fibre filling.
Mostly sold in shops.

**Artic Bunko**
260 mm x 300 mm
Edition of six.
Cream version of Bunko with detail
in turquoise and grey.
Polyester fleece with Mixed-fibre
felt details, plastic safety eyes and
polyester fibre filling. Mostly sold ir
shops.

**Angry Squared**
250 mm x 340 mm
Made as a present for Jonathan
Edwards.
Black polyester fleece, Mixed-fibre
felt, embroidery thread, card, wire
and polyester fibre filling.

**Hugh Scruntin**
350 mm x 190 mm
From the set of political candidates
for the Behemoth-on-Sea by-
Elections.
Hugh wears striped polyester fully-
lined two-buttoned single-breasted
suit, welt pockets, trousers with
crease line and slight flare and whi
cotton, wide-collared shirt with dee
cuffs, printed rayon tie with large
knot. Satin ribbon rosette.
Brushed and plain Mixed-fibre felt,
plastic safety eyes, card, wire and
polyester fibre filling.

**Leonard Groyle**
300 mm x 300 mm
From the set of political candidates
for the Behemoth-on-Sea by-Elections.
Leonard wears Mixed-fibre single-
breasted pinstriped three-piece sat
lined suit (unfastened) with wide

lar and welt pockets. Trousers with
ease line. Satin backed single-
easted waistcoat. White cotton
de-collared shirt and vintage tweed
. Satin ribbon rosette.
ushed and plain Mixed-fibre felt,
stic safety eyes, card, wire and
yester fibre filling.

dy Jemimarraggh Grunk
0 mm x 170 mm
om the set of political candidates
the Behemoth-on-Sea by-Elec-
ns.
dy J wears white cotton Broderie
glaise blouse with high-neck frilled
lar and frilled cuffs. Fully-lined Vin-
e tweed wool box jacket with braid
tail and matching lined A-line skirt
h back split and braided hemline.
rrying felt, clasped handbag. Satin
bon rosette.
ushed and plain Mixed-fibre felt,
stic safety eyes, card, wire and
yester fibre filling.

dster Male
0 mm x 180 mm
wears fully-lined three-buttoned
y gabardine suit with three welt
ckets, single back vent and narrow
trousers with crease line. High
ared button-down gingham shirt
h deep cuffs and black skinny
Retro bowling shoes with white
pe. Mixed-fibre felt, card, plastic
ety eyes, wire and polyester fibre
ng.

dster Female
0 mm x 180 mm
e wears polyester black polo-neck,
Art print poly-cotton shift dress,
waist belt with vintage plastic
ckle. Black shoes with double
ton detail. Mixed-fibre felt, card,
stic safety eyes, wire and polyes-
fibre filling.

kler
laboration with Jon Burgerman
de for Jon's Show "I Can't Sit Still"
ndon
mm x 330 mm
ton of two.
ed-fibre felt, card, wire and poly-
er fibre filling.

ke
laboration with Jon Burgerman
de for Jon's Show "I Can't Sit Still"
ndon
mm x 500 mm
tion of two.
ed-fibre felt, card, wire, and
yester fibre filling.

routhead
laboration with Jon Burgerman
de for Jon's Show "I Can't Sit Still"
ndon
mm x 250 mm
tion of three.

---

Mixed-fibre felt, card, wire and polyester fibre filling.

2009

Takeshi Kerouac
410 mm x 250 mm
Edition of six.
Made for the shop Tokyo Jazz Panda.
Takeshi wears a black felt beret.
Polyester fleece, Mixed-fibre felt,
plastic safety eyes and polyester fibre
filling.

Professor Skeffington
750 mm x 330 mm
Edition of 30
Polyester fibre fleece, Mixed-fibre
felt, plastic safety eyes, and polyester
fibre filling. Mostly sold through
shops.

Kaiju West
310 mm x 160 mm
Special Edition; the 150th Kaiju. Details based on the Kanye West/ Kaws
album artwork.
Prince of Wales Check Mixed-fibre
suiting, with Mixed-fibre felt.

Mad Hatter
800 x 500 mm
Made for the "Go Ask Alice" show at
Paul Cumes Gallery, Santa Barbara.
MH wears white cotton shirt with
oversized cuffs and vintage button
cufflinks, red polkadot cravat,
double-breasted tweed suit with
welt pockets, single back vent, and
trousers with creases and slight flare.
Blue socks and brown pointy heeled
boots. Brown top hat with curved
crown, ribbon and feather. He carries
a china cup of tea.
Mixed fibres, felt, plastic safety eyes,
wire, card and polyester fibre filling.

Marcel
600 mm x 200 mm
Marcel wears black and white skinny-
knit jumper and white pointy-heeled
boots.
Mixed fibres, felt, fleece, plastic
safety eyes, wire, card and polyester
fibre filling.

Andre Krunkle
500 mm x 250 mm
Member of "The Beastniks" made for
"Plush You" Show, Seattle.
Andre wears Mixed-fibre polo-neck
jumper, straight-legged black denim
jeans with turn-ups. Carrying portfolio
of work (original ink drawings by
Jonathan Edwards).
Mixed-fibre fake fur, Mixed-fibre felt,
card, paper, plastic safety eyes, wire
and polyester fibre filling.

Jean-Paul Schmunkle
660 mm x 200 mm
Member of "The Beastniks" made for

---

"Plush You" Show, Seattle.
Jean-Paul wears acrylic polo-neck,
straight-legged black jeans with turn-
ups. Carrying LP - "Five Horns" by
Munchy Gribbs and The Jazz Brutes.
Cover artwork by Jonathan Edwards.
Mixed-fibre felt, card, plastic safety
eyes, wire and polyester fibre filling.

Chet Krink
240 mm x 180 mm
Member of "The Beastniks" made for
"Plush You" Show, Seattle.
Chet wears woollen polo-neck ribbed
jumper and black denim straight-
legged jeans with deep turn-ups. He
carries a poetry book, "Growl" by
Allen Grimsberg, with original poems
written by Jonathan Edwards, Jon
Burgerman, Drew Webster and Darryl
Cunningham.
Mixed-fibre felt, card, plastic safety
eyes, wire and polyester fibre filling.

Tippy Winkles
480 mm x 180 mm
Made to star on our Christmas cards,
now travels with us.
Tippy wears orange lace-up winter
boots with rick-rack braiding and ribbon details. He wears a wool knitted
scarf with fringed ends but also has
two other scarves, a wool tweed scarf
and a fleece scarf with appliqued
felt pattern. Tippy also has a ski-ing
outfit complete with skis, woollen hat,
woollen polo-neck and body warmer.
He won gold with this outfit in the
Schmancy Winter Plush Olympics,
Seattle.
Mixed-fibre felt, card, plastic safety
eyes, wire and polyester fibre filling.

Tommy Floom
840 mm x 350 mm
Tommy wears blue denim jeans with
double turn-up, studded leather belt
and key chain. White collar and pink
and black satin skinny tie. Red high
top lace-up baseball style boot and
bike chain bracelet.
Mixed-fibre felt, card, plastic safety
eyes, wire and polyester fibre filling.

General Dombolo
550 mm x 200 mm
Member of "Voodoo Tron" made for
the Inky Goodness Show "Wonderland", Vaad Gallery, Birmingham
(stolen from gallery).
Mixed-fibre felt, card, plastic safety
eyes, wire, embroidery thread and
polyester fibre filling.

Topo
900 mm x 480 mm
Member of "Voodoo Tron" made for
the Inky Goodness Show "Wonderland", Vaad Gallery, Birmingham.
Mixed-fibre felt, card, plastic safety
eyes, plastic, wire, embroidery thread
and polyester fibre filling.

---

Doblolanomi
700 mm x 420 mm
Member of "Voodoo Tron" made for
the Inky Goodness Show "Wonderland", Vaad Gallery, Birmingham,
Mixed-fibre felt, card, plastic safety
eyes, wire, embroidery thread and
polyester fibre filling.

Señor Gonzalez
770 mm x 220 mm
Made for "Animals Take Over Berlin"
aka "Animal Stampede", exhibited at
various locations in Berlin, Germany.
Señor Gonzalez wears black woollen
ribbed polo-neck. Skinny blue jeans
with turn-ups. He has three pin
badges, Adam Ant, an ant, and 'I
heart Berlin'.
Mixed-fibre felt and fleece, plastic
safety eyes, and polyester fibre filling.

Travis
690 mm x 180 mm
Commissioned by an uncle whose
niece had lost her dog.
Mixed-fibre fleece and felt card,
plastic safety eyes, and polyester
fibre filling.

Tweed Travis
690 mm x 180 mm
Vintage wool tweed, Mixed-fibre felt,
card, plastic safety eyes, and polyester fibre filling.

Tweed Pandas
410 mm x 250 mm
Edition of two.
Made as presents for our godchil-
dren.
Vintage wool tweed, Mixed-fibre felt,
card, plastic safety eyes, and polyester fibre filling.

Little Blue (prototype)
designed by Jon Burgerman
250 mm x 90 mm
Fleece, felt, card, embroidery thread
and polyester fibre filling.

Anton (prototype)
designed by Jon Burgerman
260 mm x 130 mm
Fleece, felt, card, embroidery thread
and polyester fibre filling.

K8ty
Collaboration with Jon Burgerman
450 mm x 200 mm
Made for Jon's show "My American
Summer", Giant Robot NYC..
K8ty wears pink headband, white vest
top, ribbon belt with vintage buckle.
Short denim skirt, leg warmers and
pink heeled boots. Vintage button
necklace and plastic bracelets and
bangles.
Mixed fibres, felt, card, plastic, and
polyester fibre filling.

---

Grrf
Collaboration with Jon Burgerman
320 mm x 200 mm
Made for Jon's show "My American
Summer", Giant Robot NYC.
Grrf wears diamond-patterned hand
knitted tunic.
Mixed fibres, felt, card, and polyester
fibre filling.

Hammel
Collaboration with Jon Burgerman
320 mm x 170 mm
Made for Jon's show "My American
Summer", Giant Robot NYC.
Hammel wears white t-shirt with pink
detail and appliqued felt letter. Faded
blue denim jeans, knitted blue acrylic
cardigan.
Mixed fibres, felt, card, and polyester
fibre filling.

Brott
Collaboration with Jon Burgerman
320 mm x 170 mm
Made for Jon's show "My American
Summer", Giant Robot NYC.
Brott wears yellow vest top, cropped
grey sweatpants, belt and vintage
buckle. Fake leather flight jacket with
brown trim.
Mixed fibres, felt, card, and polyester
fibre filling.

Mickey
Collaboration with Jon Burgerman
450 mm x 270 mm
Made for Jon's show "My American
Summer", Giant Robot NYC.
Mickey wears white vest top, faded
blue denim jeans. Red baseball shoes,
sweatband and red neckscarf.
Sunglasses.
Mixed fibres, felt, card, embroidery
thread, plastic and polyester fibre
filling.

Randel
Collaboration with Jon
Burgerman
450 mm x 180 mm
Made for Jon's show "My American
Summer", Giant Robot NYC.
Randel wears black and white
slashed-neck t-shirt, narrow-legged
indigo denim jeans, red baseball
shoes and a blue jacket with red
sleeves (varsity style).
Mixed fibres, felt, card, and polyester
fibre filling.

Joshua
Collaboration with Jon
Burgerman
320 mm x 180 mm
Made for Jon's show "My American
Summer", Giant Robot NYC.
Joshua wears pink top with two-
button detail at neckline and white
piping.
Mixed fibres, felt, card, and polyester
fibre filling.

## Piccalilicus And The Magical Cardy Of Wonder and Wonderment.

400 mm x 170 mm
Collaboration with Jon Burgerman.
Made for Art Basel, Miami
Piccalilicus wears a diagonal, patterned knitted cardigan, and woollen pink and blue patterned legwarmers, with pink shoes. He also has his own boombox.
Mixed fibres, wool, felt, card, and polyester fibre filling.

## Fawkward

Collaboration with Jon Burgerman
250 mm x 180 mm
Mixed fibres, felt, card, embroidery thread and polyester fibre filling.

## Pickle

Collaboration with Jon Burgerman
230 mm x 400 mm
Edition of four.
Mixed fibres, felt, card, embroidery thread and polyester fibre filling.

## Anton

Collaboration with Jon Burgerman
250 mm x 150 mm
Mixed fibres, felt, card, embroidery thread and polyester fibre filling.

## Little Blue

Collaboration with Jon Burgerman
250 mm x 18mm
Mixed fibres, felt, card, embroidery thread and polyester fibre filling.

## Skull

250 mm x 170 mm
Made as a birthday present for Jonathan.
Fleece, felt , plastic safety eyes, polyester fibre filling.

## Tweedocaster

Custom Fender Stratocaster cover.
Made for a friend who wanted his guitar to look less "rock'n'roll" and more "geography teacher".
Vintage herringbone tweed.

## Choux Choux

200 mm x 160 mm
Winner of the Momiji Couture Competition, shown at Royal Tea, Los Angeles, USA
Silk, Mixed-fibre fleece and felt, embroidery thread, vintage buttons and beads, ribbons, card and polyester fibre filling.

## Serge Gainsbourg

360 mm x 190 mm
Edition of two
Made as Louise's entry for the blog "Draw Serge".
Serge wears black woollen polo-neck, charcoal gabardine trousers, and black shoes. He smokes a cigarette complete with smoke.
Mixed fibres, felt, card, and polyester fibre filling.

## 2010

## Herzog

740 mm x 320 mm
Herzog wears high waisted denim jeans, yellow belt and yellow and grey striped tie.
Fake fur, Mixed fibres, felt, plastic safety eyes, and polyester fibre filling.

## Wilbur Grumph

580 mm x 250 mm
Wilbur wears fully-lined brown checked three-button sports jacket with elbow patches. Purple woollen polo-neck and beige straight-legged corduroy trousers. He also smokes a brown pipe.
Fake fur, Mixed fibres, felt, plastic safety eyes, and polyester fibre filling.

## Brunhilde

1000 mm x 300 mm
and Little Geoff
150 mm x 180 mm
Brunhilde wears a high-collared printed cotton dress, short puff sleeves, a gathered skirt, nipped-in at the waist with grosgrain ribbon tied in a bow. Her hemline, sleeve edge and collar are trimmed with white Rick-rack braiding. A silver metal skull and crossbones decorates the neckline, as well as a neoprene choker with square studs. She also wears striped knee-length socks and white lace-up brothel creepers. Her undergarments include lace pants and a net petticoat. Geoff wears a leather collar and chain lead.
Mixed fibres, felt, fake fur, metal, wire, card, wooden doweling, plastic safety eyes, leather,studs, and polyester fibre filling.

## Lady Garrrgghh Garrrgghhh!

1160 mm x 450 mm
Lady G wears fake leather dress with ruff and feather inserts at the neckline and diagonally across the front, exaggerated hip shaping. Gunmetal lace headpiece with studs. Gunmetal lace fingerless gloves and long metal cat claw studs. Knee-high PVC boots with metal toe-tips and chain details. Undergarments include black PVC tape crossed over nipple area, PVC pants and ripped thigh-length fishnet tights.
Mixed fibres, felt, fake fur, fake leather, metal, wire, chain, card, lace,

wooden doweling, studs, PVC and polyester fibre filling.

## Dwight Klugg

620 mm x 350 mm
Dwight wears FM trucker cap and black padded body warmer with red trim and embroidered patch.
Mixed fibres, fleece, felt, plastic safety eyes, polyester wadding and polyester fibre filling.

## Elspeth Frond

710 mm x 160 mm
Elspeth wears black silk organza dress with layered circle skirt and neck frill. Black high-heeled knee-length boots with cuff. Undergarments: lace pants.
Mixed fibres, fleece, felt, beads and polyester fibre filling.

## Terry

500 mm x 350 mm
Terry wears sleeveless "This Nation Saving Grace - The Fall" t-shirt, studded leather collar and lead. He also has a growl box inside.
Mixed fibres, fake fur, felt, plastic safety eyes, leather studs and polyester fibre filling.

## Clem

610 mm x 200 mm
Clem wears a patterned knitted v-neck tank top and a furry Russian-style hat with matching boots.
Mixed fibres, fake fur, fleece, felt, plastic safety eyes and polyester fibre filling.

## Kipston

440 mm x 250 mm
Kipston wears a black bowler hat, and a black skinny tie.
Mixed fibres, distressed fake fur, felt, plastic safety eyes and polyester fibre filling.

## Zeep

300 mm x 250 mm
Zeep wears a leather-studded collar.
Mixed fibres, fake fur, felt, plastic safety eyes and polyester fibre filling.

## Peacock Wrangler

950 mm x 330 mm
Mixed fibres, fleece, felt, plastic safety eyes and polyester fibre filling.

## Flamingo Wrangler

950 mm x 330 mm
Mixed fibres, fleece, felt, plastic safety eyes and polyester fibre filling.

## Scrimpton Fleeps

650 mm x 350 mm
Scrimpton wears a yellow vest top with monster badge. Narrow-legged indigo denim jeans, rainbow stripe snake belt, orange and lime green trucker cap, high-top trainers, white framed wayfarer-style glasses, big

orange headphones and pink satchel-style back pack.
Mixed fibres, fake fur, felt, plastic safety eyes, wire, card, metal and polyester fibre filling.

## Snapper Duval

810cm x 300 mm
Snapper wears short sleeved checked button-down collared shirt with red bow tie, red framed aviator-style glasses, skinny indigo blue denim jeans with turn-ups and a red leather belt.
Mixed fibres, fake fur, felt, leather, plastic safety eyes, wire and polyester fibre filling.

## Fez-wearing Pincushion Head

140mm x 100mm
Olive green polkadot cotton head with felt fez. The base is a wooden sake box.
Cotton, felt, plastic safety eyes, embroidery thread, polyester fibre filling, card and wood.

## Tabitha Snark

770 mm x 420 mm
and Rolando
190 mm x 15mm
Tabitha wears dogtooth check dress with pussycat bow at neckline. Gathered skirt, nipped-in at waist with grosgrain ribbon bow and vintage buckle. Three-quarter length fluted sleeves with button details. Rick-rack braiding details on sleeve edge, hem and bow. Matching bow hair clip. Undergarments: lace pants.
Rolando wears fake leather studded collar and chain lead.
Mixed fibres, wool tweed, fake fur, felt, plastic safety eyes, wire, card and polyester fibre filling.

## Wilko Roby

750 mm x 450 mm
Wilko wears studded sleeveless denim jacket with embroidered patches including Iron Maiden, Led Zepplin, AC/DC and FM, with pin badges including AC/DC, Slayer, Saxon, KISS and Metallica. Thick metal chain necklace and a backstage pass for The Grimble Twins.
Mixed fibres, fake fur, felt, plastic safety eyes, wire, card and polyester fibre filling.

## Frang Tootle

750 mm x 300 mm
Frang wears cream cableknit jumper, mustard jumbo cord flared trousers, black heeled pointy boots. He carries his acoustic guitar.
Mixed fibres, fake fur, felt, plastic safety eyes, wire, card, embroidery thread and polyester fibre filling.

## Rudy Froops

530 mm x 280 mm
Rudy wears yellow cotton gingham button-down collared shirt, black

skinny tie, pink knitted cardigan, narrow legged indigo denim jeans with turn-ups and yellow lace-up pointy shoes.
Mixed fibres, fake fur, felt, plastic safety eyes, card, wire and polyester fibre filling.

## Mum Treep

520 mm x 250 mm
Mrs Treep wears vintage wool tweed dress, trimmed in yellow bias binding with lace panel down centre front, a turquoise polka dot cotton apron with large pocket and hand carved wooden spoon.
Mixed fibres, fake fur, vintage tweed, felt, plastic safety eyes, card, wire, wood and polyester fibre filling.

## Dad Treep

600 mm x 330 mm
Mr Treep wears skinny yellow polo-neck, knitted turquoise v-neck jumper and charcoal grey straight-legged trousers. He smokes a pipe.
Mixed fibres, fake fur, felt, plastic safety eyes, card, wire and polyester fibre filling.

## Klipsey Treep

300 mm x 220 mm
Klipsey wears turquoise cotton polkadot dress with bow at neckline. Turquoise knitted bolero-styled cardigan with rick-rack braid edging.
Mixed fibres, fake fur, felt, plastic safety eyes, card, and polyester fibre filling.

## Fring Treep

300 mm x 240 mm
Fring wears a turquoise knitted polo-neck with FM embroidered patch and charcoal grey straight-legged trousers.
Mixed fibres, fake fur, felt, plastic safety eyes, card, and polyester fibre filling.

## Fradley Benford

780 mm x 370 mm
Fradley wears a skinny knitted grey and orange striped polo-neck, blue denim skinny jeans with yellow topstitching, Neon lace-up high-tops, thick black round-framed glasses and large blue and orange headphones.
Mixed fibres, fake fur, felt, plastic safety eyes, card, wire and polyester fibre filling.

## Austin Flisk

750 mm x 340 mm
Austin wears four-button, red-striped single-breasted blazer with single back vent and two welt pockets. Black cotton shirt with narrow button-down collar and silver jacquard tie. Black narrow legged trousers, black pointy boots and thick framed black sunglasses.
Mixed fibres, fake fur, felt, plastic

ety eyes, card, wire and polyester
re filling.

eechy Dwippford
0 mm x 400 mm
eechy wears skinny black polo-
ck, dogtooth check tweed dress
th side bow and vintage buckle,
tching bow hair clip. Black shoes
th black and white double button
tail.
ked fibres, fake fur, felt, card, wire
d polyester fibre filling.

ahhl Lagerfurr
0 mm x 370 mm
aal wears black three-button suit
th narrow lapels, welt pockets,
gle back vent and narrow-legged
users. Black silk shirt with white
ep collar, large cuffs with diamante
tton cuff links and a silver & black
iped satin tie with diamante button
pin. He has long metallic silver
d claws and silver fingerless
ves. Black pointy shoes and black
nglasses. Adorned with numerous
ver necklace chains and pendants
luding a decorative key. He also
ries a "Grahhl Who?" canvas tote
g and has a black satin ribbon bow
his pony tail.
ked fibres, fake fur, felt, card, wire
d polyester fibre filling.

Snooks & Rondo
0 mm x 350 mm
wears faded blue denim jeans
th double turn-ups, and loosely tied
nted rayon cravat. He always car-
s his walking stick, Rondo.
ked fibres, fake fur, felt, plastic
ety eyes, card, wire and polyester
re filling.

dy Persephone
imm-Fribbington
00 mm x 300 mm
d Minkles
0 mm x 190 mm
dy P wears black and white vintage
eed coat dress with circular
ckets, fluted sleeves with pleats at
eve head and a waist belt. Hand
nted FM pink silk scarf tied in a
ssycat bow. Fake black leather fin-
rless gloves with six button detail.
nkles wears matching coat, leather
lar and chain lead.
ked fibres, fake fur, felt, plastic
ety eyes, wire and polyester
re filling.

ps Winkles
0 mm x 28mm
os wears checked woven wool scarf.
ked fibres, fake fur, felt, plastic
ety eyes, card, wire and polyester
re filling.

otling
0 mm x 200 mm
otling wears thick black round-

framed glasses.
Mixed fibres, fake fur, felt, plastic
safety eyes, card, wire and polyester
fibre filling.

Alfred Krimpling
350 mm x 300 mm
Alfred wears black double-breasted
uniform jacket with gold buttons and
braid trim, felt, peaked hat with embroidered FM patch and gold braid.
Mixed fibres, fake fur, felt, plastic
safety eyes, card, wire and polyester
fibre filling.

Alfonso
260 mm x 190 mm
Alfonso wears black felt top hat with
polkadot bow.
Mixed fibres, fake fur, felt, plastic
safety eyes, card, wire and polyester
fibre filling.

Professor Roofle Dwent
520 mm x 330 mm
Prof. Dwent wears beige lightweight
three-button suit jacket with single
vent and welt pockets, brown woollen
jumper, brown needlecord straight-
legged trousers and bronze oval wire-
framed glasses.He carries his pipe.
Mixed fibres, fake fur, felt, plastic
safety eyes, card, wire and polyester
fibre filling.

Dr. Pumford Russett
750 mm x 350 mm
Dr Pumford Russett wears a brown
striped three-button sports jacket
with single back vent and welt pockets, beige jumbo corduroy straight-
legged trousers, white cotton wide
collared shirt, vintage tie and square
black-framed glasses. He carries a
pipe.
Mixed fibres, fake fur, felt, plastic
safety eyes, card, wire and polyester
fibre filling.

Professor Gussy Flenderman
600 mm x 290 mm
Prof. Gussy Flenderman wears
vintage herringbone tweed three-
button sports jacket with single back
vent and welt pockets. White cotton
shirt with vintage tie and dark green
needlecord straight-legged trousers.
Mixed fibres, fake fur, felt, plastic
safety eyes, card, wire and polyester
fibre filling.

Terry Grunts
750 mm x 330 mm
Terry wears a silver jaquard tie.
Mixed fibres, fake fur, felt, plastic
safety eyes, and polyester fibre filling.

Frimptom Wallis
410 mm x 300 mm
Frimpton wears chunky knit fisherman-style jumper, denim work jeans
and carries a corn-cob pipe.
Mixed fibres, fake fur, felt, plastic

safety eyes, wire, card and polyester
fibre filling.

Client A (Female)
700 mm x 350 mm
She wears black large reverse collared tailored jacket with exaggerated shoulders, welt pockets and
single back vent. Metallic gunmetal
silver sleeveless top, skinny black
jeans, fake leather fingerless gloves
and knee-high pointy heeled boots.
Jewellery includes: Chanel jet bead
belt (worn as necklace) and diamanté
choker (supplied by client) She has a
pet "monster turtle" with diamanté
collar and chain lead.
Mixed fibres, felt, wire, card and
polyester fibre filling.

Client B (Male)
800 mm x 350 mm
He wears black three-button suit
jacket with welt pockets and single
back vent. White cotton shirt with
button-down collar and large cuffs
worn with diamanté button cufflinks.
Black Rayban sunglasses (supplied
by client). Black satin tie, faded grey
denim straight-legged jeans and black
lace-up shoes. Jewellery includes:
rosary beads (worn as bracelet),
circular metal pendant necklace,
diamanté CND bracelet (all supplied
by client) and a handmade metallic
skull ring with Micky Mouse ears.
He also wears large headphones
and carries a selection of handmade
record sleeves, designed by Jonathan
Edwards and based on the client's
favourite records.
Mixed fibres, felt, wire, card and
polyester fibre filling.

The Elder
Collaboration with Pete Fowler
500 mm x 400 mm
Made for the music video "I'm
Aware", by Clinic
Mixed-fibre felt, embroidery thread,
card and polyester fibre filling.

Cosmic Owl
Collaboration with Pete Fowler
500 mm x 400 mm
Made for the music video "I'm
Aware", by Clinic
Mixed-fibre felt, embroidery thread,
card and polyester fibre filling.

Guitarist
Collaboration with Pete Fowler
500 mm x 400 mm
Made for the music video "I'm
Aware", by Clinic
Mixed-fibre felt, embroidery thread,
card and polyester fibre filling.

Cult Member
Collaboration with Pete Fowler
500 mm x 400 mm
Made for the music video "I'm
Aware", by Clinic

Mixed-fibre felt, embroidery thread,
card and polyester fibre filling.

Pepper
Collaboration with Jon Knox
620 mm x 260 mm
Made for Jon's show "Teen Dream",
Chicago, USA
Pepper wears white cotton vest top,
faded grey denim shorts with double
turn-ups, turquoise trainers and white
thick framed sunglasses.
Mixed fibres, felt, fleece, embroidery
thread, card, and polyester fibre
filling.

Dillon
Collaboration with Jon Knox
620 mm x 280 mm
Made for Jon's show " Teen Dream",
Chicago, USA
Dillon wears grey and purple striped
polo-neck, blue denim straight-legged
jeans and purple trainers.
Mixed fibres, felt, fleece, embroidery
thread, card, and polyester fibre
filling.

Jeffrey
Collaboration with Jon Knox
650 mm x 240 mm
Made for Jon's show "Teen Dream",
Chicago, USA
Jeffrey wears black and white striped
t-shirt, black narrow-legged jeans,
blue trainers and black thick framed
glasses.
Mixed fibres, felt, fleece, embroidery
thread, card, and polyester fibre
filling.

Enchanter Of Mushrooms, Lover
Of No One
Collaboration with Jon Burgerman
700 mm x 450 mm
Made for Jon's show "Brain Drain",
Winchester
Mixed-fibre felt, embroidery thread,
card and polyester fibre filling.

Three-Eyed, Two-Faced Rabbit
Collaboration with Jon Burgerman
550 mm x 350 mm
Made for Jon's show "Brain Drain",
Winchester
Mixed-fibre felt, embroidery thread,
card and polyester fibre filling.

Helmot Cirsium (Woodland
Mushroom)
Collaboration with Jon Burgerman
550 mm x 200 mm
Made for Jon's show "Lossy Botany
Lab", Hamburg, Germany.
Mixed-fibre felt, embroidery thread,
card, terracotta plant pot and
polyester fibre filling.

Laciniaria Punctata (Lion Root)
Collaboration with Jon Burgerman
800 mm x 270 mm
Made for Jon's show "Lossy Botany
Lab", Hamburg, Germany.

Mixed-fibre felt, embroidery thread,
card, wire, terracotta plant pot and
polyester fibre filling.

Headlenium Armarummy (Bitter
Sneezeweed)
Collaboration with Jon Burgerman
600 mm x 260 mm
Made for Jon's show "Lossy Botany
Lab", Hamburg, Germany.
Mixed-fibre felt, embroidery thread,
card, terracotta plant pot and polyes-
ter fibre filling.

Bignoniodes Snapla (Diggut Biter)
Collaboration with Jon Burgerman
350 mm x 200 mm
Made for Jon's show "Lossy Botany
Lab", Hamburg, Germany.
Mixed-fibre felt, embroidery thread,
card, terracotta plant pot and polyes-
ter fibre filling.

Doodlichos Aipen (Charinky)
Collaboration with Jon Burgerman
770 mm x 450 mm
Made for Jon's show "Lossy Botany
Lab", Hamburg, Germany.
Mixed-fibre felt, embroidery thread,
card, terracotta plant pot and polyes-
ter fibre filling.

Aubergine Genie
Collaboration with Jon Burgerman
170 mm x 120 mm
Made for Jon's show "Lossy Botany
Lab", Hamburg, Germany.
Mixed-fibre felt, embroidery thread,
card, and polyester fibre filling.

Aubergine with Maggot
Collaboration with Jon Burgerman
250 mm x 180 mm
Made for Jon's show "Lossy Botany
Lab", Hamburg, Germany.
Mixed-fibre felt, embroidery thread,
card, and polyester fibre filling.

Chilli Baby
Collaboration with Jon Burgerman
200 mm x 60 mm
Edition of two
Made for Jon's show "Lossy Botany
Lab", Hamburg, Germany.
Mixed-fibre felt, embroidery thread,
card, and polyester fibre filling.

Wild Onion
Collaboration with Jon Burgerman
150 mm x 100 mm
Made for Jon's show "Lossy Botany
Lab", Hamburg, Germany.
Mixed-fibre felt, embroidery thread,
card, and polyester fibre filling.

Spotted Lemon
Collaboration with Jon Burgerman
120 mm x 100 mm
Made for Jon's show "Lossy Botany
Lab", Hamburg, Germany.
Mixed-fibre felt, embroidery thread,
card, and polyester fibre filling.

**The Last Pear In The World**
Collaboration with Jon Burgerman
150 mm x 120 mm
Made for Jon's show "Lossy Botany Lab", Hamburg, Germany.
Mixed-fibre felt, embroidery thread, card, and polyester fibre filling.

**Pea Pods (Sad, Sad, Happy)**
Collaboration with Jon Burgerman
120 mm x 70 mm
Made for Jon's show "Lossy Botany Lab", Hamburg, Germany.
Edition of three
Mixed-fibre felt, embroidery thread, card, and polyester fibre filling.

**Dog/Mother**
Designed by Karine Bernadou
690 mm x 210 mm
Made for Nobrow.
Exhibited at "Pick Me Up" Somerset House, London.
Mixed fibres, felt, embroidery thread and polyester fibre filling.

**Father/Daughter**
Designed by Karine Bernadou
710 mm x 310 mm
Made for Nobrow.
Exhibited at "Pick Me Up" Somerset House, London.
Mixed fibres, felt, embroidery thread and polyester fibre filling.

**Daughter/Father**
Designed by Karine Bernadou
460 mm x 200 mm
Made for Nobrow.
Exhibited at "Pick Me Up" Somerset House, London.
Mixed fibres, felt, embroidery thread and polyester fibre filling.

**Jim & Jon Anxieteam Hand Puppets**
collaboration with Jon Burgerman
400 mm x 230 mm
Made for Anxieteam Music Video.
John carries a microphone and Jim a Ukulele.
Mixed fibres, felt, card, embroidery thread and polyester fibre filling.

**Green Green** (named by owner)
450 mm x 230 mm
Made as a present for our godson.
Mixed fibres, fake fur, felt, plastic safety eyes, and polyester fibre filling.

**Pokey** (named by owner)
450 mm x 230 mm
Made as a present for our goddaughter.
Mixed fibres, fake fur, felt, plastic safety eyes, and polyester fibre filling.

**Undetermined Wrangler**
550 mm x 180 mm
Made as a present.
The Wrangler wears a skinny knit, grey and yellow polo-neck.
Mixed fibres, fake fur, felt, plastic safety eyes, and polyester fibre filling.

**Thug Life**
Collaboration with Jon Boam
800 mm x 270 mm
Commissioned by Nobrow for the Jon Boam/Matthew The Horse show "Doom 3.0".
Mixed fibres, fleece, felt, wire, card and polyester fibre filling.

**Flink Strothers**
700 mm x 280 mm
Member of The Furry Mayhem, made for "Tales From The Sock Drawer" Show, touring UK Art Centres.
Flink wears black denim skinny jeans with turn-ups, yellow and back sleeveless t-shirt, studded leather belt and wrist bands, a plectrum neckace and black high-top baseball boots. He carries his black flying V guitar.
Mixed fibres, fake fur, felt, plastic safety eyes, wire, card and polyester fibre filling.

**Groobo Tubbs**
600 mm x 360 mm
Member of The Furry Mayhem, made for "Tales From The Sock Drawer" Show, touring UK Art Centres.
Groobo wears black denim jeans with double turn-ups, a leather belt with cross-shaped buckle and studded wrist bands. He carries his black and yellow bass guitar.
Mixed fibres, fake fur, felt, plastic safety eyes, wire, card and polyester fibre filling.

**Thrubb**
650 mm x 260 mm
Member of The Furry Mayhem, made for "Tales From The Sock Drawer" Show, touring UK Art Centres.
Thrubb wears skinny-legged black jeans with turn-ups, yellow leather belt, and grey marl sleeveless "Motorthread" t-shirt. He carries his wooden drum sticks.
Mixed fibres, wood, fake fur, felt, plastic safety eyes, wire, card and polyester fibre filling.

**Promotional Malibu Bottle Custom**
330 x 190 mm
MacGregor Emilio Snowcone is Emeritus Professor of Grooming at Arctic Tech.
His name was picked in a competition run on the Felt Mistress Blog, by winner Laurie Pink.
Fake fur, felt, plastic safety eyes, card and polyester fibre filling.

2011

**Demetri**
500 mm x 320 mm
Made for Pictoplasma's "Missing Link", Berlin, Germany.
Demetri wears indigo denim jeans with double turn-up and leather belt. He smokes a pipe.
Mixed fibres, fake fur, felt, plastic safety eyes, wire, card and polyester fibre filling.

**Looboo**
650 mm x 330 mm
Part of the Totem Pole made for "Inky Goodness Totem" show, Pictoplasma, Berlin.
Wool, Mixed fibres, felt, embroidery thread, plastic safety eyes, card, and polyester fibre filling.

**Shaboo**
600 mm x 700 mm
Part of the Totem Pole made for "Inky Goodness Totem" show, Pictoplasma, Berlin.
Wool, Mixed fibres, felt, embroidery thread, plastic safety eyes, card, and polyester fibre filling.

**Bulbobo**
850 mm x 350 mm
Part of the Totem Pole made for "Inky Goodness Totem" show, Pictoplasma, Berlin.
Wool, Mixed fibres, felt, embroidery thread, plastic safety eyes, card, and polyester fibre filling.

**Rombondo**
600 mm x 700 mm
Part of the Totem Pole made for "Inky Goodness Totem" show, Pictoplasma, Berlin.
Wool, Mixed fibres, felt, embroidery thread, plastic safety eyes, card, and polyester fibre filling.
When stacked/interlocked the Full Totem measures 1950 mm x 700 mm.

**Barnaby Grangle**
700 mm x 350 mm
Made during artist residency at Head-space Gallery, Japan and shown at Head Space Arts And Music Festival, Osaka, Japan.
Barnaby wears narrow-legged black jeans with turn-up, studded belt and red high top baseball shoes. He carries his black and red electric guitar.
Mixed fibres, fake fur, felt, plastic safety eyes, and polyester fibre filling.

**Pooky Snooks**
530 mm x 300 mm
Made during artist residency at Head-space Gallery, Japan and shown at Head Space Arts And Music Festival, Osaka, Japan.
Pooky wears vintage welsh tweed trapeze-line cape with high mandarin collar and frog fastenings. She carries her felt Leica.
Mixed fibres, fake fur, felt, plastic safety eyes, and polyester fibre filling.

**Dwink**
500 mm x 240 mm
Made during artist residency at Head-space Gallery, Japan and shown at Head Space Arts And Music Festival, Osaka, Japan.
Dwink wears a printed cotton cravat and a yellow diver's watch.
Mixed fibres, fake fur, felt, plastic safety eyes, and polyester fibre filling.

**Tammy**
500 mm x 300 mm
Made during artist residency at Head-space Gallery, Japan and shown at Head Space Arts And Music Festival, Osaka, Japan.
Tammy wears striped chunky roll-neck jumper and washed out denim jeans with turn-ups.
Mixed fibres, wool, fake fur, felt, plastic safety eyes, wire, card and polyester fibre filling.

**Tupsy Winkles**
480 mm x 180 mm
Made during artist residency at Head-space Gallery, Japan and shown at Head Space Arts And Music Festival, Osaka, Japan.
Tupsy wears a embroidered Kimono fabric bow.
Mixed fibres, fake fur, felt, plastic safety eyes, and polyester fibre filling.

**Tippy Head Mascot**
Edition of two
90 mm x 100 mm
Made as gifts for Japanese Team Tippy members Aiko & Noriko
Fake fur, felt, plastic safety eyes, wire, card, cord and polyester fibre filling.

**Gilbert Twang**
780 mm x 350 mm
Made during artist residency at Head-space Gallery, Japan and shown at Head Space Arts And Music Festival, Osaka, Japan.
Gilbert wears black half-rimmed glasses, skinny faded grey denim jeans, black leather belt, checked cotton shirt with button-down collar, black satin tie and grey slip-on shoes. He carries a vintage grey tweed bag with black felt shoulder strap and smokes a cigarette.
Mixed fibres, fake fur, felt, plastic safety eyes, and polyester fibre filling.

**Albert Krang**
580 mm x 320 mm
Made during artist residency at Head space Gallery, Japan and shown at Head Space Arts And Music Festiva Osaka, Japan.
Albert wears a hand knitted welsh wool arran jumper, black denim jea with turn-ups and thick black-frame glasses.

**Hubert Grumph**
580 mm x 380 mm
Made during artist residency at Hea space Gallery, Japan and shown at Head Space Arts And Music Festiva Osaka, Japan.
Hubert wears a beige knitted polo-neck jumper, dark green needle cor trousers, vintage tweed three-but toned sports jacket with welt pocke elbow patches and single back vent Thick angular black-framed glasses He smokes a pipe.
Mixed fibres, wool tweed, fake fur, felt, plastic safety eyes, wire, card and polyester fibre filling.

**Fenella Snark**
710 mm x 300 mm
Made during artist residency at Hea space Gallery, Japan and shown at Head Space Arts And Music Festiva Osaka, Japan.
Fenella wears a long-sleeved printe kimono with red trim and a black sa Obi. Fabric pattern illustration by Jonathan Edwards. Print designed b Tomatsu Shimada. Fenella also has living ponytail with hidden cats' eye
Mixed fibres, fake fur, felt, plastic safety eyes, wire, card and polyeste fibre filling.

**Edwin Crepuscule Flenk**
900 mm x 330 mm
Made for a Halloween show, Kidrob London.
Edwin wears skinny black jeans wit turn-ups, white cotton button-down collared shirt, wide cuffs with vinta button cuff links and ribbon bow at neck, a double-breasted black pea coat with welt pockets and single back vent. He smokes a cigarette.
Mixed fibres, fake fur, felt, plastic safety eyes, wire, card and polyeste fibre filling.

**Benji**
260 mm x 200 mm
Designed as a kit for workshops.
Mixed-fibre felt, fake fur, embroider thread, plastic safety eyes, card, an polyester fibre filling.

**Gustav**
200 mm x 260 mm
Designed as a kit for workshops.
Mixed-fibre felt, embroidery thread plastic safety eyes, card, and polyes ter fibre filling.

...n

...mm x 200 mm

...igned as a kit for workshops.
...ed-fibre felt, fake fur, embroidery
...ead, plastic safety eyes, card, and
...yester fibre filling.

...donaargghhh
...mm x 300 mm
...vate commission.
...donaargghhh wears metallic
...e leather conical bra, lace-up
...set. Fishnet tights, knee-length
...e leather boots and pvc fingerless
...ves.
...ed fibres, fake leather, PVC, fake
...felt, wire, card and polyester fibre
...ng.

...mer
...mm x 320 mm
...mmissioned by Kärnhuset Sweden
...star on Arla Milk vending machines
...posters.
...mer wears blue denim dungarees,
...on checked shirt and trucker cap.
...ed fibres, felt, plastic safety eyes,
...e, card and polyester fibre filling.

...w
...mm x 450 mm
...mmissioned by Kärnhuset Sweden
...use on Arla Milk vending machines
...posters.
...ed-fibre felt, embroidery thread,
...stic safety eyes, card, and polyes-
...fibre filling.

...mm x 190 mm
...mmissioned by Kärnhuset Sweden
...use on Arla Milk vending machines
...posters.
...ed-fibre felt, embroidery thread,
...stic safety eyes, card, and polyes-
...fibre filling.

...d (large)
...mm x 260 mm
...mmissioned by Kärnhuset Sweden
...use on Arla Milk vending machines
...posters.
...ed-fibre felt, embroidery thread,
...stic safety eyes, card, and polyes-
...fibre filling.

...ds (small)
...mm x 180 mm
...tion of two.
...mmissioned by Kärnhuset Sweden
...use on Arla Milk vending machines
...posters.
...ed-fibre felt, embroidery thread,
...stic safety eyes, card, and polyes-
...fibre filling.

...ound Dwellers
...mm x 150 mm
...tion of two.
...mmissioned by Kärnhuset Sweden
...use on Arla Milk vending machines
...posters.
...ed-fibre felt, embroidery thread,

---

plastic safety eyes, card, and polyester fibre filling.

Rabbit
300 mm x 120 mm
Commissioned by Kärnhuset Sweden
for use on Arla Milk vending machines
and posters.
Mixed-fibre felt, embroidery thread,
plastic safety eyes, card, and polyester fibre filling.

Big Arm/Hand
700 mm x 200 mm
Commissioned by Kärnhuset Sweden
for use on Arla Milk vending machines
and posters.
Mixed-fibre felt, embroidery thread,
plastic safety eyes, wire, and polyester fibre filling.

Grûber
260 mm x 200 mm
Magazine tutorial commissioned by
Mollie Makes Magazine
Mixed-fibre felt, embroidery thread,
plastic safety eyes, vintage buckle,
ribbon and polyester fibre filling.

Sebastien
800 mm x 220 mm
Puppet
Sebastien wears white thick-framed
sunglasses, skinny jeans with turn-
ups, black and white stripey skinny-
knit jumper and a black and white
checked fringed scarf.
Mixed fibres, fake fur, felt, plastic
safety eyes, wire, card and polyester
fibre filling.

Giant Hoopoe
350 mm x 200 mm
Made for the "Ghosts Of Gone Birds"
show, London.
Mixed-fibre felt, embroidery thread,
plastic safety eyes, card, and polyester fibre filling.

Bishops 'O
Collaboration with Ben Newman
260 mm x 200 mm
Made for the "Ghosts Of Gone Birds"
show, London.
Mixed-fibre felt, embroidery thread,
plastic safety eyes, card, and polyester fibre filling.

Tippy Tea Custom
100 mm x 100 mm
Made for Lunartik's "Custom Tea
Tour", Pictoplasma Berlin and touring
show.
Mixed-fibre felt, embroidery thread,
fake fur, card, plastic, metal and
polyester fibre filling.

Spyghetti Western
180 mm x 120 mm
Made for Mad Magazine's Celebra-
tion "50 years of Spy vs Spy Custom
Show", San Diego, California.
Mixed-fibre felt, cotton, embroidery

---

thread, card, spray paint, and plastic.

Taimatsu Maru
Collaboration with Ben Newman
650 mm x 330 mm
Made for Ben's show "Masks",
Nobrow Gallery, London.
Mixed-fibre felt, embroidery thread,
card, and polyester fibre filling.

Dateotoko Fishu San
collaboration with Ben Newman
1400 mm x 360 mm
Made for Ben's show "Masks",
Nobrow Gallery, London.
Mixed-fibre felt, embroidery thread,
card, and polyester fibre filling.

Neko Mata
Collaboration with Ben Newman
975 mm x 300 mm
Made for Ben's show "Masks",
Nobrow Gallery, London.
Mixed-fibre felt, embroidery thread,
card, and polyester fibre filling.

Willow
Collaboration with Neil McFarland
(Paris Hair)
300 mm x 750 mm
Made for ustwo, the makers of the
game "Whale Trail", designed by
Neil McFarland. Also featured in
the video promo for the Gruff Rhys
single "Whale Trail", directed by Neil
McFarland.
Mixed-fibre felt, embroidery thread,
and polyester fibre filling.

Hilda
Collaboration with Luke Pearson
750 mm x 260 mm
Commissioned by Nobrow.
Mixed-fibre felt, embroidery thread,
card, plastic safety eyes, wood, and
polyester fibre filling.

The Mope
400 mm x 230 mm
Character designed by John Allison,
made as a present for John.
Mixed-fibre felt, fake fur, plastic
safety eyes, embroidery thread, card,
and polyester fibre filling.

Wendigo
440 mm x 230 mm
Edition of two (one fake fur, one fleece).
Designed by John Allison, made as a
present for John.
Mixed-fibre felt, fleece, fake fur, embroidery thread, plastic safety eyes,
card, and polyester fibre filling.

Mack
330 mm x 170 mm
Designed by Joe List, made as a gift
to Joe to celebrate The Annotated
Weekender's birthday.
Mixed-fibre felt, embroidery thread,
plastic safety eyes, and polyester
fibre filling.

---

Goth Panda (renamed Patchy by
owner)
450 mm x 230 mm
Made as a present for our goddaughter.
Panda wears black sleeveless A-line
dress with white lace trim and matching bow hair clip.
Mixed fibres, brushed and plain felt,
plastic safety eyes, wire, card and
polyester fibre filling.

Bernard
450 mm x 230 mm
Made as a present for our godson.
Bernard wears hand knitted round-
neck arran tank top, shirt with
embroidered collar and checkered
bow tie.
Mixed fibres, brushed and plain felt,
plastic safety eyes, wire, card and
polyester fibre filling.

Codey
Collaboration with Pete Fowler
750 mm x 270 mm
Made for the puppet show "The
Stuffs", shown both online and on
Cartoon Network.
Codey wears indigo denim jeans with
turn-ups, blue striped long-sleeved
t-shirt, hand printed neck-scarf, baseball shoes and spotted trucker cap.
Mixed fibres, felt, foam, plastic safety
eyes, wire, card and polyester fibre
filling.

Trendy Boy
Collaboration with Pete Fowler
800 mm x 270 mm
Made for the puppet show "The
Stuffs", shown both online and on
Cartoon Network.
TB wears brown cord trousers, white
plimsoles, black v-neck t-shirt and
orange hoody with pin badges.
Mixed fibres, felt, foam, plastic safety
eyes, wire, horn, card and polyester
fibre filling.

Rogue Girl
Collaboration with Pete Fowler
800 mm x 270 mm
Made for the puppet show "The
Stuffs", shown both online and on
Cartoon Network.
RG wears shot pink/purple A-line
sleeveless dress with RG felt appliqued logo, striped knee-high socks
and two-tone lace-up dance shoes, a
heart-shaped crystal ring, diamante
bracelet and orange watch. RG also
wears a brace.
Mixed fibres, felt, foam, plastic safety
eyes, wire, card and polyester fibre
filling.

Dooder McTavish
Collaboration with Pete Fowler
800 mm x 270 mm
Made for the puppet show "The
Stuffs", shown both online and on
Cartoon Network.

---

Dooder wears cut off faded denim
shorts with frayed hems, plaited
leather belt, slip-on blue boat shoes,
cotton hawaiian shirt (never buttoned
up) and a shark's tooth necklace.
Mixed fibres, felt, foam, plastic safety
eyes, wire, card and polyester fibre
filling.

Pepperdelica
950 mm x 300 mm
Made for the Jim Henson tribute
show "The Lovers, The Dreamers
and Me", Gallery Nucleus, Alhambra,
California.
Pepperdelica wears purple trousers,
cowboy boots, a military Sgt. Pepper-
style jacket with frog fastenings and a
peaked cap. He carries his left-handed bass guitar.
Mixed-fibre felt, foam, wire, embroidery thread, card and polyester fibre
filling.

Geraint
800 mm x 220 mm
Prototype Puppet
Geraint wears short sleeve checked
cotton shirt with button down collar,
indigo straight-legged jeans with turn
up. Black belt and aviator sunglasses.
Mixed fibres, fake fur, felt, wire, card
and foam and polyester fibre filling.

Zultantara
300 mm x 220 mm
Made for the Rabbids "Eeerz" Custom
Vinyl Invasion Tour, London and Paris.
Mixed-fibre felt, embroidery thread,
card, and polyester fibre filling.

Beetle Prototype (Big)
230 mm x 100 mm
Felt, embroidery thread, plastic safety
eyes and polyester fibre.

Beetle Prototype (small)
120 mm x 70 mm
Felt, embroidery thread, plastic safety
eyes and polyester fibre.

Frilled Arizona Beetle
250 mm x 250 mm (Framed)
Mixed-fibre felt, embroidery thread,
card, wire, and polyester fibre filling.
Wooden glass-fronted box frame.

Wide-Eyed Mint Winter Beetle
250 mm x 250 mm (Framed)
Mixed-fibre felt, embroidery thread,
card, wire, and polyester fibre filling.
Wooden glass-fronted box frame.

Ruby-Booted Petal Wing Beetle
250 mm x 250 mm (Framed)
Mixed-fibre felt, embroidery thread,
card, wire, and polyester fibre filling.
Wooden glass-fronted box frame.

Ice-Winged Polar Beetle
250 mm x 250 mm (Framed)
Mixed-fibre felt, embroidery thread,
card, wire, and polyester fibre filling.

Wooden glass-fronted box frame.

### Flame-Frilled Red Amber Beetle

250 mm x 250 mm (Framed)
Mixed-fibre felt, embroidery thread, card, wire, and polyester fibre filling. Wooden glass-fronted box frame.

### Smoke-Frilled Maru Maru Beetle

250 mm x 250 mm (Framed)
Mixed-fibre felt, embroidery thread, card, wire, and polyester fibre filling. Wooden glass-fronted box frame.

### Hot-Footed Booted Beetle

250 mm x 250 mm (Framed)
Mixed-fibre felt, embroidery thread, card, wire, and polyester fibre filling. Wooden glass-fronted box frame.

### Curl-Toed Sweetheart Beetle

250 mm x 250 mm (Framed)
Mixed-fibre felt, embroidery thread, card, wire, and polyester fibre filling. Wooden glass-fronted box frame.

### Stripey-Legged Paku Paku Beetle

250 mm x 250 mm (Framed)
Mixed-fibre felt, embroidery thread, card, wire, and polyester fibre filling. Wooden glass-fronted box frame.

### Monochromatic Chelsea Booted Beetle

250 mm x 250 mm (Framed)
Mixed-fibre felt, embroidery thread, card, wire, and polyester fibre filling. Wooden glass-fronted box frame.

### Gold-Frilled Cherry Boot Beetle

250 mm x 250 mm (Framed)
Mixed-fibre felt, embroidery thread, card, wire, and polyester fibre filling. Wooden glass-fronted box frame.

### 2012

### Aubodo Burger

Collaboration with Jon Burgerman
800 mm x 500 mm
Made for Jon's show "Fast Food", Sergeant Paper, Paris
Mixed-fibre felt, embroidery thread, card, and polyester fibre filling.

### Goom

Collaboration with Ben Newman
580 mm x 400 mm

Made for Ben's show "Masks", Pictoplasma, Berlin.
Mixed-fibre felt, embroidery thread, card, plastic safety eyes and polyester fibre filling.

### Inugami

Collaboration with Ben Newman
580 mm x 270 mm
Made for Ben's show "Masks", Pictoplasma, Berlin.
Mixed-fibre felt, embroidery thread, card, plastic safety eyes and polyester fibre filling.

### Tigraaarrr

Collaboration with Ben Newman
580 mm x 450 mm
Made for Ben's show "Masks", Pictoplasma, Berlin
Mixed-fibre felt, embroidery thread, card, plastic safety eyes and polyester fibre filling.

### Secret Seven Record Sleeve

118 mm x 118 mm
Stitched record cover for DJ Shadow 7" single - 'Come On Riding (Through The Cosmos)'
made for the Secret Seven show in aid of The Teenage Cancer Trust at Idea Generation Gallery Shoreditch
Felt, embroidery thread and plastic safety eyes, card

### Purple Hearted Petal Wing Beetle

250 mm x 250 mm (Framed)
Mixed-fibre felt, embroidery thread, card, wire, and polyester fibre filling. Wooden glass-fronted box frame.

### Scalloped Wing Cherry Heart Beetle

250 mm x 250 mm (Framed)
Mixed-fibre felt, embroidery thread, card, wire, and polyester fibre filling. Wooden glass-fronted box frame.

### Purple Hearted Petal Wing Beetle

250 mm x 250 mm (Framed)
Mixed-fibre felt, embroidery thread, card, wire, and polyester fibre filling. Wooden glass-fronted box frame.

### Scalloped Wing Cherry Heart Beetle

250 mm x 250 mm (Framed)
Mixed-fibre felt, embroidery thread, card, wire, and polyester fibre filling. Wooden glass-fronted box frame.

### Anton Trenche

1120 mm x 300 mm
Made for "Hey! Who's This Guy?", Nobrow Gallery.
Anton wears white "Stallion" kinetic sunglasses by Kirk Originals, white cotton wide collared shirt with deep collar and cuffs, knitted yellow and grey striped tie. Grey two-buttoned jacket with narrow lapel, single back vent, welt pockets and 3 button cuff detail. Narrow legged black

denim jeans with turn up, pointy black heeled boots and a yellow leather belt. Button badge by SeaHawks music. He smokes a cigarette.
Mixed-fibre felt, card, wire and polyester fibre filling.

### Hester Flent

1070 mm x 340 mm
Made for "Hey! Who's This Guy?", Nobrow Gallery.
Hester wears orange "Dione" glasses by Kirk Originals. Black crepe a-line, button-back dress, with long fluted sleeves edged with lace and vintage button detail. Black petersham ribbon belt fastened with vintage button. She also wears her orange live tentacle scarf/pet.
Mixed-fibre felt, card, plastic safety eyes, wire and polyester fibre filling.

### Lester Flent

1240 mm x 450 mm
Made for "Hey! Who's This Guy?", Nobrow Gallery.
Lester wears orange "Janus" glasses by Kirk Originals., a black, high-fastening double-breasted suit with large lapels, welt pockets and single back vent. His trousers have a slight flare. Also wearing orange gingham shirt with wide collar and cuffs, black satin bow tie and black shiny pointy boots with a heel.
Mixed-fibre felt, card, plastic safety eyes, wire and polyester fibre filling.

### Amphibina De Lorian

900 mm x 320 mm
Made for "Hey! Who's This Guy?", Nobrow Gallery.
Amphibina wears black, "Chip" kinetic glasses by Kirk Originals, aubergine slash-neck knitted jumper with button detail at neckline, paisley-printed silk scarf, skinny indigo jeans with turn-ups and white lace-up brothel creepers.
Mixed-fibre felt, card, plastic safety eyes, wire and polyester fibre filling.

### Hector Bunford

1000 mm x 430 mm
Made for "Hey! Who's This Guy?", Nobrow Gallery.
Hector wears brown "Janus" glasses by Kirk Originals, wool tweed three-button sports jacket with patch pockets, a single back vent and elbow patches, a light brown knitted polo-neck, green needlecord straight-legged trousers and brown dealer boots. He smokes a pipe.
Mixed-fibre felt, card, plastic safety eyes, wire and polyester fibre filling.

### G'goob

1380 mm x 480 mm
Made for "Hey! Who's This Guy?", Nobrow Gallery.
G'goob wears Turquoise "Marvin" glasses by Kirk Originals.

Mixed-fibre felt, card, plastic safety eyes, wire and polyester fibre filling.

### Giant Japonica Yosemite Ocular Beetle

520 mm x 520 mm
Made for "Hey! Who's This Guy?", Nobrow Gallery.
Mixed-fibre felt, embroidery thread, card, wire, and polyester fibre filling. Wooden glass-fronted box frame.

### Giant Cavalry-caped Kitchener Beetle

520 mm x 520 mm
Made for "Hey! Who's This Guy?", Nobrow Gallery.
Mixed-fibre felt, embroidery thread, card, wire, and polyester fibre filling. Wooden glass-fronted box frame.

### Heliotrope-headed Honky tonk Beetle

250 mm x 250 mm (Framed)
Made for "Hey! Who's This Guy?", Nobrow Gallery.
Mixed-fibre felt, embroidery thread, card, wire, and polyester fibre filling. Wooden glass-fronted box frame.

### Reckless Running Rhomboid Beetle

250 mm x 250 mm (Framed)
Made for "Hey! Who's This Guy?", Nobrow Gallery.
Mixed-fibre felt, embroidery thread, card, wire, and polyester fibre filling. Wooden glass-fronted box frame.

### Sighing Cyan Serrated Sundown Beetle

250 mm x 250 mm (Framed)
Made for "Hey! Who's This Guy?", Nobrow Gallery.
Mixed-fibre felt, embroidery thread, card, wire, and polyester fibre filling. Wooden glass-fronted box frame.

### Grey-tongued Lichen-licking Beetle

250 mm x 250 mm (Framed)
Made for "Hey! Who's This Guy?", Nobrow Gallery.
Mixed-fibre felt, embroidery thread, card, wire, and polyester fibre filling. Wooden glass-fronted box frame.

### Fuegondo

Custom for Dudebox Launch Show, Village Underground, London
260 mm x 250 mm
Vinyl toy custom with felt covering.
Felt, embroidery thread, polyester fibre filling, card, plastic safety eyes.

### Rishikesh George

George Harrison, made for "All Together Now", The Beatles tribute show at Gallery Nucleus, Alhambra, California.
1200 mm x 360 mm
Sitar 690mm x 260mm
George wears a short, orange,

embroidered kurta with matching loose fitting trousers and has flowe garlands around his neck. His right hand has an appliquéd eye detail.
Felt, plastic safety eyes, embroider thread, card and polyester fibre filli

### Crimp-frilled Kayamori Kicking Beetle

520 mm x 520 mm
Mixed-fibre felt, embroidery thread card, wire, and polyester fibre filli Wooden glass-fronted box frame.

### Silver-booted Midori-winged Sakurai Beetle

520 mm x 520 mm
Mixed-fibre felt, embroidery thread card, wire, and polyester fibre fillin Wooden glass-fronted box frame.

### John Evans

designed by Pete Fowler
1250mm x 350mm

Made for Gruff Rhys' investigative film, photography and music tour through North America, "American Interior".
John wears 18th century inspired grey felt breeks and matching grey jacket with covered buttons detailin on turn-back collar, deep cuffs and large welt pockets. Cream cotton shirt with gathered sleeve head, de cuffs and centre-front frills with a self fabric tie at neck. Black belt wi metallic buckle, grey over-the-knee socks, black shoes with metal buck and a black felt tricorn hat trimmed with grey felt binding. He also has change of clothes, which include a fake fur sleeveless tunic waistcoat and some feather and bead native American inspired jewellery.
Mixed fibres, felt, cotton, polyester fibre filling, embroidery thread, wire, wood, card, foam, fake fur an feathers.

### Drain The Red (Marceline)

1300mm x 350mm
made for the Cartoon Network Adventure Time anniversary show Gallery Nucleus, Alhambra, Californ
Marceline wears red and black mix fibre slash-neck skinny knit jumper, skinny-legged indigo denim jeans a deep red pointy calf-length boots. She carries her axe bass, wears an FM plectrum necklace around her neck and a "Nocturnal Romantic" Edwin pin badge on her guitar stra
Mixed fibres, felt, fake fur, metal clasps and rings, embroidery threa polyester fibre filling, wire, card an wood.

## Shows/Exhibitions

Oootopia: An Artgebraic Tribute To
Adventure Time
Gallery Nucleus
Alhambra
California
18 August – 9 September 2012

Konnichiwa Japan – solo show
Soma Gallery
Bristol
19 July – 8 September 2012

Monster workshop at Foyles
The Gallery at Foyles
Foyles Bookshop
London
30 June 2012

Monster London
The Gallery at Foyles
Foyles Bookshop
London
25 June – 4 July 2012

All Together Now: A Tribute To The
Beatles
Gallery Nucleus
Alhambra
California
7 – 29 July 2012

"Hey! Who's This Guy?"
Nobrow Gallery
London
18 May – 23 June 2012

Dudebox Launch
Village Underground
London
11 May 2012

Secret Sevens
Idea Generation Gallery
London
21 – 22 April 2012

Pictoplasma Berlin
Masks
Berlin-Weekly.com Gallery Space
Berlin
11 – 15 April 2012

Jon Burgerman "Fast Food"
Sergeant Paper
Paris
28 January – 25 February 2012

The Lovers, The Dreamers, and Me:
A Jim Henson Tribute
Gallery Nucleus
Alhambra
California
10 December – 2 January 2012

Eeerz Custom show
Artoyz
Paris
26 January – 25 February 2012
+
Forbidden Planet
London
25 November – 28 December 2011

Ghosts Of Gone Birds
Rochelle School
Arnold Circus
London
2 – 23 November 2011

Ben Newman - Masks
Nobrow
London
16 September - 11 November 2011

Tales From the Sneaky Crypt
Kidrobot
Earlham Street
London
28 – 31 October 2011

Lunartik's Mini Tea Tour Custom
Show
Forbidden Planet
London
5 – 31 August 2011

Sixxa
Vienna
1 – 31 May 2011

43 degrees
Berlin
6 – 10 April 2011

Totem Homecoming
Zellig Gallery
Birmingham
19 – 30 July 2011

Japan Residency – Head Space Gallery
Nara, and
Head Space Arts and Music Festival
Osaka
10 May – 9 June 2011

Pictoplasma Berlin
InkyGoodness Character Totem
Neurotitan Gallery
Berlin
6 – 10 April 2011

Tales From The Sock Drawer
York College
Bishopthorpe
York
28 February – 1 April 2011
+
20-21 Visual Arts Centre
Scunthorpe
North Lincolnshire
13 November 2010 – 29 January 2011

Selfridges Window Display &
Selfridges Wonder Room
Oxford Street
London
28 October – 24 December 2010

Start London
Instore installation for London
Fashion Week
Rivington Street
London
17 – 22 September 2010

Jon Boam & Mathew The Horse:
Dooom 3.0
Nobrow
London
22 July – 23 September 2010

Jon Burgerman – The Lossy Botany
Lab
Heliumcowboy
Kaiser-Wilhelm-Str. 81
Hamburg
1 July – 5 August 2010

Jon Burgerman – Brain Drain
The Gallery
Winchester Discovery Centre
14 May – 11 July 2010

Pick Me Up
Contemporary Graphic Art Fair
In Association with Nobrow
Somerset House
London
23 April – 3 May 2010

Hello Brute – Teen Dream
Rotofugi
1953-55 West Chicago Avenue
Chicago
Illinois
9 – 25 April 2010

Momiji Couture
Royal T
Los Angeles
California
20 December 2009 – 18 January 2010

Multiversal Group Show
Art Basel, Miami
Florida
3 December 2009

Go Ask Alice – Doll & Plush Show
Paul Cumes Fine Art
131 East Anapamu Street
Santa Barbara
California
5 December 2009 – 7 January 2010

Plush You!
Bluebottle Gallery,
415 East Pine Street,
Seattle
Washington
October 2009

Inkygoodness Wonderland
Vaad Gallery
Birmingham
11 – 27 September 2009

Animals Take Over Berlin
Various locations
Berlin
31 August – 7 September 2009

Jon Burgerman – My American
Summer
Giant Robot New York
437 East 9th Street
New York City
15 August 2009

Jon Burgerman – "I Can't Sit Still"
Coningsby Gallery
London
21 October – 1 November 2008

# Index

Louise Evans and Jonathan Edwards would like to thank:

Both our families
Woodrow & Bridget – the captain and first mate!
Jon Burgerman, Pete Fowler, Ben Newman, Jon Knox, Luke "Chops" Pearson, Jon Boam
Alex & Sam at Nobrow, Jason & Karen at Kirk Originals, Jakob Westman
Craig & Chris, Dan Berry, John Allison, Brix Smith-Start, Theo Vanderzalm, JAKe, Joe & Lynn, Neil McFarland
Aiko, Jamie & Lee at Headspace (& the rest of the Kansai Tippy Street Team), Kyoko, Hario, Kozo and Tomatsu - どうもありがとう
Kenny, Martin & Iz at Blank Slate, Channel Flip, Cartoon Network, Selfridges, Kärnhuset, Foyles, Gallery Nucleus
Cafe Absinthe, ustwo™, Welsh Artists International, Clinic, Gruff Rhys, Bruno Vincent, Paddy Steer
Drew, Julia, Ava & Bertie, Ben & Maki at Tokyo Jazz Panda, Ilya, Zeel, Darryl Cunninghan, Will Kane, Ian Carney, Steve Martin
Louise Turner & Betty, Jason Bennion, Simon Gane, Matt Macabre, Matt Patt, Rachel Smart, Raymond (Doc 18) Kan
Mike and Katie TADO, Sarah Habershon, Richard and Fran, David & Heidi, Jackie, Steffi, Marc Stipling for fringe maintenance
Kuniko, Mrs Ivy Payne, Peter Haylock, Ian Robertson, Jeremy Brautman, Andy Woo at Crazy Label, Andy Heng at ToysREvil
Peter & Lars at Pictoplasma, Ryan & Dave at Mad Magazine
Toby Jones (I miss you my furry best friend), Tippy Winkles and Twitter

Sorry if we've missed anyone out. Your name goes here _____

If you've ever commented, retweeted, blogged, reblogged or 'liked' – thank you.

Photographs by Louise Evans and Jonathan Edwards except:

10, 14, 80, 81, 83, 112, 113, 116, 117, 120, 121, 127, 210, 211, 212, 213, 214, 215,
222, 232, 233, 244, 245, 248, 255, 258, 259, 284, 285, 326, 329, 374, 375, 398, 399 Woodrow Phoenix
24–37, 63, 64, 66, 118, 119, 124, 125, 129, 130, 132, 133, 164,
169, 202, 204, 209, 224, 225, 240, 286, 287, 329, 332, 333, 345 Dan Berry
6, 12 Imagine
12 Agan
43, 44, 45 Daniel Lundkvist
87 Nathan Beddows
93 Sergeant Paper
107 Heliumcowboy
134, 135, 136, 144 Bruno Vincent
145 Frames from Clinic video courtesy of Domino records
147, 149, 151, 153 Frames from 'The Stuffs' courtesy of Channel Flip
181, 227, 308, 309, 312, 313, 314, 315 Doc 18/Raymond Kan
185 Kozo Ono
204 Rotofugi
232 Paul Cumes Fine Art
276, 278, 282 Nobrow
263, 265, 267 Dunstan Baker
318, 319 Megan Hindley
372, 373 Frames from 'Whale Trail' courtesy of ustwo™
394 Gruffington Post

Designed, written, compiled, photoedited and finessed by Woodrow Phoenix
Can't rock the house without the party people, can't make a book without Bridget rocking the pages  x
Props to Kenny in the two-seater for declaring it ON and making it all (relatively) painless | salutations to Steenton and Ultravision Iz
San-Kyu mista Double-C Craig Conlan and Sky High Chris
Team Detonator, thrillas from the winnas, home of the hits

Interviews by Woodrow Phoenix Interview transcriptions by Woodrow Phoenix and Bridget Hannigan
Ben Newman Bristol, Monday, 14 May 2012
Alex Spiro and Sam Arthur Nobrow Shop, London, Tuesday, 15 May 2012
Pete Fowler Nobrow Shop, London, Thursday, 17 May 2012
Louise Evans Institute of Contemporary Arts, London, Friday, 18 May 2012
Jonathan Edwards Institute of Contemporary Arts, London, Friday, 18 May 2012